A Long Week in March

The 36th (Ulster) Division in the German Spring Offensive, March 1918

Michael James Nugent

Helion & Company

Helion & Company Limited
Unit 8 Amherst Business Centre
Budbrooke Road
Warwick
CV34 5WE
England
Tel. 01926 499 619
Fax 0121 711 4075
Email: info@helion.co.uk
Website: www.helion.co.uk
Twitter: @helionbooks
Visit our blog http://blog.helion.co.uk/

Published by Helion & Company 2019
Designed and typeset by Mach 3 Solutions (www.mach3solutions.co.uk)
Cover designed by Paul Hewitt, Battlefield Design (www.battlefield-design.co.uk)
Printed by Hobbs the Printers, Totton, Hampshire

Text and maps © Michael James Nugent 2018
Images © as individually credited

ISBN 978-1-912390-57-1

British Library Cataloguing-in-Publication Data.
A catalogue record for this book is available from the British Library.

For details of other military history titles published by Helion & Company Limited contact
the above address, or visit our website: http://www.helion.co.uk.

We always welcome receiving book proposals from prospective authors.

This book is dedicated to the brave officers and men who fought against overwhelming odds with the 36th (Ulster) Division during the German Spring Offensive, March 1918.

Remembering in particular two connections our family have to the Division at that time:

My Great Grandfather, 19446 Serjeant James Greer MM, Machine Gun Corps, formerly 16504 8th (Service) Battalion Royal Irish Rifles (East Belfast Volunteers)

And my wife's Great Uncle, 23292 Corporal James (Jim) Donaghy MBE, 9th (Service) Battalion Royal Inniskilling Fusiliers (Tyrone Volunteers) formerly 10th (Service) Battalion Royal Inniskilling Fusiliers (Derry Volunteers)

Contents

Due to the volume of appendices attached to this volume it has been decided to make the extensive appendix 'Fatalities attached to 36th (Ulster) Division 21-31 March 1918' available as a free download. Please follow the link below to access the file:

http://www.helion.co.uk/LWiM_Appendix.pdf

List of Illustrations

List of Maps

Author's Note

Before proceeding it would be of value to give the reader some understanding of the structure of the Armies engaged in the conflict. In the Infantry of the British Army throughout the Great War, the basic formation was the Platoon. This numbered around fifty men and was commanded by a Lieutenant or Second Lieutenant assisted by a Serjeant. The Platoon was divided into four sections each commanded usually by a Corporal. There were four platoons in a Company which was commanded by a Captain and four Companies – normally identified as A, B, C and D and a Headquarters Company in a Battalion which was commanded by a Lieutenant Colonel. Within the Headquarters Company was the Battalion second-in-command known as the Adjutant, who usually held the rank of Major, the Regimental Sergeant Major and the battalion Medical Officer. At full strength a battalion numbered around 1,000 officers and men and throughout the narrative where accurate figures are available, they have been included.

At the time of the German Spring Offensive the Infantry of the British Army had undergone a reorganisation with three battalions now forming a brigade instead of four as had been the case since the outbreak of war. The brigade was commanded by a Brigadier General and there were three Infantry Brigades in a Division which was commanded by a Major General. Divisions were organised into Corps. In the case of the 36th (Ulster) Division, along with 30th and 61st Divisions they formed part of XVIII Corps commanded by Lieutenant General Sir Ivor Maxse. There were four Corps in the Fifth Army commanded by General Sir Hubert Gough. From a British and Commonwealth perspective, there were five Armies holding the front line, all commanded by Field Marshal Sir Douglas Haig, the Commander-in-Chief British Expeditionary Force.

On the German side, at battalion level the German structure was much the same with each battalion containing four companies and numbering around 1,000 Officers and men. There were three battalions and a Machine Gun Company in a Regiment. Two Regiments comprised a Brigade and there were three Brigades in a Division. Five Infantry Divisions comprised an Army Corps, one of four such Corps which were part of the German Eighteenth Army which was directly opposite the 36th (Ulster) Division. This Army was commanded by General der Infanterie Oskar von Hutier.

British ranks and their German equivalent are as follows:

Private	Grenadier/Jager/Musketier
Lance Corporal	Gefreiter
Corporal	Unteroffizier
Serjeant	Feldwebel
Staff Serjeant	VizeFeldwebel
Second Lieutenant	Leutnant
Lieutenant	Oberleutnant
Captain	Hauptmann
Major	Major
Lieutenant Colonel	Oberstleutnant
Colonel	Oberst

To simplify the narrative, I have abbreviated the titles of units. An infantry battalion will be identified by its full title in the first instance and in abbreviated form thereafter. So for example, the 9th (Service) Battalion Royal Inniskilling Fusiliers (County Tyrone Volunteers) will become 9th Inniskillings or simply the Inniskillings as appropriate. At Brigade level for example, 107th Infantry Brigade will become 107th Brigade and the 36th (Ulster) Division will become, the 36th or Ulster Division. On the German side, *Regiment der Infanterie 463* will become IR 463.

Some French place names also appear in various forms in records and publications from the time. For example, the village of Seraucourt-le-Grand frequently appears as Grand Seraucourt and Essigny-le-Grand as simply Essigny. In the narrative I have included them as they appear in records from the time.

Summer Time for the British Expeditionary Force began on the night of 9-10 March 1918, but the German Army was not scheduled to switch to summer time until the night of 14-15 April. Therefore, the clock times of the two Armies were the same during the period of the offensive.

Acknowledgements

Compiling a book can be a long and sometimes solitary process. In this instance, I could not have reached the goal of publication without the advice, practical help and assistance from a large number of people who I am delighted to acknowledge here.

Firstly, I would like to thank Duncan Rogers, Dr Michael LoCicero and the staff at Helion & Company for having the belief in this project and for their valuable advice and support which is greatly appreciated.

No account of the Ulster Division in this defining week of the war would be complete without examining the role played by the German units in direct opposition. Having obtained the German history of the offensive and the Regimental history of *Regiment der Infanterie 463*, I am greatly indebted to Jane Kenny for her meticulous translation of the relevant sections. Through her outstanding work it was possible to match accounts from the opposing forces and clarify the course of incidents particularly on the first day. In a similar vein, the use of maps and sketches provides the reader with an understanding of the area which the Ulster Division held and the wider area over which they withdrew. In creating these, I was exceptionally fortunate in being able to engage the services of Heather Browne, a gifted Graphic Designer whose interest and attention to detail has added immeasurably to the quality of this book.

In my day to day research work I often rely on the expertise of my colleague Nigel Henderson, for advice and assurance and in relation to this book I am indebted to Nigel for the provision of images of servicemen from his extensive Great War Ulster Newspaper Archive and for cross-checking the fatality figures. The ability to see a photograph of those who engaged in such momentous events one hundred years ago personalises the narrative in a unique way.

The Regimental Museums of the battalions who comprised the Division continue to be a valuable source of material and I am extremely grateful to Natasha Martin at the Royal Inniskilling Fusiliers Museum, Jonathan Maguire at the Royal Irish Fusiliers Museum and Gavin Glass at the Royal Ulster Rifles Museum, for making me feel welcome and for efficiently answering the countless questions that I posed. To Gavin at the Rifles Museum, Neil Armstrong, Curator Inniskillings Museum and Caroline Corvan, Curator Royal Irish Fusiliers Museum, many thanks for permission to use material held by each Museum. Thanks are also due to Savina Donohoe, Curator of Cavan County Museum for making me feel welcome and for answering my many questions about the Farnham family.

The various repositories of information from the Great War situated throughout these islands have proved a vital source of research material and requests for assistance and for permissions have without exception been met with a positive response. In this regard, I would like to acknowledge the assistance of the following; The National Archives, Kew, London, for unit war diaries and personal records, the Imperial War Museum, London for access to the personal papers of men attached to the Ulster Division and to Mrs Rose Hunt (nee Miller) for permission to quote from her late father Captain Charles Cecil Miller's, *A Letter to my Daughters* held by the IWM. The National Archives of Ireland, Dublin, for details of Soldiers Wills, the Commonwealth War Graves Commission for permission to use information held by them to construct the fatalities appendix and The Public Records Office Northern Ireland (PRONI) for permission to use and quote from papers held by them.

I am also especially grateful to Damien Burke at the Irish Jesuit Archives in Dublin for his assistance regarding the exceptionally detailed diaries of Father Henry Gill SJ DSO MC, Chaplain attached to 2nd Battalion Royal Irish Rifles and to Jimmy Taylor, author of histories of both 1st and 2nd Battalions Royal Irish Rifles in the Great War, whose help and advice have been invaluable.

Information contained within *The History of The 36th (Ulster) Division* (1922) by Cyril Falls has been vital to this project and I am indebted to Roy Baillie of W&G Baird for permission to use material and to quote from this iconic book. One of my favourite books concerning the Great War is *Three Cheers for the Derry's*, by Gardiner Mitchell. First published in 1991, it is exceptionally well researched in a time when some veterans were still alive and able to give first-hand accounts and the internet was a far off dream. I would like to thank Gardiner for permission to quote from some of the accounts in this excellent work.

Thanks are also due to Chris Baker, author of the Long Long Trail website, which has proved exceptionally useful for checking material, particularly unit affiliations, and the assistance of the members of the Great War Forum cannot be overlooked. I am constantly amazed by the depth of knowledge out there!

As expected, family have shown immense support throughout this project. To my sons-in-law Bill and Chris, I am indebted for your technological brilliance in relation to spreadsheets and photos which was far beyond the skills of this old Luddite. To my daughters Basti (who deftly sub-contracted work where possible) and Gaby, many thanks for your support and practical advice.

Finally, I could not have completed this work without the support of my wife Alison, whose patience knows no bounds. An excellent companion on trips to the battlefields of France. Even though the shopping opportunities in the villages around St Quentin were sparse, she never failed to source good coffee!

Michael Nugent

Introduction

Having had my first attempt at writing published in 2015, I was encouraged by the positive feedback I received from all quarters, but particularly from acknowledged experts in the Great War and the wider Inniskillings family. This encouraged me to look for a new project. With the centenary of the Somme fast approaching, I was consciously looking for an aspect of the Great War that had not been investigated in detail. I initially considered the involvement of the 16th (Irish) and 36th (Ulster) Divisions in the disastrous attack at Langemarck on 16 August 1917 however, realised quickly that the timeline would be much too short to do such a project justice. Looking beyond this, I then gave considerable thought to the March Offensive of 1918 and through initial research, realised that this was not a clear-cut defeat as has often been portrayed. As I continued to research, I became intrigued by the background factors which led to the Ulster Division facing the main thrust of the German attack on that foggy March morning. I quickly realised that there was a story to be told which heretofore has been neglected in Great War literature.

The officers and men of the 36th (Ulster) Division rightfully retain a revered place within Ulster folklore and culture. It could be argued that this is due solely to the disastrous losses suffered by the Division on the 1st July 1916 and the following days during the Battle of Albert. The losses suffered at that time had a disproportionately catastrophic impact due to the recruiting pattern of the Division at its formation in the autumn of 1914. The Ulster Volunteer Force formed the nucleus of the Division and in practice entire UVF units – men who were neighbours and work colleagues enlisted together, ensuring that in July 1916, whole neighbourhoods were decimated similar to many towns (particularly in the north of England) where 'Pals' battalions had been raised. The Ulster Division lost 1935 men killed[1] on the 1st and 2nd July and it is estimated that total casualties for the Division (dead, wounded and missing) totalled 5500. Due to the impact on the British Army and British society of the devastating casualties of that day, countless books have been devoted to every aspect of the battle,

---

1   Figures compiled by Nigel Henderson following extensive research. Further research results can be found at History Hub Ulster <http://historyhubulster.co.uk/ulster-division-somme/>.

whilst in contrast there are few devoted to the German Spring Offensive of March 1918.

What are the reasons for this? According to Brigadier General Sir James Edmonds' *The Official History of the War, Military Operations France and Belgium 1918*, (London: MacMillan & Co, 1935) the 36th (Ulster) Division sustained 7,310 casualties (dead, wounded and missing) during its period of involvement in the offensive of March 1918.[2] This figure was later revised in the following days when stragglers and those mixed up with other units returned, to 6,109. This figure may not be even correct, but what is undisputed is that the 36th sustained the greatest casualties of any Division in XVIII Corps during their seven days of fighting. It is obvious also, that this figure is greater than the highest estimate of casualties suffered at the Somme in 1916.

Is it the fact that the sacrifices of the Ulster Division were 'hidden in plain sight' due to the fact that the Ulster ethos of the Division by 1918 was much diminished and the impact of the losses had a lesser effect in the communities throughout the Province? This could be a reason, especially as the numbers killed in 1918, slightly less than 1,000, were around half the total killed in 1916. What negates this argument however, is the fact that when compared to 1916, the 1918 battle is neglected not only in relation to accounts relating to the Ulster Division, but also in relation to other units throughout the British Army.

War weariness is another factor which could be considered. By the Spring of 1918, the war had been raging for three and a half years, hundreds of thousands of men had been killed and even more seriously wounded. For the British public, after a series of bloody and ultimately exhausting offensives in 1917, there appeared to be no end in sight. Those who had lost loved ones – perhaps the sole breadwinner, or an only son, could have been forgiven for expressing little continued interest in a conflict which had torn families apart and caused untold ongoing hardship. The original battle cry of 'protecting gallant little Belgium' was long forgotten by early 1918 and the increasing appeal of Pacifism and more prevalent throughout Europe, Communism, were concrete indicators that affected populations wished to see radical change.

However, what is possibly the greatest indicator of why this is neglected subject, is that it was perceived as a defeat. For a British public inured to three years of major offensives by the Allies with varying degrees of success and subsequent jingoistic proclamations of the press, to suddenly find that your forces had lost 40 miles of ground (when offensives were judged a success when yards were gained) and that this ground had been previously painstakingly won over a number of years at the cost of countless thousands of lives, and that the Army had sustained around 160,000 casualties in the process, was sobering news. Quite simply, the British Army was not meant to retreat.

---

2   Brigadier General Sir James Edward Edmonds. *History of the Great War based on Official Documents. Military Operations France and Belgium 1918* (London: MacMillan & Company, 1935), Volume 2, p. 491.

It was not part of the fighting culture of the Empire and more disturbingly, the idea of surrendering to the hated Boche was seen as an anathema.

In the Great War, the best available records indicate that from 1914-1918 around 180,000 British officers and men were taken prisoner by the Germans. Around 21,000 of that figure were taken on the opening day of the German offensive, 21 March 1918, alone. This gives some idea of the scale of the perceived disaster. In the culture (particularly in the military) pertaining at the time, to surrender was seen as dishonourable, a sign of inherent weakness and something less than manly. In fact, as will be seen, the military had strict regulations and procedures around the subject, which impacted particularly on officers. So why publicise and herald to a war weary public that the Germans had very nearly overrun the British Army? It is for this reason I would contend that the experiences of the British Army during the Spring Offensive have been conveniently disregarded both at the time and since.

However, perception is all important here. As will be demonstrated throughout the book, this was not a catastrophic military defeat, but perhaps one of those occasions where in the main, the finest fighting qualities of the British soldier, including improvisation, loyalty and heroism were displayed. In the words of Brigadier General Sir James Edmonds, compiler of the *Official History of the War* (1935):

> The Fifth Army grew smaller owing to casualties. It bent but it never broke and all its components remained in being.[3]

This view coincides with that held by Paul Maze, a French Liaison Officer attached to the staff of General Sir Hubert Gough, Commander Fifth Army:

> All that remained of the Fifth Army were men whose bodies were tired out but whose spirits were unbroken. Not one of them looked upon himself as a beaten man.[4]

Of the publications which deal with the involvement of the Ulster Division, *The History of the 36th (Ulster) Division* by Cyril Falls – a Staff Officer with the Division and published in 1922, gives a detailed account of the experiences of the Division and although it contains some personal experiences to illustrate particular actions, it is written from a strategic military point of view. The most comprehensive contemporary account concerning the 36th (Ulster) Division I have come across is contained within Tom Johnstone's excellent, *Orange Green and Khaki. The Story of the Irish Regiments in the Great War, 1914-18*. In this book, the author gives as detailed an account as space permits, given that he also covers the experiences of the 16th (Irish) Division as well as covering the rest of the war.

---

3   Edmonds, *Military Operations France and Belgium 1918*, p. 458.
4   Edmonds, *Military Operations France and Belgium 1918*, pp. 458, 483.

The Kaiser's Battle, by Martin Middlebrook, deals comprehensively with the first day of the battle and although the Ulster Division features in the narrative, the book by necessity deals with the entire British defensive effort. In a similar vein, Jerry Murland's impressive: *Retreat and Rearguard Somme 1918. The Fifth Army Retreat,* covers as the title suggests the Fifth Army however, it contains informed accounts of the Ulster Division, particularly during actions on 21 and 24 March. Some of the experiences of the Division have also been included by Lyn MacDonald in her outstanding, *To the Last Man. Spring 1918.* The use of interviews with veterans to illustrate the course of the battle making for an easy reading style. MacDonald's primary source of information concerning the experiences of the 36th (Ulster) Division during the battle comes from Lieutenant (Later Captain) Thomas Hastings Witherow, 2nd Battalion Royal Irish Rifles.[5] Lieutenant Witherow however, was not present in the lead up to, or the commencement of the battle as he was attending a course of instruction in a town to the rear of the front lines. On answering the call to return, he arrived into a confused situation and was temporarily attached to the 9th (Service) Battalion Royal Inniskilling Fusiliers (Tyrone Volunteers) for the latter part of the battle.

Regimental and Battalion Histories by their raison d'etre, concentrate solely on their subject matter and in this regard, there are some excellent publications which draw heavily on battalion war diaries where they exist. *The Royal Inniskilling Fusiliers in the World War,* by Sir Frank Fox and published in 1928 covers the Regular 1st and 2nd Battalions as well as the 9th (Service) Battalion. Being a Regimental History of the entirety of the war however, does not afford the space for detailed analysis of the experiences of these three battalions during the 1918 offensive. This aspect in respect of the 9th Inniskillings is covered by William Canning in his informative 2006 publication, *A Wheen of Medals. The History of the 9th (Service) Battalion The Royal Inniskilling Fusiliers (The Tyrones) in World War One.* In relation to the Royal Irish Fusiliers, *The 1st Battalion The Faugh-A-Ballaghs in the Great War,* by Brigadier General Burrows was compiled shortly after the war and again whilst dealing with the entirety of the war, devotes four pages to the experiences of the 1st Battalion in March 1918. The most comprehensive and detailed narrative relating to the Royal Irish Fusiliers is contained in Nick Metcalfe's exceptional *Blacker's Boys. 9th (Service) Battalion Princess Victoria's (Royal Irish Fusiliers) (County Armagh) & 9th (North Irish Horse) Battalion, Princess Victoria's (Royal Irish Fusiliers).* The detailed description of the activities of the battalion during the offensive enhanced by personal experiences, enlighten the reader and are an enjoyable read.

A similar level of attention to detail is to be found in James Taylor's two impressive books; *The First Royal Irish Rifles in the Great War* and *The Second Royal Irish Rifles*

---

5   Thomas Witherow was born at Belfast in 1890 and educated at Campbell College and Queens University. After the war he was ordained as a Presbyterian Minister and died in 1989 aged 99.

in the Great War. The biographical detail contained within both provides a welcome human dimension to the experiences of these regular battalions of the Regiment.

Whilst there are other publications which touch on the experiences of the Division, those mentioned above contain the most detail. This however raises an issue. There are no publications which give detailed accounts of two Service battalions of the Royal Irish Rifles who played crucial roles particularly on the opening day of the offensive, the 12th (Service) Battalion Royal Irish Rifles (Central Antrim Volunteers) and the 15th (Service) Battalion Royal Irish Rifles (North Belfast Volunteers). This leaves a yawning gap in outlining the experiences of two battalions facing the initial German assault. It has been acknowledged by other commentators that relating the true story as to the events of March 1918 is impossible due to the absence of original records. Indeed Murland (2014) comments:

> There were of course hundreds of individual and unit encounters during the March retreat that never found their way into any written format and sadly remain untold to this day. Typical of these is the story of the forward posts and redoubts in the British Forward Zone on 21 March. Many of these so-called strong-points were overcome extraordinarily quickly. If they had not been subdued by the preliminary artillery bombardment then the first waves of attacking German infantry quickly overwhelmed them, often surrounding them in the fog before they had any opportunity to retaliate.[6]

The 12th and 15th Royal Irish Rifles were two such battalions who found themselves in the Forward Zone on 21 March and were the first to experience the German advance. Similarly, there are no published accounts of the 16th (Service) Battalion Royal Irish Rifles (Pioneers) many of whose members were in the front-line positions during the German attack, nor of the Entrenching Battalions – formed during the reorganisation of the army in 1918 when many of the Division's original battalions were disbanded or amalgamated. The vital role played by non – infantry units including Artillery, Engineers, Machine Gun Corps and Medical personnel also remains hidden.

The complete picture of the experiences of the 36th (Ulster) Division during the German Spring Offensive of March 1918, exists therefore in a fragmentary manner. What my intention is through this book is to draw on the existing published accounts, supplemented by research which has uncovered information which has never been presented to a wider audience to explain how the officers and men of the 36th (Ulster) Division faced the largest German offensive of the War.

Through carrying out research over a number of years, it rapidly became apparent that it would be impossible to solely concentrate on the events of the penultimate week of March 1918, without considering the issues which placed the 36th (Ulster) Division in the invidious position in which they found themselves. Research identified

---

6   Jerry Murland, *Retreat and Rearguard: Somme 1918* (Barnsley: Pen & Sword, 2014), p. xi.

a number of factors, none of which the officers and men of the Division had any influence over, which when combined created a 'perfect storm' from which the events of 21-28 March unfolded.

Each of these issues will be analysed in depth and their impact on the Division evaluated as the book progresses. They include;

- The lack of reinforcements being sent to the British Army in France due to Government intransigence.
- The reorganisation which the British Army was forced to undertake, primarily due to the above state of affairs in January 1918.
- The political as opposed to military agreement which led to the British taking over a greater proportion of the front line in February 1918.
- The imposition of a new defensive system which few at the front comprehended or had any faith in.
- The inexplicable lack of urgency displayed when it was evident that a massive German attack was imminent.
- The weather.

The Ulster Division found themselves heavily outnumbered at the opening of the battle. The peace treaty with Russia in 1917 had released hundreds of thousands of seasoned German troops who had spent the winter carrying out specialised training. The German Eighteenth Army opposite the Ulster Division were led by one of Germany's leading Generals, Oskar von Hutier, who had commanded the German forces which crushed the Russian Army at Riga the previous year. The post-war history of *Infanterie Regiment 463* who were in the vanguard of the assault on the Ulster Division has been obtained and relevant passages translated which provide a remarkable account of the experiences of the ordinary German soldier. In some instances, these records match exactly the corresponding accounts from men of the Ulster Division battalions – evidence that it is still possible to obtain a reasonably accurate view of certain events.

Research has uncovered sufficient records to construct a narrative of the experiences of the officers and men of the 36th (Ulster) Division in that fateful week in March 1918. Whilst it is impossible to give a blow by blow account of the entire seven days, the major important engagements involving the Division are examined and evaluated. These include:

- The attack on the British frontline positions on the morning of 21 March
- The fighting at the Somme crossings and in the villages south of the river on 23/24 March focusing especially on the situation on the afternoon of 24 March, when what until then had been an organised withdrawal, threatened to turn into a rout
- Fighting around the villages of Erches, Andechy and Guerbigny on 26/27 March

Some valuable accounts from men who were taken prisoner have also been obtained and these give an extraordinary insight into life as a prisoner and the various ways that the Germans dealt with a massive influx of prisoners, the numbers of which threatened to overwhelm the structures put in place for dealing with them. Research has identified all the officers taken prisoner during the offensive and these appear as an appendix.

The issue of casualties is also addressed. As highlighted above, it is extremely difficult to obtain an exact figure of casualties. However, research has been carried out to identify the number of fatalities who fell whilst serving with the Division in their involvement in the offensive and their origin – important in establishing to what extent at that time that the Division could have been described as an 'Ulster' Division. For reasons of space, the full list could not be included as an Appendix however, can be accessed via this link http://www.helion.co.uk/LWiM_Appendix.pdf

The heroism of the men of the Division during the offensive was recognised by the award of two Victoria Crosses won on 21 and 22 March 1918. The first was awarded posthumously to 2nd Lieutenant Edmund De Wind 15th Royal Irish Rifles, a native of Comber, Co. Down and the second by Lieutenant Cecil Leonard Knox, 150th Field Company, Royal Engineers[7] from Nuneaton, Warwickshire. Awards of the Distinguished Service Order, Military Cross, Distinguished Conduct Medal and Military Medal were also made and it is of no doubt that many who deserved awards went unrecognised due to the confusion existing at the time. Research indicates that it was only after the repatriation of officers who were prisoners of war that steps were put in place to recognise some of the acts of bravery which took place during the offensive. An example of this were the heroic actions of C Company, 12th Royal Irish Rifles on the opening day of the offensive which resulted in the award of one Military Cross, two Distinguished Conduct Medals and four Military Medals – all awarded after the Armistice.

When I was undertaking the task of writing my first book, *It was an Awful Sunday: The 2nd Battalion Royal Inniskilling Fusiliers at the Battle of Festubert, 15-17 May 1915*, my motivation was to tell the stories of brave men who had until now been neglected in Great War literature. On this occasion, the motivation remains the same – to bring to the attention of a wider public the exploits of ordinary men doing an extraordinary job in the face of immense odds.

---

7   121st, 122nd and 150th Field Companies Royal Engineers provided the engineering complement to 36th Division.

1

The Politics of War

War is too serious a matter to entrust to soldiers.
Georges Benjamin Clemenceau, French Prime Minister 1917-20.[1]

By the beginning of 1917, the 36th (Ulster) Division had been at the front for just over 15 months and had been severely tested at the Somme in July of the previous year. The Division was based at Ploegsteert in Belgium and was able to operate with two brigades in the line with a third able to rest and carry out training. In January, 108th Brigade were in reserve and the War Diary of the 9th (Service) Battalion Princess Victoria's (Royal Irish Fusiliers) gives some insight of how this time was spent. As well as route marches, bomb and musketry training, there was also plenty of time for recreational activities. On 17 January 1917, the war diary records the results of inter – battalion competitions:

B Coy won Football & Bayonet fighting
C Coy won Boxing
D Coy won Cross Country running[2]

The following evening, the officers held a battalion dinner in the Canon D'Or restaurant at Bailleul. Guests from the Brigade staff and other units were invited and the war diary records that following dinner, there were toasts to the King and the French President and then speeches. Then:

1 Quoted in *Clemenceau and the Third Republic,* by John Hampden Jackson (London: Hodder & Stoughton/English Universities Press, 1946) p. 228.
2 The National Archives (TNA) WO 95/2502/2: 9th (Service) Battalion Princess Victoria's (Royal Irish Fusiliers) war diary.

After dinner a few choruses were sung, and the proceedings terminated at 10:30
p.m. with Auld Lyne Sang, the Marseillaise and God Save the King.[3]

At the end of the month it was back to the front line. Following a harsh winter, preparations were underway for the forthcoming first summer offensive which would become
known as the Battle of Messines. Little did the officers and men of the Division know
as they toiled erecting barbed wire defences through and around Ploegsteert Wood,
that strategic events taking place across Europe at that time would have consequences
for them a year further down the line.

By the beginning of 1917, the war had been grinding on for close to two and a half
years with the stalemate of trench warfare ongoing for two years. From mid-1915 on
the Western Front, British and Allied forces had embarked on a 'War of Attrition'.
This was a long term plan to wear out the enemy and exhaust his resources before
embarking on a decisive offensive action. Key to this plan was the keenly awaited
arrival of the vast resources of the United States to bolster the war effort.

The United States had been initially reluctant to be dragged into the ongoing conflict
and had adopted a position of armed neutrality, a position that became increasingly
untenable in early 1917 due to repeated attacks on United States flagged ships by
German submarines. The United States finally declared war on Germany and her
allies on 6 April 1917. Whilst it could be justifiably claimed that Britain was unpre-
pared at the start of the war, the United States was even more unready. The United
States Army numbered just under 250,000 and was untrained and ill-equipped to
go to war. It was estimated that by April 1918, 10 to 12 American Divisions would
be available, with these only suitably trained to relieve troops in quiet areas. It was
also estimated that it would be a year before American troops took part in any offensive action. Whilst the Allies were frustrated at this estimate, the German High
Command were acutely aware that the clock was ticking.

Russia meanwhile, had been part of the Entente Cordiale since the outbreak of
war and were engaging (with various degrees of success) large numbers of German
troops on the Eastern Front. Disillusionment with the war amongst the populace
was compounded by the exceptionally harsh winter of 1916-17. Food and the means
to distribute it to civilians across the country were subservient to the war effort and
the needs of the Army. This caused increasing disenchantment to a populace who had
endured two years of war with no apparent hope of a breakthrough and this resent-
ment was seized upon by political agitators who encouraged dissent amongst civilians
and soldiers alike. By April 1917, the Russian Provisional Government declared in
favour of self-determination of peoples and a durable peace.

By May, even whilst the British Army was still engaged at Arras, the Chief of the
Imperial General Staff General Sir William Robertson, presented a paper to the War

3   TNA: WO 95/2502/2. 9th Royal Irish Fusiliers war diary

Cabinet entitled, '*The Military Effect of Russia Seceding from the Entente.*'[4] In this paper he stated:

> While it may yet be too early to despair altogether of further military assistance from her, if these disintegrating tendencies (pacifist and revolutionary ideas) continue, they must greatly impair her capacity for continuing the War, and may ultimately render it impossible for her to do so; for it is folly to suppose that an army without discipline and efficient services of maintenance can have any fighting value worthy of the name.

Further on in the paper he issued the following prescient warning:

> It must be assumed that the whole of the German Army on the Eastern Front will be available for operations in the West.

This was the first warning that political events elsewhere would conspire against the British military effort. This warning was effectively ignored and no action was taken until General Robertson raised the issue again in July of 1917, but again the warning fell on deaf ears. By this time, the Russian military had continued to show a marked lack of enthusiasm to continue the fight against the Germans. Finally, on 26 October 1917, Lenin signed a decree for peace and proposed the immediate withdrawal of Russia from the war which came into effect in December 1917. This gave the Germans the important boost that they were looking for, as it freed up hundreds of thousands of troops from Russia who could be directed to the Western Front, prior to the arrival of the Americans.

The effect of the Russian action had implications for the French Army also. By the beginning of 1917 the strain of war was beginning to show on the French Army. This was characterised by extended periods in the trenches, too short or cancelled periods of leave, inadequate or irregular pay and poor medical and hospital arrangements. Allied to this, subversive and defeatist propaganda was directed at the army by activists and agitators emboldened by the success of protests in Russia. This had the effect of a further deterioration in morale and a situation that was ripe for revolt.

Aware of the unrest, General Robert Nivelle the French Commander in Chief, gambled on a successful offensive to win the troops over. The offensive began on 16 April and was known as the Battle of Chemin-des-Dames after the ridge of the same name, one of the objectives for the battle. Although initially successful, heavy casualties and the absence of a decisive victory pushed the Army into mutinous actions. The mutiny was widespread with many men deserting and others refusing to go back

---

4   Brigadier General Sir James E Edmonds, *History of the Great War based on Official Documents. Military Operations France and Belgium 1918* (London: MacMillan & Co Ltd, 1935) p. 2.

into the lines. In total the mutiny affected 68 French Divisions. As a result, General Nivelle was sacked and replaced by General Philippe Petain, who placated the mutineers by personally touring Divisions and listening to grievances. One gesture he made to resolve the situation was to implement a scheme to ensure that soldiers received 10 days leave every four months – a much greater allocation than that afforded to British troops who were lucky to get 10 days leave in a year. In a move which had massive implications for the British on the Western Front, Petain implored the British Commander in Chief, Field Marshal Sir Douglas Haig, to take over the main thrust of offensives on the Western Front throughout 1917 to give the French Army time to recover and reorganise. Of strategic interest is the fact that the German Army never realised that the French Army was in a state of mutiny. Had it done so, the course of the war could have been very different. From a British point of view, the approval given by the War Cabinet to Field Marshal Haig to continue the Flanders campaign in 1917 was on the express condition that the French army would participate. This was now not the case, but Field Marshal Haig, buoyed by intelligence reports indicating that German casualties were running at a rate that would eventually prove untenable, decided to continue the campaign regardless.

On 25 September 1917, the British and French Prime Ministers, David Lloyd George and Paul Painleve met at Boulogne accompanied by their respective Chiefs of Staff – General Sir William Robertson and General Ferdinand Foch. At this meeting, Robertson's concerns about Russia were again raised and it was agreed to investigate the situation further. Reporting on the state of the French Army following the mutiny, Prime Minister Painleve pointed out that French casualties after successive failed offensives had reached a precarious state, 54,000 per month, amounting to 650,000 in a year and that only 225,000 reinforcements were available to replace them.[5] What Painleve was trying to achieve was something that the French had been pressing for since the British Expeditionary Force had landed in France in August 1914, a promise that the British would commit more to the war effort. His suggestion was that the British should take over more of the front line to enable the French Army to recuperate.

Lloyd George was sympathetic to Painleve and saw this as a means to restrict the offensive capabilities of Sir Douglas Haig. The relationship between the Prime Minister and his Commander in Chief was frosty at best. An avowed Westerner, Douglas Haig had been wedded to a policy of attrition since he was an Army Commander in 1915 and held the belief that the Germans could only be defeated by victory on the Western Front. He saw other campaigns such as Gallipoli and Salonica as sideshows with no inherent value which only served to deplete valuable resources required for the Western Front. Whilst the policy of attrition combined with the naval blockade of German ports was having a degree of success, progress was slow and the casualty rate was horrendous. By contrast, Lloyd George saw the opportunity of

5   Edmonds, *Military Operations France and Belgium 1918*, p. 11.

opening other fronts against the Germans as a key to 'knocking the props' from under the German war effort and he was keen not to provide his Commander in Chief with further resources, which in his opinion would be utilised in costly offensives for no appreciable gain.

Without recourse to consultation with Haig, the conference recorded:

> The British Government, having accepted in principle the extension of the line by the British Army on the Western Front, the two Governments are agreed that the question of the amount of the extension and the time at which it should take place, should be left for arrangements between the two Commanders in Chief.[6]

The following day, Lloyd George visited Sir Douglas Haig. Revisiting General Robertson's concerns, he asked for the submission of options in the event of Russia ceasing to be a viable ally. He mentioned the French desire that the British should take over more of the line – neglecting to say that this course had already been decided. To this suggestion, Haig replied that the Government should oppose doing anything of the sort until plans for 1918 were decided.

Haig's reaction when he received a letter from General Robertson outlining the decision that the British were to take over more line from the French can only be imagined. In his diary entry of 3 October 1917, he recorded:

> A great bombshell arrived in the shape of a letter from CIGS stating that the British Government had 'approved in principle' of the British Army...taking over more line from the French, and details are to be arranged by General Petain and myself. This was settled at a conference at Boulogne on 25 September at which I was not present. Nor did either LG or Robertson tell me of this decision at our interview. All the PM said was that 'Painleve was anxious that the British should take over more line.'[7]

Incensed by what he saw as interference in his prosecution of the war, Douglas Haig incorporated his frustrations into his response to the request for the options should Russia disengage from the war submission. In an eight-page letter, Sir Douglas Haig reiterated his view that the Germans must be dealt with on the Western Front and that the offensives to date in 1917 had degraded the German defenders substantially, to the extent that intelligence indicated that replacements were of an inferior quality. Striking an optimistic note, he continued:

---

6   Ibid.
7   Gary Sheffield & John Bourne (eds.) *Douglas Haig. War Diaries and Letters 1914-1918* (London: Weidenfeld & Nicholson, 2005) p. 331.

Under such conditions, we should enter next year's offensive on the Western Front with excellent prospects of decisive success if we throw onto the scale wholeheartedly the full weight of the empire's strength and if Russia can contain on her front even the number of German Divisions now there.[8]

On the request from the French for the British to take over a further stretch of front line he gave vent to his frustrations:

The French authorities will no doubt insist strongly on an extension of our front, but the weight of argument is all against it and our troops are entitled to be protected against what is really an unfair demand on them. They are in a foreign country, the French are at home. They get little leave and at long intervals. The French soldiers get ten days leave every four months and their Government dare not refuse it. Our men have borne more and accomplished more than the French this summer and though France may plead that the weight of the war has fallen on her, it cannot be expected that the British soldiers in the field who have done so much and borne so much and who have come voluntarily from the ends of the earth to fight in France will be content to see preferential treatment given to our allies.[9]

Countering the argument from the French that the length of front line held by them was much greater, he stated:

The actual extent of front measured by miles is no test of what we should hold. The true test is the relative number of enemy divisions engaged by us and still more, the role to be allotted to us in next year's campaign. For all these reasons, it is necessary in my opinion to refuse to take over more line and to adhere resolutely to that refusal, even to the points of answering threats with threats if necessary.[10]

Haig's opinion fell on deaf ears. In Lloyd George, he faced a man who was implacably opposed to Haig's strategy of attritional warfare. The Prime Minister was horrified by the massive casualties sustained during the 1917 offensives and particularly the slog at the Third Battle of Ypres, which was just drawing to an ineffective conclusion. He adhered to the French view that having been on the offensive throughout 1917, it would be better for the allies to take a defensive posture on the Western Front for the six months or so that it would take American forces to be prepared for action.

Lloyd George's position was given a boost on 24 October 1917 by a surprise attack by Austro-Hungarian forces strongly supported by German troops, which routed the

8   Edmonds, *Military Operations France and Belgium 1918*, Appendix 1.
9   Ibid.
10   Ibid.

Italian Army at Caporetto.[11] This necessitated urgent action by the Allies to support the Italians and forced Douglas Haig to despatch two Divisions from the Western Front on 27 October, followed by a further two on 7 November accompanied by Artillery and two squadrons of the Royal Flying Corps.

The Battle of Caporetto is of significance when the fate of the 36th (Ulster) Division and the prosecution of the German Spring Offensive is considered. The Austro-Hungarian forces who were barely managing against the Italians, were supplemented at the end of September by six Divisions released from the command of General von Hutier on the Eastern Front. These troops were fresh from success at the Battle of Riga on 3 September 1917, when German troops routed the Russian Army aided by a precise Artillery barrage. This bombardment was designed and managed by Colonel Georg Bruchmuller, Artillery Commander 8th Army, of whom we will hear substantially more in relation to the Spring Offensive.

The attack at Caporetto was a portent of things to come in March 1918. German and Austrian troops attacked in misty conditions following a bombardment of high explosive, gas and smoke. Infiltration tactics used at Riga were again employed, utilising groups of lightly armed soldiers making maximum use of grenades, light machine-guns and flamethrowers to advance as far as possible. By the end of the first day the joint force had advanced 15 miles, an astounding achievement in the context of the war at that time.

Having had to send resources to bolster the Italians which he could ill-afford, Haig received another hammer blow on 3 November with the arrival of a letter from the War Office concerning reinforcements for the forthcoming year. The contents of the letter indicated that recruiting would be unable to keep pace with demands and that by 1 October 1918, the deficit in troops would reach 259,000.[12] To add to Haig's exasperation was the statement that only 140,000 troops would be available in France by 1 April 1918. The problem was that Divisions were already running on limited manpower and few frontline battalions were anywhere near their active service strength of 1,000 officers and men. Haig was aware however, that the slow release of replacements for the front was another manoeuvre by Lloyd George to negate his ability to plan and commence any large-scale offensives in the early months of 1918. The rationale of the War Office, fully supported by the Prime Minister, was based on the following:

1.   There were other theatres to consider as well as the Western Front.
2.   A majority of the reserves currently in training were 'lads' under 19.[13]
3.   If men were sent to the front they would only be used in indecisive operations.

---

11   Caporetto is now named Kobarid and is located in what is now Slovenia.
12   Edmonds, *Military Operations France and Belgium 1918*, Appendix 4.
13   Following a furore in 1915 over the numbers of soldiers under 18 who had been killed, principally at Neuve Chapelle, Aubers Ridge and Festubert, a campaign was begun which resulted in the War Office directing that those under 19 years of age should not serve overseas.

Where Lloyd George's rationale was deficient however, was in the failure to take into account the fact that reserves were not only needed to bolster Divisions for offensive action, but also to maintain the strength of those units simply holding the line at the front. Towards the end of 1917 after the major offensives of that year, all Divisions were understrength and whilst holding positions still had to deal with men sick, on leave and on courses, further weakening their strength and their ability to successfully perform even the most routine defensive actions. What was lost on the Prime Minister was the fact that newly recruited men required time to acclimatise and to be taught the realities of front-line fighting – markedly different than anything experienced in training. The Prime Minister's decision-making was ridiculed by General Sir Hubert Gough, Commander Fifth Army. In his 1934 book *The March Retreat*, he stated:

> Nevertheless, hundreds of thousands of men were still retained under arms in England – kept there partly from a ridiculous fear of a German invasion, and partly because the cabinet did not desire to trust Haig with any more men, blaming him for all that 1917 had cost the British. This seems both a weak and an unjust attitude for Mr Lloyd George and his colleagues to have taken up. The battles of 1917 had been fought with the knowledge and consent of the Cabinet and at the particular demand of the French.[14]

In his reply to the War Office dated 24 November 1917, Sir Douglas Haig highlighted that:

> It is evident from calculations based on previous experience that the British Infantry in France will be approximately 250,000 or about 40 percent below establishment on the 31st March next. It will be fully recognized that under such conditions not only will the offensive power of the British Armies in France be completely paralysed, but their defensive power will be curtailed, and they will not be able to hold the same amount of line as heretofore.[15]

Further on in his reply, the Commander in Chief illustrated how the deficiency in manpower would affect the Infantry down to battalion level, where he reasoned that an infantry battalion would be reduced to 542 officers and men – just over half its active service strength. To manage this deficiency, Sir Douglas Haig advised that it would be necessary to break up five Corps and 15 Divisions, a drastic move which he was loathe to contemplate, as the Division was the basis of the Infantry and had stood

---

14   General Sir Hubert Gough, *The March Retreat* (London: Cassell, 1934) p.39. Seen as an unfortunate scapegoat by many for the events of March 1918, Gough had a particular axe to grind with both the Prime Minister at the time and his administration.

15   Edmonds, *Military Operations France and Belgium 1918*, p. 17.

the test of time in extremely demanding conditions. In conclusion, he stressed the necessity of swift action:

> My plans for holding the line and the dispositions of the troops for the winter depend on this matter being settled <u>now</u>. Moreover, arrangements cannot be made for divisions to take their turn for rest and training out of the line until the number of divisions to be maintained has been decided, whilst Divisions themselves cannot train properly if they are very much below establishment. It is all important that no time should be lost to put into effect such measures of re-organisation as may be considered necessary, and if the additional men to keep divisions up to their establishment will not be forthcoming, I shall be glad if I might be informed as early as possible in order that I may forthwith submit definite proposals for the disbandment of certain divisions. Meanwhile, I trust that the gravity of the situation and the effect the shortage of men has already had and will continue to have in the conduct of the campaign on the Western Front is fully appreciated by His Majesty's Government.[16]

In his final sentence, Sir Douglas Haig hinted pointedly that those directing efforts from the War Office were ignorant of the issues of managing an Army in the field. Whilst he was most likely correct, Lloyd George had set his face against releasing adequate numbers of replacements and so Field Marshal Haig's impassioned plea fell on deaf ears. Lloyd George's decision also ran contrary to the advice of the Army Council, a body comprising senior military and civilian figures which was established to advise the War Cabinet on military issues. In a report to the War Cabinet they gave the following prophetic warning:

> There is every prospect of heavy fighting on the Western front from February onwards and the result may be that even if the divisions successfully withstand the shock of the earlier attack, they may become so exhausted and attenuated as to be incapable of continuing the struggle until the Americans can effectively intervene.[17]

On 7 December, having received no positive news on reinforcements, Field Marshal Haig chaired a conference of Army Commanders at Doullens, northern France, the main topic for discussion being the reorganisation of the defensive line in view of the Russians having dropped out of the war. Highlighting the efforts of the British and Commonwealth forces throughout 1917, he noted in his diary:

16   Ibid.
17   Edmonds, *Military Operations France and Belgium 1918*, p. 53.

It is just 6 months today since I held the last conference with Army Commanders at Doullens (7 May) and issued orders for the offensive against Messines etc. We expected at that time help from Russia, Italy and France!! In reality the British Army has had to bear the brunt of it all. I added that we (Commanders) might well be proud of the achievements of the Armies this year and I thanked them one and all for their help and support.[18]

With no prospect of the required resources being allocated and time very much of the essence, there was no alternative but to undertake the massive task which had been imposed upon him for political reasons, to restructure the Army.

18   Gary Sheffield and John Bourne (eds.) *Douglas Haig. War Diaries and Letters 1914-1918* (London: Weidenfeld & Nicolson, 2005) p. 358.

2

Reorganisation

We trained hard, but it seemed that every time we were beginning to form up into teams we would be reorganized. Presumably the plans for our employment were being changed. I was to learn later in life that, perhaps because we are so good at organizing, we tend as a nation to meet any new situation by reorganizing; and a wonderful method it can be for creating the illusion of progress while producing confusion, inefficiency and demoralisation.

Charles Ogburn[1]

The full implications of the scheming taking place at a strategic level were about to be visited on the unsuspecting Ulstermen of the 36th Division. It would be a massive undertaking to reorganise an entire branch of the Army in peacetime. It would certainly involve committees and lengthy meetings where the pros and cons of each action would be discussed at length. In the prevailing circumstances, to undertake such a task in the middle of a war, in a finite timescale, where you had been recently let down by your allies and were basically standing alone, could be described as bizarre at best.

However, this was the situation facing Field Marshal Douglas Haig at the end of 1917. He had the added urgency of the expectation that a German offensive was looming, as was the decision imposed upon him to arrange to take over more of the front line currently held by the French. There was no time to lose and critical decisions had to be made to arrange an effective Infantry structure without the benefit of time to reflect and consider.

Manpower and levels of recruitment had always been an issue for the 36th (Ulster) Division. In the first days of the war in August 1914, the recently appointed Secretary

---

1   Charles Ogburn was a US Journalist who had served in Burma during World War II. The quote is taken from an article which he had written entitled 'Merrill's Marauders' which appeared in the January 1957 edition of Harper's Magazine. <https://www.harpers.org/archive/1957/01/merrill's-maurauders/ > (Accessed 9 October 2017).

of State for War, Field Marshal Lord Kitchener, requested that the Ulster Volunteers raise a Brigade for service overseas. The then Captain James Craig,[2] assured him that a Division could be recruited and he and Colonel Thomas Edgecumbe Hickman, a Conservative MP and Inspector General of the Ulster Volunteer Force, were appointed as Recruiting Officers to make good their promise. Recruiting began at the beginning of September 1914 however, they faced an immediate problem. On 5 August 1914, the day after the outbreak of war, Sir Edward Carson had sent a telegram to the Secretary of the Ulster Unionist Council:

> All officers, non-commissioned officers and men who are enrolled in the Ulster Volunteer Force and who are liable to be called out by His Majesty for service in the present crisis, are requested to answer immediately His Majesty's call, as our first duty as loyal subjects is to the King.[3]

This led to numbers of experienced officers and men enlisting in established Irish Regiments and also travelling to the mainland to enlist in Scots and English regiments with whom they had a connection. This early enlistment led to a shortage of experienced officers and non-commissioned officers which was to bedevil the Ulster Division in its early days.

Craig's boast that he could raise a Division was fairly easy to achieve. An Infantry Division at full strength numbered around 17,500 men. In his respected *History of the 36th (Ulster) Division*, Falls (1922) states:

> At the outbreak of war, the Ulster Volunteer Force contained over 80,000 men between the ages of seventeen and sixty-five, and a number of women, enrolled not only as nurses but for many of those supplementary services which were not allotted to women in the European War until a comparatively late period.[4]

Progressive it may have been, but it could be argued that even with those enlisting in regular Army battalions and if those towards the upper end of the age scale were discounted and remained as a form of Home Guard, the Ulster Volunteer Force should have been able to put not one, but two complete Divisions in the field. There were however competing priorities, both practical and cynical. As the local economy focused heavily on agriculture, there were many Farmer's sons, eminently eligible to enlist, but who remained at home to manage the farms which may not have survived or been productive had they enlisted. There were also those who saw the Ulster Volunteer

---

2   Later to become Sir James Craig, the first Prime Minister of Northern Ireland.
3   David R. Orr and David Truesdale, *Ulster will fight…The 36th (Ulster) Division from Formation to the Armistice* (Solihull: Helion and Company, 2016) p. 25.
4   Cyril Falls, *The History of the 36th (Ulster) Division* (Belfast: McCaw, Stevenson and Orr, 1922) p. 2.

Advertisement for recruits
for the Ulster Division.
(*The Ballymena Observer*,
31 December 1915)

ULSTER DIVISION.

The General Officer Commanding the Ulster Division, now at the Front, writes as follows :—

"On behalf of Ulstermen in the Field, I beg you will tell our Ulstermen at home that we are counting on them to keep us up to our numbers in trained men.

"We must not let it be said of us that we failed in the undertaking that we took on ourselves, to give an Ulster Divi·ion for service of the King."

RALLY TO THE COLOURS
AND JOIN THE
20th Reserve Battalion Royal Irish Rifles

Now being formed at BALLYKINLAR CAMP, Co. Down, under the Command of LIEUTENANT-COLONEL T. V. P. M'CAMMON.

Exceptional opportunities are afforded to smart men who join a new Battalion at the commencement.

Men enlisting in the above Battalion, when trained, will as far as possible be sent to join either the 13th Batt. Royal Irish Rifles (Down Volunteers), or the 16th Batt. Royal Irish Rifles (Pioneers).

GOD SAVE THE KING.

52-53

Force as the last line of defence against the imposition of Home Rule. Their argument was that if everyone enlisted, who would be left to defend the country? To these people, contrary to Carson's call, country came first, not King.

If only one Division was to be formed, it is evident that there should have been adequate numbers to sustain it throughout the war, even given the worst projected casualty figures. This however, appears not to have been the case and concerns over recruiting in Ireland were evident even before the Battle of the Somme.

The advertisement pictured appeared in *The Ballymena Observer* on 31 December 1915. The quote from the General Officer Commanding leaves the reader in no doubt as to the severity of the situation, and this was only 11 weeks after the Division had arrived on the Western Front and were yet to take part in any major engagements.

On 1 May 1916, the Adjutant General of the British Army Sir Nevil Macready,[5] wrote a conciliatory letter of his concerns to Sir Edward Carson:

> As you are no doubt aware the recruiting situation in Ireland has been far from satisfactory and has given the War Office authorities a good deal of anxiety...I

5   Affectionately known as 'Make Ready', Sir Nevil had been General Officer Commanding Belfast District in 1914, prior to the outbreak of War.

venture to ask whether you could see your way to attend a small conference which I thought of holding in my office to discuss the whole question. I propose to ask Mr Redmond to attend, as I feel that if in full possession of your view and his views, it would be a great way to help us to overcome the difficulties that exist.[6]

The mention of John Redmond, MP for the Irish Parliamentary Party and leader of the Irish National Volunteers, who had been largely responsible for exhorting the Irish Volunteers to enlist – most notably in the 16th (Irish) Division, set alarm bells ringing for Carson. He immediately used his political connections to approach the Prime Minister, David Lloyd George, who replied to his concerns on 7 June 1916:

> There is no intention of breaking up the Ulster Division and I hope there never will be. There is some difficulty regarding the provision of drafts and on this question the Adjutant General hopes to see you shortly...[7]

Following the catastrophic casualties suffered by the 36th (Ulster) Division in July 1916 and the 16th (Irish) Division in September of 1916, the need for some form of action on recruiting gathered impetus. In September 1916, the Adjutant General reported that the Irish Divisions were 17,194 men understrength,[8] and one of the options being actively considered in the absence of extending conscription to Ireland, was the amalgamation of the 36th (Ulster) Division with the 16th (Irish) Division. This was a solution that was clearly an anathema to both Carson and Redmond. If such a decision was unacceptable to those in the political sphere, to those entrusted with the actual fighting, such a course of action made sense. In a letter to Sir Nevil Macready on 6 October 1916, the commander of the 36th (Ulster) Division, Major General Oliver Nugent (a Cavan man who had been instrumental in raising the Cavan Ulster Volunteer Force) struck a conciliatory tone – perhaps aware that any dallying could see both Irish Divisions disappear:

> You may remember telling me that Carson had said he would prefer to see the Ulster Division absorbed in a Highland Division instead of seeing them amalgamated with the 16th should the necessity arise. I have thought this over and I am sure that it would be disastrous from the point of view of Ireland. It would mean the complete disappearance of two Irish Divisions and it would be read as an admission that the two Irish Divisions could not combine, that Irish creeds and politics were carried into the firing line. It would be a libel on both Divisions. There are no politics whatever and I am sure that there would be no better cure

6   PRONI: D1507/A/16/2.
7   PRONI: D1507/A/17/10.
8   Timothy Bowman, *Irish Regiments in the Great War, Discipline and Morale* (Manchester: Manchester University Press, 2003) p. 141.

for Irish home troubles than that Protestants and Catholics should fight together in the same unit. If we do get compulsory service in Ireland, I sincerely hope that the Ulster Division will not be exclusively supplied from one creed. I hope that all creeds and politics will be drafted into it. It will then be really representative and not as at present with too much flavour of a time which I hope is dead and buried. If however the question of amalgamation becomes imperative, I hope the 16th and 36th will be amalgamated and that there may be at least one Irish Division. I am sure that this will be the view of Officers and men of both Divisions and I have written to Carson to tell him so.[9]

Sir Edward Carson remained wedded to his position and with the issue rumbling on with no sign of progress being made, an increasingly exasperated Adjutant General again wrote to Sir Edward Carson on 16 October 1916:

I am truly sorry to read from your letter of 10th inst. that you think there is no hope of compulsory service being extended to Ireland. The position therefore as regards the future of the Irish Divisions and Regiments appears to be one of the following alternatives. 1. Amalgamation, 2. Drafts from Great Britain, 3. The Divisions should be allowed to waste away or 4. Transferring Irish units from non-Irish to Irish units.[10]

Sir Edward Carson was right in one thing – there was no hope of conscription being extended to Ireland, being opposed by all shades of political opinion and many in high office, most notably King George V himself.[11] In the event, as in many other situations pertaining to Ireland, the path of least resistance was taken and the issue was resolved by a combination of options 2 and 4 above.

Little action was taken in this regard until after the Battle of Messines in June 1917, ironically the attack where the Division suffered the least casualties of any of the attacks they participated in during the war. Even before the attack, in May of 1917 a decision had been taken by the War Office to reduce the number of Cavalry units across the army, as unable to carry out their traditional role, they had been utilised as guides and for reconnaissance duties. One of the units earmarked to be dismounted was the 2nd North Irish Horse.[12] By mid-July 1917 the officers and men

9   PRONI: D1507/A/19/16.
10   PRONI: D1507/A/19/19.
11   In a meeting with Sir Douglas Haig at GHQ in France on 29 March 1918 the King stated that he was opposed to forcing conscription on Ireland. This was contrary to the view of Sir Douglas Haig who was in favour, not only to get the extra men, but for the good of Ireland. Gary Sheffield and John Bourne (eds.) *Douglas Haig, War Diaries and Letters 1914-1918* (London: Weidenfeld and Nicholson, 2005) p. 395.
12   The North Irish Horse was a part-time yeomanry regiment formed in 1908. It had deployed with the BEF in August 1914. For further details see Phillip Tardif, *The North*

of the unit were informed that they were to be transferred to Infantry duty. Soon afterwards they dismounted and travelled to the 36th Division depot at Harfleur near Le Havre for training as infantry. Training completed, they were posted with a few exceptions en masse to the 9th (Service) Battalion Royal Irish Fusiliers. A total of 569 officers and men joining in September and October 1917. In deference to their origins, the battalion was renamed the 9th (North Irish Horse) Battalion Princess Victoria's (Royal Irish Fusiliers).

Other units also received non-Ulster reinforcements. On 2 July 1917, the War Diary of the 14th (Service) Battalion Royal Irish Rifles (Young Citizen Volunteers) recorded in a none to complimentary manner:

> One officer and 78 other ranks, mostly men 'combed out' from the Army Service Corps at home reported for duty.[13]

It may have been some of these men who became known in the 14th as the 'Gawd blimey brigade' in reference to their London origins. Around the same time the 15th Battalion Royal Irish Rifles also received a draft from the 25th (London) Regiment. Such drafts rarely received a warm welcome to their new units and were regarded as outsiders, especially within the tightly knit Ulster Division. Those who had been conscripted were looked down on particularly by those who had volunteered from the outbreak of war.

A few days later on 4 July, Major General Nugent met with King George V at Kemmel in Belgium, in an event staged for the King to meet his Divisional Commanders and Brigadiers. The King enquired if the Ulster Division was receiving any Ulstermen to which General Nugent replied, 'None'. When asked why it was still called the Ulster Division, General Nugent replied, 'any Englishmen coming to us were as keen to belong to us as any Ulsterman and were quite proud of being in the 'Ulsters'.[14]

The first movement of an Irish unit into the Division took place at the end of July 1917, when a regular Army battalion, the 1st Battalion Royal Irish Fusiliers joined the 36th (Ulster) Division, being initially posted to 107th Infantry Brigade. There was little warning of the move, with the battalion war diary recording:

> 31 July. Working parties as usual. The Commanding Officer was informed that the battalion was to leave the Division at short notice.[15]

Irish Horse in the Great War (Barnsley: Pen & Sword, 2015)
13   TNA: WO 95/2511/1: 14th Battalion Royal Irish Rifles war diary.
14   PRONI: D3835/E/2/13/22.
15   TNA: WO 95/1482/1: 1st Battalion Royal Irish Fusiliers war diary.

It was short notice indeed. Having been part of 4th Division since embarking for France on 23 August 1914, two days after being informed of the move, the battalion marched to the railway station at Arras, being played there by the pipes and drums of battalions they were leaving behind. The Fusiliers joined the 36th Division at Poperinghe, west of Ypres in Belgium and commenced a period of training.

It was following the involvement of the Ulster Division in the Battle of Langemarck on 16 August 1917, that the issue of reinforcements became critical. The Division was intended to take part in this battle as fresh troops, with the original date for the battle being 14 August. However, from the beginning of the offensive (known as the 3rd Battle of Ypres or more commonly, Passchendaele) on 31 July 1917, unseasonal torrential rain began and continued for days. The Divisions involved in the initial advance became so exhausted by the conditions that the 36th (Ulster) Division was moved up to the front to assist. They remained there in horrendous conditions and under more or less continuous shellfire for 12 days, until their turn came to carry on the advance. In a letter to his wife on 4 August, Major General Nugent described the conditions endured by the troops:

> We have all moved up and taken the place of the Division which was in front of us, so we are now in the front and the next move falls to us. The weather conditions are simply indescribable. I went up this morning to the front and it is really pitiful to see the conditions in which these unlucky men are living. The whole country has been ploughed up by shellfire, all drains stopped and there is nothing but water and mud everywhere.[16]

The advance which the Division was due to undertake on 14 August was postponed due to the weather conditions until 16 August. Unsurprisingly, the battalions were severely depleted even before they advanced and the attack carried out in a sea of mud made no appreciable gains. Such were the casualties in these first two weeks of August and the lack of suitable reinforcements, that urgent action had to be taken to reinforce the Division. On 28 August 1917, the 8th and 9th Battalions Royal Irish Rifles were amalgamated to become the 8/9th Royal Irish Rifles and at midnight on 13 November 1917, the 11th and 13th Battalions Royal Irish Rifles amalgamated to become the 11/13th Royal Irish Rifles.

On the same date, another regular Irish Battalion joined the Division. The 2nd Battalion Royal Irish Rifles had embarked for France as part of the original British Expeditionary Force on 13 August 1914 and at the time of transfer were attached to 25th Division. As a regular Army battalion which recruited from across the island, not all were impressed by the thought of the move. The battalion Roman Catholic Chaplain, Father Henry Gill noted:

16   PRONI: D3835/E/2/13/22.

Our repose was disturbed by some bad news which reached us. We were to be transferred into the 36th (Ulster) Division. This news came as a surprise and disagreeable shock to almost everyone in the battalion... The prospect of a change into a political division was not pleasant, nor did the outlook appear very bright. Everything possible was done to have the decision changed, but without success.[17]

There were those within the 2nd Rifles who were keen to emphasise their nationality. Second Lieutenant John Lucy from Cork who had enlisted as a private soldier in Belfast before the war, described his return to the battalion after a period of leave which coincided with the move:

I had all kinds of commissions to perform for my fellows in France, one special request being to bring out a supply of Irish flags with harps only inscribed on them. I bought them in an umbrella shop in Cork. Our battalion was due to be transferred to the Ulster Division, which was considered poisonously loyal by many of our southern officers, hence the flags. The battalion was in bivouac east of Arras in reserve for the battle of Cambrai when I got back, and it had already been transferred to the Ulster Division. We gave a great dinner the night before the battle and invited a good many officers of the Ulster Division to join us. They came and affected no surprise at our very Irish table, decorated with green flags and other national emblems, and we had a very merry evening.[18]

The regular battalions took some time to bed in with their new comrades and a perceived slight by the Divisional Commander did not help matters, as Father Gill recorded:

The most important domestic event of this time was the inspection of the Divisional Commander. Since our arrival into the Division, he had taken no notice of the battalion. Having been through so much and being accustomed to compliments, this action was resented. When he did come, his speech was such as to still further annoy the men. Some of them had decorated their billets with the sign of the Division – a red hand. He had hardly gone when it was noticed that the red hands disappeared and in their place was put the sign of the 25th Division which they had just left![19]

17   Irish Jesuit Archives (IJA) CHP 1/28 p. 154.
18   John Francis Lucy, *There's a Devil in the Drum* (Uckfield: Naval & Military Press, 1993 reprint of 1938 edition), p. 378.
19   IJA CHP 1/27 p. 153.

Until the end of 1917, the reorganisation which had taken place had been to solve the issue of the lack of reinforcements coming from Ireland. Now came the impact of the reorganisation of the Infantry battalions of the British Army.

At Divisional command level, it was an open secret that massive changes were coming to the Infantry Divisions. Major General Nugent had serious concerns about the future composition of his Division and shared these views candidly in a letter to the Adjutant General, Sir Nevil Macready on 11 December 1917 in which he obviously hoped to influence the decision-making process:

> Is there any prospect of anything being done to make up the three battalions of Inniskilling Fusiliers in the 109th Brigade of this Division? Their average strength is now under 660 giving a trench strength of about 350. They are first rate fighting battalions and it is a pity to see them dwindling. Would the following suggestions meet with approval? 1. To give the Division two Inniskilling Fusilier battalions, one of which would be a regular battalion and the other to be broken up to make up the other four battalions of the Inniskilling Fusiliers. The 109th Brigade would then be a homogenous Brigade of Inniskillings. 2. The 14th Royal Irish Rifles, now in 109th Brigade, to be broken up and used to make up casualties in the Royal Irish Rifles battalions in the Division. This battalion should in my opinion be broken up in any case. About a year ago, I reported them as totally wanting in military spirit and asked for a CO and a large draft of Englishmen to try to create a fighting spirit in them. You gave me both and while Cheape[20] was in command they certainly improved, but since he left they have been tried and found wanting. It is significant that the present CO told me two days ago that most of the English draft sent to them a year ago have become casualties. The brigadier says that he cannot trust them and I know that he is right. They are poor stuff, either as workers or fighters, and have been a constant source of anxiety during the past three weeks.[21]

It is unclear why Major General Nugent had taken such an umbrage against the 14th Rifles. The last sentence of the letter above referred to the performance of the battalion following the Battle of Cambrai in November 1917. On 11 December, the same day in which the Divisional Commander penned his letter to the Adjutant General and no doubt fresh in his mind, the Battalion war diary stated:

> As a result of the cold, wet, exposure and the lengthy period without a proper rest, the health of the battalion is much below par. The Medical Officer's sick parades are very largely attended, no less than 118 men reported sick today.

---

20 Lieutenant Colonel George Ronald Hamilton Cheape. Commanding Officer 4 March 1917 to 19 August 1917.
21 PRONI: D3835/E/10/8/24.

Working parties of 160 were requested in the afternoon, but only 75 were passed by the Medical Officer as passed fit to be on it. We are to go into the line again on the 12th and strong representations are being made to Higher Authorities to alter this and to have the Battalion (and the Brigade and the Division whose health is equally impaired) back somewhere for a complete rest. The men are cold in billets and their clothes are still wet, it is small wonder that there is much sickness.[22]

In his excellent *Irish Regiments in the Great War, Discipline and Morale*, Bowman (2003) comments on the disciplinary record of the Battalion which was very good and continues:

However, there is strong evidence to suggest that both discipline and combat effectiveness were considerably worse than courts martial statistics suggest.[23] At Langemarck in August 1917 the 14th Royal Irish Rifles appear to have retreated precipitately when facing German machine-gun fire.[24]

Available records however, indicate that the 14th Rifles have been unfairly treated in this instance. Captain Cyril Falls, in *The History of the 36th (Ulster) Division*, Falls (1922), commented on the 14th Rifles experience at Langemarck:

On the right of the 109th Brigade, the 14th Rifles had to cross ground far worse even than the ordinary, completely under water in fact. In their passage they came under withering machine-gun fire from Pond Farm. Lieutenant Ledlie[25] made a fine attempt to capture this place, surrounding it on three sides with the few men remaining to him when he reached it, and killing any Germans who showed themselves. With his numbers so greatly depleted, he waited for support before making an attempt to rush it, sending back two messages. But no supports came; the men could not face the machine-gun fire. They had already suffered greatly from the artillery barrage, which the leading waves had avoided. At eight o'clock, seeing that his position was hopeless, he withdrew his men 150 yards, covering his retirement with Lewis-gun fire.[26]

---

22   TNA: WO 95/2511/1: 14th Battalion Royal Irish Rifles war diary.
23   Bowman, *Irish Regiments in the Great War. Discipline and Morale*, p. 113. Table 4.1 'The number of men tried by courts martial whilst serving in the 36th (Ulster) Division 1 Oct 1915-30 Sept 1916'. The figures in this table show that the 14th Rifles had the second lowest number of men tried, with eight. The highest was the 10th Royal Irish Rifles with 38.
24   Ibid, p. 146.
25   Second Lieutenant, later Captain Edwin Reade Ledlie MC was born at Belfast in 1897 and lived on the Crumlin Road in the north of the city. He later transferred to the Royal Air Force in August 1918 and survived the war.
26   Falls, *The History of the 36th (Ulster) Division*, pp. 118-119.

On that day, the battalion went into action with a strength of 19 officers and 480 men. Their total casualties, dead, wounded and missing were 10 officers and 222 other ranks, a similar percentage to other battalions in the Division.[27] The Battalion war diary entry for the day was critical of those in command, praising the Divisional and Brigade Staff in what could be perceived as a sarcastic manner and this may have been one reason for Major General Nugent's enduring antipathy:

> The whole thing has been a miserable failure for reasons which are obvious to us all. Our men did all that was asked of them, but the peculiar attitude of the enemy and his methods were not properly appreciated by the powers that be. Our Divisional and Brigade Staff did everything that was humanly possible as we know from past experience how well they look ahead and the splendid system they work on. Even with all our losses our confidence is not shaken in our Division and the aim and object of us all will be to bring back to our men the splendid fighting spirit which we have always had. We went into this battle knowing that things were not right and that spirit is fatal, but all around us the signs were very clear and we could not blame either officers or men. They did their best and from our point of view could have done no more.[28]

Perhaps it was just a case of unfortunate timing that the 14th Rifles were brought to the General's attention for large numbers sick and for requesting a rest on the day that he wrote to the Adjutant General, but whatever the reason, the 14th Rifles were destined to be amongst the battalions to be disbanded.

The ongoing situation in relation to the reorganisation obviously caused Major General Nugent great anxiety which was reflected when he wrote to his wife on 15 December 1917:

> My next trouble will be how to make up the Division. There are no recruits to be had and we have got to the end of absorbing Irish battalions from other Divisions because there are no more. It is really time to drop all pretence of being an 'Ulster' Division and become just the 36th.[29]

Whilst the Divisional Commander was aware that the reorganisation was to take place, the actual order from the War Office was only issued on 10 January 1918 – the same day that Sir Douglas Haig had agreed to take over an extra portion of front line from the French. The instructions to the Commander in Chief, including a list of 145 battalions from which he was to choose those to be disbanded stipulated the following:

27   TNA: WO 95/2511/1: 14th Battalion Royal Irish Rifles war diary.
28   Ibid.
29   PRONI: D3835/E/2/15/31.

No Regular, First-Line Territorial or Yeomanry battalions were to be disbanded; the most recently raised Territorial (Second-Line) and Service (New Army) Battalions were to be broken up first.[30]

Following the reorganisation, any surplus men were to be organised into 'Entrenching Battalions' which were to be used for work on defences until they were required to replace casualties. Entrenching Battalions had been used earlier in the war as 'holding battalions', not attached to any Division but under Corps control before men were sent to the front, but the practice had ceased to exist by the autumn of 1917.

The plan settled upon was to reduce the strength of an Infantry Division from 12 battalions to nine. However, this was not as straightforward as it sounds. The 145 Battalions identified were not evenly distributed throughout the Infantry. Some Divisions had as many as six, whilst others had none. In all, 47 Divisions were affected. Given the familiar ties and history, it was envisaged that there would be protests, which indeed there were in the case of many Divisions including the Ulster Division. However, orders had been given so it was decided to proceed as quickly as possible to avoid dragging the process out. Details were settled by 18 January, with the reorganisation to begin on 29 January and to be completed by 15 February. In the 5th Army to which the 36th Division belonged, the process was completed on 25 February.

Apart from the massive upheaval engendered by the process, there was a more serious practical consideration which would have consequences in the coming months. From a tactical point of view, the reorganisation caused serious difficulties. The Brigade of four battalions was the traditional British formation, just as the Regiment of three was the continental. It was the formation which British Commanders had handled in training and practice since the British Expeditionary Force had landed in France in August 1914 and under which their concepts of infantry in war were based. Now, at a critical time in the war they were being asked to adopt a completely new structure – which none had trained for. Added to this was the fact that the soldier on the ground disliked change. Particularly in the New Army Divisions such as the 36th, men had been recruited from close knit, geographical areas. They had developed a sense of comradeship and belonging and in the offensives to date had proved that they fought well with men they knew and could rely on. These structures were about to be disrupted and it is of no doubt that morale suffered as a result.

The fact that the War Office instruction that New Army or Service Battalions were to bear the brunt of the disbandment, did not augur well for the Ulster Division. Although they had recently received two Regular Army Battalions, this meant that they still had 10 Service Battalions.[31] The reorganisation affected the Division as follows:

---

30   Edmonds, *Military Operations France and Belgium 1918,* p. 54, footnote 1.
31   The instruction from the War Office indicated that no Pioneer Battalions were to be disbanded, therefore ensuring the continued existence of the 16th (Service) Battalion

107th Infantry Brigade

8/9th (Service) Battalion Royal Irish Rifles (East & West Belfast Volunteers) was disbanded on 31 January 1918.

10th (Service) Battalion Royal Irish Rifles (South Belfast Volunteers) went into Brigade Reserve on 31 January with a strength of 42 Officers and 730 other ranks. Most of the officers and men of this battalion and the majority of the 8/9th Rifles formed the 21st Entrenching Battalion on 18 February 1918, under the command of Major JDM McCallum DSO, formerly 8/9th Royal Irish Rifles. This Battalion effectively left the Division and came under the command of 8 Corps. At the end of February, the battalion strength was 74 officers and 1236 other ranks.[32]

The 15th (Service) Battalion Royal Irish Rifles (North Belfast Volunteers) remained in the Brigade and was joined by the 1st Battalion Royal Irish Rifles and their sister Regular Army battalion the 2nd Battalion Royal Irish Rifles.

The thoughts of those involved in the move gave some idea of their feelings and some idea of the effect on morale. Captain Gerald Whitfield from Essex, who had been with the 1st Battalion Royal Irish Rifles since 1915 commented:

> Definitely settled that the battalion will leave that fine Division, the 8th and go to the 36th (Ulster) Division as we know it. The 86th[33] have already joined it I believe. Everyone seems very sick over the move.[34]

Lieutenant Thomas Witherow[35] 8/9th Royal Irish Rifles, was one of those who was transferred to the 2nd Royal Irish Rifles instead of going to the 21st Entrenching Battalion. Even then, he was not enamoured with the move:

> That day the 6th February, I will always remember as one of the most depressing I have ever come through. We received orders to join the 2nd Battalion Royal Irish Rifles, which had some time previous come into our Division… We were such a happy crowd that it is difficult to realise the feeling of depression that settled on everybody at the prospect of parting… I was by no means favourably impressed by my first visit to my new unit…We were looked upon as strangers by most of

Royal Irish Rifles (Pioneers).
32   TNA: WO 95/828/10: 21st Entrenching Battalion war diary.
33   The 86th refers to the 1st Battalion Royal Irish Rifles who originated from the 83rd and 86th Regiments of Foot.
34   James W Taylor, *The First Royal Irish Rifles in the Great War* (Dublin: Four Courts Press, 2002) p. 123.
35   Lieutenant, later Captain Thomas Hastings Witherow, was born at Belfast the son of a Presbyterian Minister and was educated at Campbell College. He survived the war and followed his father into the Ministry being ordained in 1922. He retired in 1963 and died in 1989 aged 99.

the officers who were not originally Ulster Division officers at all and who were not inclined to look at things from the Ulster point of view. They were most careful to distribute us all over the battalion so that we could not collect together in a clan. Although I was senior to several Company Commanders and therefore ought to have got a Company, things were so arranged that I should only be a Platoon Commander. Only Officers from Sandhurst were fit to command companies in a regular Battalion.[36]

108th Infantry Brigade

The 11/13th Battalion Royal Irish Rifles, the amalgamation of the South Antrim and County Down Volunteers, went into Brigade Reserve on 31 January 1918. At the time, the strength of this battalion was 45 Officers and 1014 other ranks.[37] For the next two weeks they continued training and providing working parties for the 171st Tunnelling Company. On 18 February, the battalion travelled by motor lorries to the aptly named village of Misery, 19 miles east of St Quentin and became the 22nd Entrenching Battalion under the command of Lieutenant Colonel Philip Laurence Kington-Blair-Oliphant, formerly 11th Royal Irish Rifles.[38] The 22nd Entrenching Battalion also left Divisional control and came under the command of 18 Corps, having a strength of 40 officers and 907 other ranks.[39]

The 12th (Service) Battalion Royal Irish Rifles (Central Antrim Volunteers) were untouched in the reorganisation and remained in 108th Brigade.

One of the recently arrived regular army battalions, the 1st Battalion Royal Irish Fusiliers, moved to 108th Brigade from 107th Brigade and joined the 9th (North Irish Horse) Battalion Princess Victoria's (Royal Irish Fusiliers) and 12th Rifles to complete the Brigade.

109th Infantry Brigade

Major General Nugent's plea to Sir Nevil Macready of 11 December 1917 in relation to this Brigade came to fruition with the two regular battalions of the Royal Inniskilling Fusiliers, 1st and 2nd joining 109th Brigade. The 2nd Battalion arrived on 1 February from 32nd Division which had been based in the Ypres sector. On first impressions, Captain Charles Cecil Miller of the 2nd Inniskillings was reasonably content with the move:

---

36   James W Taylor, *The Second Royal Irish Rifles in the Great War* (Dublin: Four Courts Press, 2005) p. 112.
37   TNA: WO 95/2506/4: 11/13th Royal Irish Rifles war diary.
38   Lieutenant Colonel Philip Laurence Kington-Blair-Oliphant had been with the Division since it embarked for France and died of wounds on 8 April 1918.
39   TNA: WO 95/957/4: 22nd Entrenching Battalion war diary.

Very early in 1918 there was a big reshuffle of Corps, Divisions and Brigades and my battalion went south to St Quentin area to join the 36th Division of the 5th Army under General Gough. In this case we were taking over trenches from the French, and as I could talk the language to a certain extent, I was sent on ahead to spend a few days in the trenches with the French Battalion which we were to relieve and to facilitate the transfer... The French ideas of cleanliness and sanitation in trenches were not ours, but nevertheless they appeared to thrive on them. When we first arrived there the St Quentin area was a paradise compared to Ypres, but it was obvious to any soldier that we had a desperately long line to hold for the forces at our disposal.[40]

The 1st Battalion Royal Inniskilling Fusiliers joined the Ulster Division from 29th Division. Well used to travel, the 1st Inniskillings had been in India at the start of the war and had returned to England in December 1914 to become part of 29th Division. They had taken part in the initial Gallipoli landings in April 1915, before arriving on the Western Front in the summer of 1916.

To facilitate the arrival of the regular battalions in the Brigade the 10th (Service) Battalion Royal Inniskilling Fusiliers (Derry Volunteers) and 11th (Service) Battalion Royal Inniskilling Fusiliers (Donegal and Fermanagh Volunteers) and the 14th (Service) Battalion Royal Irish Rifles (Young Citizen Volunteers) had to make way. More so in this Brigade than the others, men were transferred between battalions to ensure that those battalions remaining in the Brigade – 1st, 2nd and 9th Inniskillings were up to strength. The end for the 11th Inniskillings was reported in a matter of fact manner in the battalion war diary:

Routine work. Notification received from the Divisional Commander of the disbandment of the battalion.[41]

On 8 February, 20 officers and 400 other ranks from the battalion were posted to the 9th Royal Inniskilling Fusiliers. The close-knit ties within the Brigade and the general feeling of loss at the turn of events were evident in the war diary of the 14th Royal Irish Rifles:

The band accompanied by Company Officers marched to Happencourt and played the 11th Inniskillings as they marched past to join 9th Inniskillings. The 11th and 14th Rifles have always been good friends, have met in friendly rivalry

40   Imperial War Museum (IWM) Doc. 4118, 'A Letter to my Daughters', Captain Charles Cecil Miller papers.
41   TNA: WO 95/2510/5: 11th Royal Inniskilling Fusiliers war diary.

on the football field and have fought shoulder to shoulder in many fights. These are depressing days for the Ulster Division.[42]

On 21 February, a further 30 officers and 219 other ranks from the 11th Inniskillings amalgamated with the bulk of the 14th Royal Irish Rifles to form 23rd Entrenching Battalion. For men used to front line action and proud of their achievements, the change of duty was reported almost contemptuously, as the 14th Rifles war diary recorded on 19 February:

> We are almost immediately to become an Entrenching Battalion under the name of No 23 Entrenching Battalion. Our work will be digging trenches in the rear zone. The remains of the 11th Royal Inniskilling Fusiliers are to join us consisting of a Company Commander and about 200 other ranks, thus bringing the battalion up to full strength.[43]

On establishment, the 23rd Entrenching battalion had a strength of 73 officers and 1017 other ranks and having been detached from the Division, came under the command of 2 Corps.[44]

On disbandment, the 52 officers and 685 men of the 10th Royal Inniskilling Fusiliers were distributed to 1st, 2nd and 9th Inniskillings to bring those battalions up to strength, some were also sent to 21st Entrenching Battalion.

Whilst the men at the front were despondent at the reorganisation, at home there was also considerable unease. The Lord Mayor of Belfast Alderman James Johnston, argued that the 14th Royal Irish Rifles, drawn from the Young Citizen Volunteers which predated the formation of the Ulster Volunteer Force and having been raised as a Volunteer Rifle Unit by Belfast Corporation in 1912, should be retained. He wrote on the subject to Major General Nugent on 9 February 1918. In a tactful reply which did not hint at his antipathy towards the battalion and gave his rationale for the decisions he had taken, the Divisional Commander stated:

> In reply to your letter of 9th instant, I regret to say the break-up of the 36th Division in respect of the greater number of its original battalions is already accomplished. The Division now consists of 5 Regular North Irish battalions, and of 5 battalions of the original Division. As General Officer Commanding the Division, I had the most unpleasant duty of selecting 2 battalions of Inniskilling Fusiliers and 4 battalions of Royal Irish Rifles for disbandment. I decided that the battalions to remain in the Division should be those which were composed of the men who first came forward to form the Ulster Division. I therefore selected

---

42   TNA: WO 95/2511/1: 14th Battalion Royal Irish Rifles war diary.
43   Ibid.
44   TNA: WO 95/664/7: 23rd Entrenching Battalion war diary.

the senior of the three battalions of Inniskilling Fusiliers to remain. In the case of the Royal Irish Rifles, I selected the senior battalion to remain. This was the 15th Battalion, a Belfast Battalion originally raised as the 7th Battalion. The next senior of the original battalions of the Ulster Division would have been the 10th Royal Irish Rifles. This was also a Belfast Battalion and I decided that it would be unfair to the Counties of Down and Antrim that they should have no representation amongst the original units of the Division. I therefore selected the 12th Royal Irish Rifles as the other battalion to remain. The remaining third battalion of the Royal Irish Rifles, the Pioneer Battalion, which *(sic)* was not affected by the reorganisation of the Division. I have gone into the matter at this length because there is no reason why you should not know the principle on which I acted in naming the battalions which I considered should be abandoned. I need hardly say how deeply I regret the disappearance of so many fine battalions from the Division. The claims of the 14th Royal Irish Rifles were put before me by the OC the battalion, but in view of the principle of selection I had decided upon I felt I could not accept his views.[45]

In addition to writing to Major General Nugent, the Lord Mayor also wrote to Field Marshal Sir Douglas Haig and the Adjutant General, Sir Nevil Macready. However, the decisions had been made and there was to be no deviation from the plan. Sir Nevil Macready replied himself to the Mayor on 15 February, taking the opportunity to mention the recruiting difficulties in Ireland:

> Under the reorganisation it is necessary to break up certain battalions, the choices of which was left to the authorities in France in order that they might carry out the scheme with the least possible dislocation and to avoid throwing extra work on the already overburdened transport arrangements. Broadly, the lines laid down were that where possible, the battalions chosen should be those with the shortest life and further that those of Irish and Welsh nationalities where recruiting has failed and where it has been necessary to draft Englishmen into these units, the numbers should be reduced to a figure which would enable the national characteristics to be maintained.[46]

Macready's deputy, J Bennett Stuart replied to the Lord Mayor on behalf of the commander in chief, Field Marshal Sir Douglas Haig in a letter dated 18 February 1918. Replying to the Mayor's concern over the disbandment of 14th Royal Irish Rifles he also highlighted recruiting difficulties:

45   Nicholas Perry (ed.) *Major General Oliver Nugent and the Ulster Division 1915-1918* (Stroud: Sutton Publishing, 2007) p. 207.
46   PRONI: D961/8.

The shortage of reinforcements for all battalions of the Ulster Division for some considerable time past gave rise to the situation that in actual practice there were more Englishmen than Irishmen serving in the Division. The situation has unfortunately not improved and in spite of drafts from English districts it has not been possible to keep the Division up to its establishment.[47]

By the end of February 1918, the reorganisation of the 36th (Ulster) Division was completed and the three Brigades were comprised as follows:

107th Infantry Brigade
1st Royal Irish Rifles
2nd Royal Irish Rifles
15th Royal Irish Rifles

108th Infantry Brigade
1st Royal Irish Fusiliers
9th Royal Irish Fusiliers
12th Royal Irish Rifles

109th Infantry Brigade
1st Royal Inniskilling Fusiliers
2nd Royal Inniskilling Fusiliers
9th Royal Inniskilling Fusiliers

The reorganisation of the Division had been completed in a manner which maintained an Irish if not a wholly Ulster ethos. The regular battalions brought in to complement the Division were at least all Irish, which partially satisfied the aims of Sir Edward Carson and Major General Nugent. By this stage of the war, the original 'Ulster' Division was all but gone, a fact noted by Father Gill of the 2nd Royal Irish Rifles in his diary:

The 36th or 'Ulster' Division to which we belonged had also undergone a transformation. Battalions like that to which I was posted were moved out of other Divisions and placed in the 36th. Thus, out of the fighting battalions in the Ulster Division for some time before the 21st March, 5 were old regular battalions whose rank and file had no sympathies whatsoever with the religious and political ideals of the men they replaced... A status of religion at this time showed that in the Ulster Division at the time of the German advance there were between 3,000-4,000 Catholics.[48]

47   Ibid.
48   IJA CHP 1/27 p. 155.

As described by Father Gill, the loss of so many men from the Division's strength to the Entrenching Battalions was a grievous blow. A total of 187 officers and 3160 men had left the Division. Many had embarked for France in October 1915 and had fought at the Somme, Messines, Langemarck and Cambrai. The loss of experience, comradeship and morale to the Division was incalculable and crucially also further diminished the Ulster ethos. Of those sent to the Entrenching Battalions, it was particularly galling to be reclassified as little more than a labourer after performing in action with distinction for over two years. The mood was captured by Major GJ Apperson MC from Balmoral Avenue, Belfast who, in a letter to the Historical Section of the War Office in September 1927 commented:

> As showing the spirit of the battalion, I should like to mention that all ranks took strong exception to the title of 22nd Entrenching Battalion and never used it and that the fighting efficiency of the battalion was not allowed to be impaired by its short absence from the line.[49]

Fortunately for the Ulster Division, some of those in the Entrenching battalions were unexpectedly able to come to its aid in the imminent German Offensive.

---

49   TNA: WO 95/957/4: 22nd Entrenching battalion war diary.

3

Defences & German Plans

Lastly, instead of being deeply dug and strongly revetted and wired it was quite obvious that when the moment came to use them the strong points would hardly be strong enough to keep out a well-aimed snowball. [1]

Captain Charles Cecil Miller 2nd Battalion Royal Inniskilling Fusiliers,
lamenting the state of the defences on the battalion front.

As if the wholesale reorganisation of the infantry on the Western Front was not enough to be getting on with, it will be remembered that Field Marshal Haig had been coerced into taking over more of the front line from the French. To formalise this process, Haig met with the French Commander-in-Chief, General Petain on 17 December and agreed to relieve two French Divisions by 10 January 1918. Edmonds, *Official History of the War. Military Operations France and Belgium 1918* (1935) detailed the area to be taken over:

> The British line was to be extended farther south to a point five and a half miles east of the River Oise. The relief of the French 6th Army was punctually begun on 10 January, XVIII Corps under Lieutenant-General Maxse completing the takeover from the French III Corps of the Sector opposite St Quentin on 14 January. The 36th and 61st Divisions were sent into the line and the 30th Division held in reserve. After the takeover, the British 5th Army line stretched from the Barisis-St Gobain railway to near Gouzeaucourt (opposite Cambrai) – a distance of 42 miles.[2]

As a result of this extension, British resources especially in the Fifth Army, were spread dangerously thinly. As Martin Middlebrook highlights in his exceptional *The Kaiser's Battle*:

1   IWM Doc. 4118 Captain Charles C Miller papers.
2   Edmonds, *Military Operations France and Belgium 1918*, p. 47.

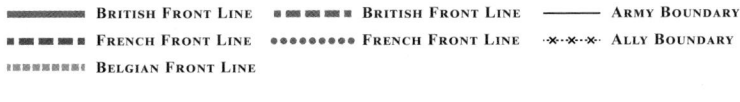

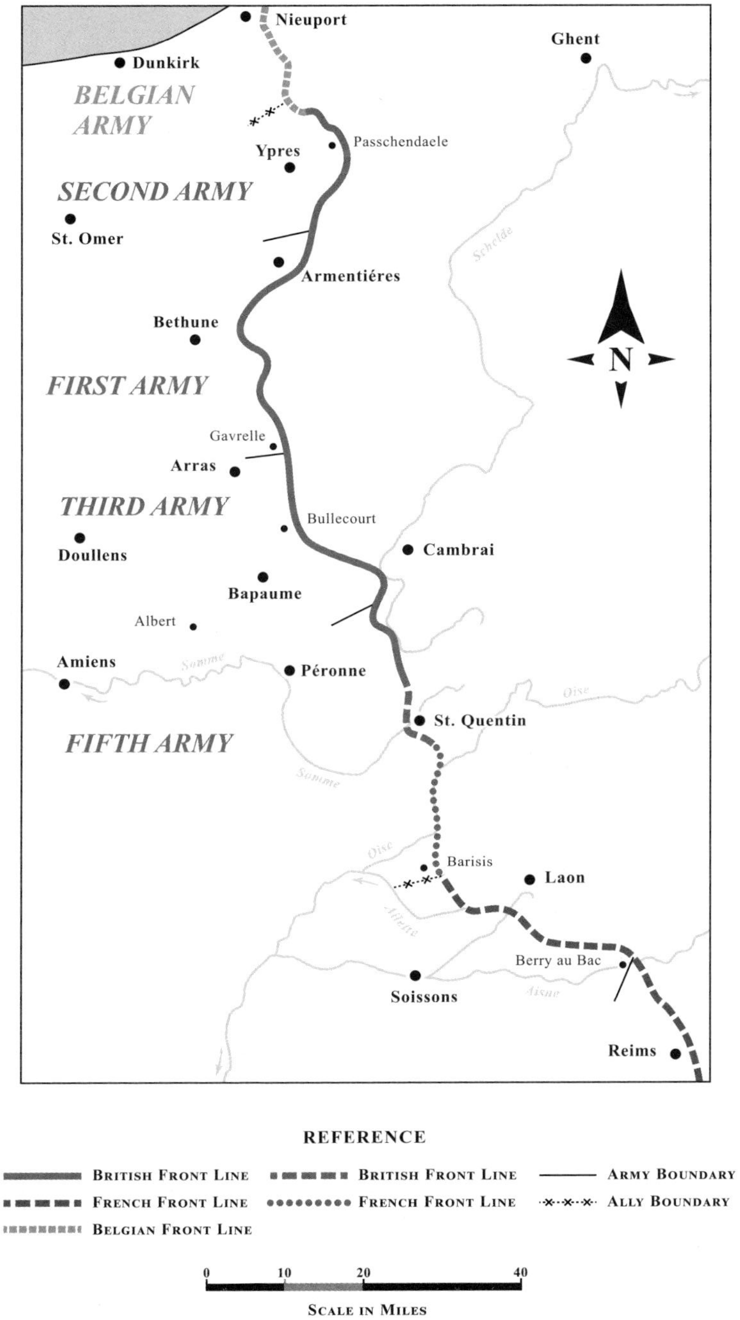

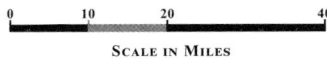

Map 1 Extension of the British front line, January 1918.

The Fifth Army frontage was 42 miles which were to be held by 12 Infantry Divisions and 3 Cavalry Divisions. Each Cavalry Division mustered the strength of an Infantry Brigade so in effect, 5th Army had the strength of 13 Divisions. This effectively meant that each Division had to cover just over three miles of frontage – over a mile per Division further than the Divisions of 3rd Army. There were eight Divisions in Reserve, however these were spread over the entire front, so to get them to a point of breakthrough in the 5th Army area for example would take time to arrange.[3]

As luck would have it, the 36th (Ulster) Division were positioned in the middle of the new stretch of line, nearly opposite the historic town of St Quentin. The stretch of line the Division held ran from Sphinx Wood, some 1200 yards west of the village of Itancourt, to a point on the St Quentin-Roisel Railway a thousand yards west of Rocourt Station.[4] This position, to the south of St Quentin saw the Ulster Division positioned straddling the River Somme and the St Quentin Canal.[5] The Somme and the St Quentin canal ran parallel to each other from north to south until they joined near the hamlet of Le Hamel and the ground between was marshy. Hardly ideal defensively, the majority of the ground held by the Division was on the eastern side of the canal, with a small portion of the 109th Brigade area on the western side. The canal as it ran south through the Ulster Division territory had a number of small hamlets, each with a bridge connecting the eastern and western banks. On the right of the Ulster Division were the 14th (Light) Division, who had recently arrived in the area after having been involved (like the Ulster Division) in the Battle of Langemarck, but also in the First and Second Battles of Passchendaele. Unfortunately, due to the geography of the landscape, the 36th Division frontage did not face the German defences head on. The disposition of the Division ran from the north-east in the Forward Zone, in a south westerly direction until it reached the St Quentin Canal.

Following the relief of the French units, the 41st Brigade of 14th (Light) Division were immediately to the right of the 36th Division's 108th Brigade. On completion of the reorganisation of infantry, the 41st Brigade was comprised of; 8th Battalion King's Royal Rifle Corps and 7th and 8th Battalions of the Rifle Brigade. On the left of the Ulster Division was the 30th Division. The 21st Brigade of this division was immediately to the left of the Ulster Division's 109th Brigade. Following reorganisation, the 21st Brigade comprised; the 2nd Battalion Wiltshire Regiment, the 2nd Battalion Yorkshire Regiment and the 17th Battalion Manchester Regiment.

By all accounts, the progress of the Division to affect the relief of French troops was leisurely and evidenced the curious lack of urgency that was to characterize actions in the following two and a half months. As Falls (1922) states:

---

3   Martin Middlebrook, *The Kaiser's Battle* (London: Penguin, 1983), p. 71.
4   Rocourt is a suburb of St Quentin.
5   The St Quentin Canal was also known as the Crozat Canal.

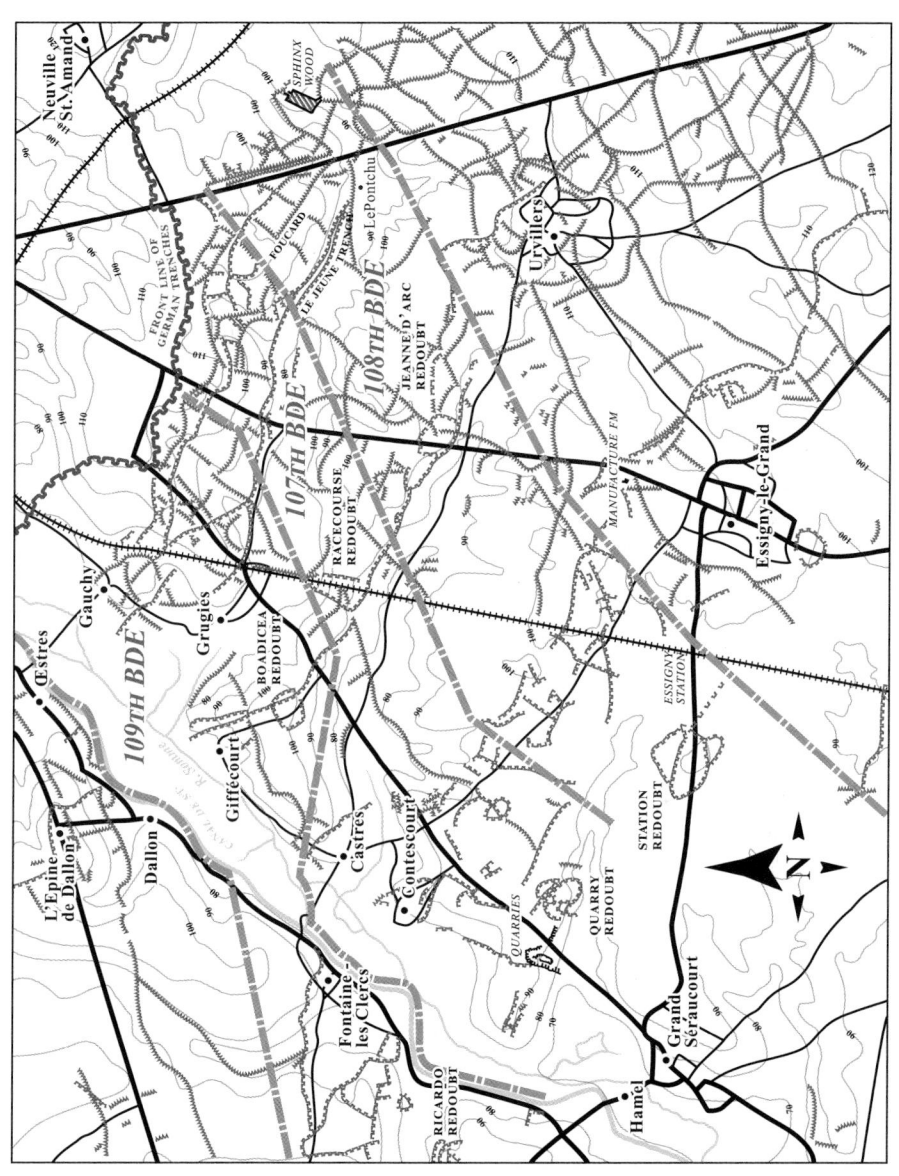

Map 2 Area of Operations, March 1918.

REFERENCE

BRITISH TRENCHES

GERMAN TRENCHES

BRIGADE BOUNDARY

SCALE IN YARDS

0   500   1000   1500

The Division remained five days at rest in the Corbie area, where it was joined by its Artillery. Then it went slowly forward, via Harbonnieres to the area of Nesle, a town left undamaged by the Germans in their retirement, into which they had herded civilians, old men, women and children from other towns and villages destroyed by them. Here Divisional Headquarters were established on January 12th.[6]

This lack of urgency does not appear to have only affected the Ulster Division. The war diary of the 8th Battalion King's Royal Rifle Corps (part of 14th (Light) Division which following the relief of the French were on the right of the 36th) recorded:

1 January. Holiday. New Year's Day spent in recovering from New Year's Eve Dinner.[7]

At this point it would be prudent to discuss further the 'retirement' to which Falls refers, as it was to have a crucial bearing on events which were to take place in March 1918. From late December 1916, the Germans had sought to realign their defences in the Somme region, reasoning that a shorter front line would be easier to defend. In a far-sighted move, they voluntarily ceded a large area of ground to retain the best defensive positions. As they withdrew, they destroyed everything in their wake – demolishing villages and bridges, tearing up railway lines, poisoning wells and slaughtering livestock. In essence, this was a scorched earth policy and one which they had previously used on a smaller scale in 1915 in Northern France. In carrying out this policy, the Germans were denying the Allies any resources with which to construct defences. Civilians were forcibly relocated from towns and villages that were not demolished in order that the German Army could utilise them as billets and reinforce them at their leisure. At St Quentin for example, the German troops were able to live in houses in the town and walk the short distance via communication trenches to the front line. The effects of the destruction that the Germans left in their wake were witnessed by Father Gill as he moved forward with the 2nd Royal Irish Rifles:

Monday January 14th, we moved into the remains of a village just off the Ham – St Quentin road called Flesquieres. Hardly anything was left of this place. Our quarters were constructed in some 'houses' constructed from the bricks of the former cottages. On the way, some of the men who had been out in the beginning of 1914 told me they remembered coming along this road in the Retreat from Mons.[8]

---

6   Falls, *The History of the 36th (Ulster) Division*, p. 182.
7   TNA: WO 95/1895/2: 8th Battalion King's Royal Rifle Corps war diary.
8   IJA/CHP1/27 p. 151.

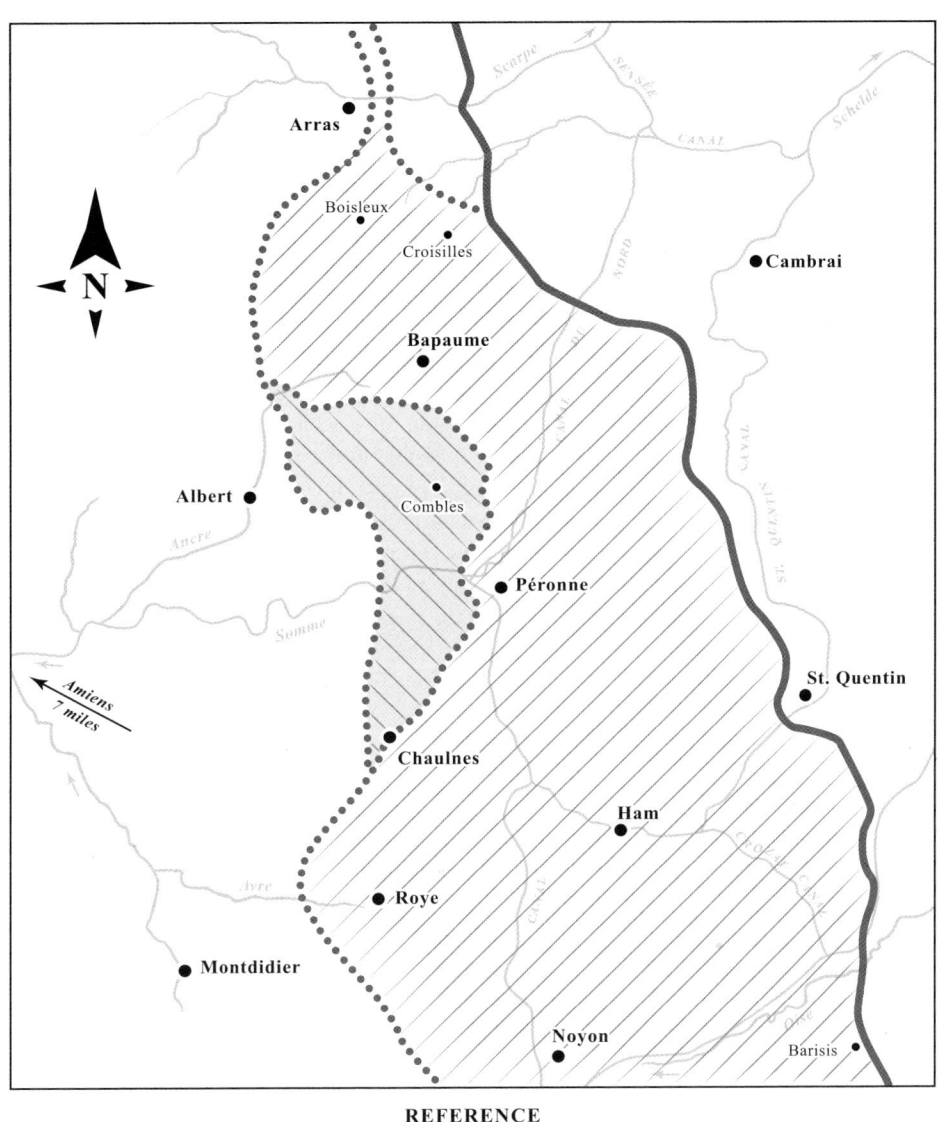

REFERENCE

/////	SOMME 1916
/////	GERMAN RETREAT TO HINDENBURG LINE 1917
▬▬▬	FRONT LINE ON 20TH MARCH 1918

0   5   10   20   30

SCALE IN MILES

Map 3 Area devastated by the Germans.

The most important element of the German withdrawal, and one which had a decisive impact during the Spring Offensive is mentioned in many personal accounts, but crucially does not appear in orders issued by those in command. In a commonsense endeavour (especially in a war in which movement forward and to the rear was key) the Germans having held the ground being ceded, accurately mapped every point of interest and in some cases left markers, a situation which Father Gill observed:

> In many ways, the months in this portion of the line were very pleasant. There was not much fighting, the country was open and dry and the weather on the whole, good. The French in this sector had just been relieved by the British and there was a lot of work to be done getting the place into proper order. In view of the attack which took place a few months later, it is interesting to recall that when we arrived at this position there was practically no second line of defence. The place was excellently chosen as a jumping off place by the Germans. There was very little cover on our side. Every possible gun position must have been mapped out to a yard by the enemy before their retirement. From St Quintin *(sic)* they could command an excellent view of our position and no doubt enjoyed our preparations for their reception. A curious thing which did not seem to trouble either French or English Staffs was the presence of certain landmarks which the Germans had evidently left for their own purposes. The most prominent of these were trees. On the main roads, they had cut down practically all the trees, but at the crossroads a tree was left standing. This was hardly accidental.[9]

The relief of the French began for the Division on the evening of 12 January. Whilst relieving another British or Dominion formation was usually a straightforward procedure, relieving the French was a different matter. In this case munitions were of a different calibre and instead of being handed over had to be transferred. There were formalities to be observed and many sumptuous dinners to be consumed. Even private soldiers were treated royally and none of the war diaries of the 36th (Ulster) Division expresses any disappointment at the way they were treated by the French.

As for the relief itself, 107th Infantry Brigade relieved the 24th French Infantry Regiment in the left sector of the line on the night of 12-13 January. The following night, 109th Infantry Brigade relieved the 119th French Infantry Regiment in the right sector. Divisional Headquarters moved to Ollezy and command passed from the French 6th Division at 10:00 a.m. on 14th January.[10]

Around the time of the relief, a review of the situation of the Army on the Western Front was under way. The review was carried out by General Jan Christiaan Smuts, a South African General who had fought against the British in the Second Boer War and subsequently agitated for self-government for the Transvaal within South

---

9   Ibid.
10 TNA: WO 95/2492/2: 36th (Ulster) Division war diary.

Africa. Following his successful command of South African forces in German South-West and East Africa, he was brought to Britain by the Prime Minister, David Lloyd George and made a member of the War Cabinet. General Smuts believed that the Germans could only be defeated on the Western Front and was a supporter of Field Marshal Haig's policy of attrition there. After a visit to the front lasting six days, he reported the following:

> I am satisfied that the morale of the Army is good. The bearing of the troops coming in and out of the line and in the large working parties all along the front is in every way satisfactory. The Army is well found and in good fettle. There is however, no question that the men are tired. This applies more especially to the Infantry. To a considerable extent the personnel of the artillery have been rested after the great fatigues of the Flanders battle. The Infantry on the other hand is not yet sufficiently rested. All the Divisions were actively engaged in in exhausting offensive operations during the whole of 1917. Much new ground has been wrested from the enemy, with the result that entirely new defences have had to be created on a large proportion of the front, and the tired Divisions had not during 1917 maintained even the old defences at the highest level. The change in the strategical situation, due to the collapse of Russia has necessitated the construction of a great new system of defence in depth, the fronts of which in most parts of the front do not correspond with the first line trenches. A defensive system that amply sufficed for an Army continually on the offensive, does not meet the defensive needs of the existing situation, and behind the elaborate system of the main battle zone, reserve defences are being constructed. The preparation of this vast but absolutely essential scheme of defence requires an enormous amount of labour. As the greater part of the work has to be done within the zone of artillery fire, native and prisoner labour cannot be employed to any considerable extent. The burden falls in the main on the infantry. Consequently, Divisions which have completed their term in the defensive line, have almost immediately to be turned on to the construction of defence works. The result is that they suffer in regard both to rest and training. In the circumstances, the surprising feature is not that they are fatigued, but that their spirits are so good.[11]

As can be seen from his report, he highlighted two main themes which proved crucial in the following months:

1. That the Infantry were tired after continued offensives throughout 1917
2. That defences sufficient for offensive action were in no way suitable for defensive purposes

---

11   Edmonds, *Military Operations France and Belgium 1918*, p. 40.

Unfortunately for the infantry, there was no prospect of any rest, a situation exacerbated by the refusal of the Prime Minister, Lloyd George to release sufficient freshly trained troops from the United Kingdom. A further aggravating factor was that the tired troops were the very ones who were going to have to carry out the labour required for the defensive system. There is no evidence that Lloyd George took any heed of the warnings implicit in the report.

The 'vast but absolutely essential scheme of defence' as described by General Smuts was disseminated as '*GHQ Memorandum on Defensive Measures*,' dated 14 December 1917.[12] It should be remembered that the British Expeditionary Force had been constantly on the offensive since the conclusion of the Retreat from Mons at the end of August 1914. Here, just over three years later, troops who were exhausted were about to be overburdened by a new military concept, which had never been tried in practice in this war to date. Worse still, the infantry had to carry out the majority of the hard labour required to make it happen. In its opening paragraph, the memorandum sets out the rationale for the defensive system:

> The general situation on the Russian and Italian fronts may enable the enemy to release a considerable number of effectives both as formed units and as reinforcements to the Western Front. At the same time the condition of our own man power and the paucity of reinforcements which we are likely to receive during the next few months will make it impossible for our units to be brought up to establishments. In consequence, the British Army in France will probably have to adopt a defensive attitude for some time to come and be prepared to meet a strong and sustained hostile offensive, adequately supported by artillery.[13]

Given that this memorandum was issued six weeks before General Smuts had completed his review, it appears obvious that Lloyd George's policy on reinforcements was going to prevail, no matter what. The memorandum goes on to describe in detail the General Scheme of Defence which due to its importance in relation to what subsequently occurred is reproduced as follows:

General Scheme of Defence
In considering the distribution of troops and the construction of defences, a careful study of the ground is necessary with a view to the main resistance being made on ground favourable to us. In accordance with this principle, a battle zone has been selected in which to prepare to meet and repel any serious attacks on the part of the enemy.

12   Ibid, Appendix 6.
13   Ibid.

The Battle Zone
The battle zone will be organized for defence in great depth, varying from 2,000 to 3,000 yards and will consist of strong successive systems of defence. Diagonal switch lines, supporting points and defended localities must be constructed within the battle zone with a view to preventing the enemy from spreading outwards and rolling up the position, should he succeed in temporarily penetrating the defences. The more important localities in the battle zone will be permanently garrisoned. Plans and preparations for the employment of troops both in the defensive battle and in counter-attack must be carefully worked out. Not only must the troops permanently allotted to the various sectors be considered in preparing schemes, but also possible reinforcements arriving from elsewhere.

The Outpost Zone[14]
The outpost zone will also be organised for defence in depth and will be sufficiently garrisoned and strengthened to guard against surprise, to break up the enemy's attacks and compel him to expend large quantities of ammunition and employ strong forces for its capture. The back bone of the defence in this zone will be machine guns skilfully concealed in combination with wire entanglements.

The Rearward Zone
In addition to the battle and outpost zones of defence, a rear zone some 4 – 8 miles behind the battle zone will be selected and prepared for defence as labour becomes available. Arrangements will be made by GHQ in conjunction with Armies to have this defensive zone reconnoitred and the projected defences spit-locked.[15]

There are a number of issues arising from this memorandum which warrant further examination. Firstly, nowhere in the memorandum, which runs to six pages, is it mentioned that in the siting of the various zones, cognizance should be taken of the fact that the Germans had held the ground for some time and would obviously be aware of its characteristics. Secondly, in the description of the role of the Outpost or Forward zone it is implicit that it existed only to hold the Germans up for as long as possible and in reality, was expendable. This is actually confirmed further on in the memorandum where it is stated:

The troops allotted to the defence of the outpost zone will do all in their power to maintain their ground against every attack… The battle zone, being the ground

14   Renamed the 'Forward Zone' in January 1918.
15   Edmonds, Appendix 6

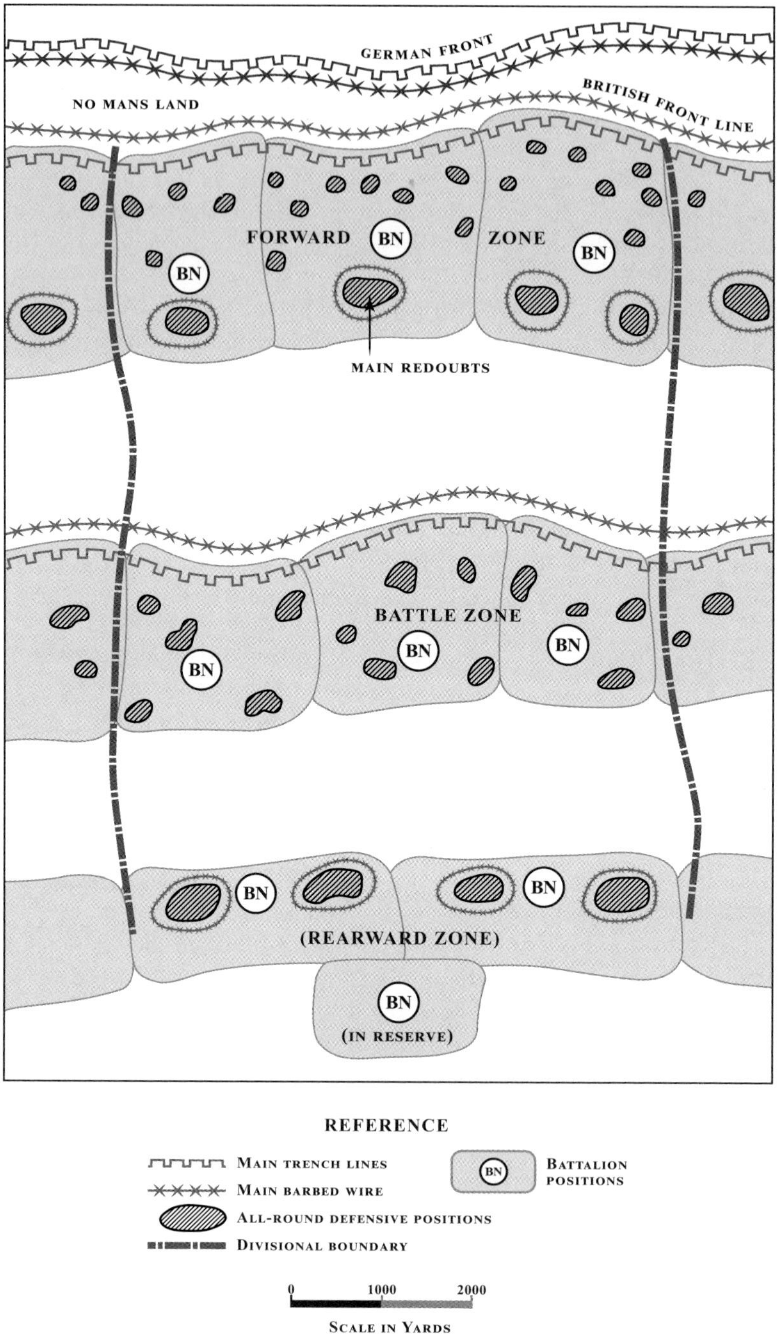

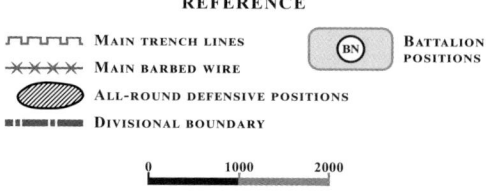

GERMAN FRONT

BRITISH FRONT LINE

NO MANS LAND

FORWARD (BN) ZONE

(BN)

(BN)

(BN)

MAIN REDOUBTS

BATTLE ZONE

(BN)

(BN)

(BN)

(BN)

(BN)

(BN)

(BN)

(REARWARD ZONE)

(BN)

(IN RESERVE)

REFERENCE

⊓⊔⊓⊔ MAIN TRENCH LINES

✕✕✕✕ MAIN BARBED WIRE

▨ ALL-ROUND DEFENSIVE POSITIONS

▬▬▬ DIVISIONAL BOUNDARY

(BN) BATTALION POSITIONS

0   1000   2000

SCALE IN YARDS

Map 4 Divisional defence system, Fifth Army.

on which it has been decided to give battle should the enemy attack in strength, must be maintained.[16]

Although Brigades rotated their battalions through the various zones, those going to the Forward Zone must have known there was little hope in the event of an attack, which must have contributed to a fatalistic state of mind in those based there. Despite the memorandum being relatively clear on this point, there were different interpretations put on it by different Armies. For the 36th (Ulster) Division, part of Fifth Army, the plan was that the Forward Zone would disrupt and hold the initial attack. Troops would then retreat to the Battle Zone, where troops based there would constitute the main defence assisted by reserves from the Reserve Zone and those who had fallen back.

Part 1 Orders of the 1st Battalion Royal Inniskilling Fusiliers dated 23 February 1918, put the situation succinctly:

> Duties of troops in the outpost line – They must give immediate warning of any attempt on the part of the enemy to attack and will resist any such attempt to the utmost of their power. The outpost line will not be reinforced.[17]

However, Fifth and Third Armies appeared to have different instructions. Third Army was told to fight for the Forward Zone whilst Fifth Army were told to concentrate defences on the Battle Zone. Hardly what was required in the face of a concerted offensive. Thirdly and finally, no-one had ever been trained in this sort of defensive warfare or had even thought defensively and so there was no template as to how to proceed, just general instructions. Battalion Commanders were used to a tried and trusted linear system of trench warfare which could be easily controlled from a Battalion Headquarters positioned slightly to the rear which could arrange support where necessary. In the new system, the point of first contact with the enemy was farther to the front and controlled by junior officers who were left to their own initiative and were not likely to receive either directions or reinforcements.

Captain Charles Miller of the 2nd Inniskillings was scathing in his criticism:

> The British Army incidentally has certain shibboleths one of which, and it has cost the lives of scores of thousands of soldiers, is that when you are attacked in overwhelming force you mustn't run away. The French, who are much more logical than we, and who consider results and not prestige, invariably run away under such circumstances, and when the right moment comes run back again and deliver a counter attack. The British shibboleth of course only extends to the

16   Edmonds, *Military Operations France and Belgium 1918,* Appendix 6.
17   The Inniskillings Museum: 1st Battalion Royal Inniskilling Fusiliers Part 1 Orders February 1918.

actual men in the line, the brigadiers and the Divisional Generals run away all right, only they call it moving their quarters. This does not apply to quite all the generals, but to the very great majority of them.[18]

The ground taken over from the French and the defences it contained had to be completely reconstructed in accordance with the new instructions. In a paragraph entitled, 'Construction of Defences' the memorandum optimistically stated:

> In the construction of defences, a careful planning of work and the suitable distribution of the available labour and material are the chief means of achieving good results. Comprehensive plans, covering a considerable period ahead should be drawn up, and should not be departed from, otherwise waste and delay are inevitable. In order further to ensure continuity of work, officers should be placed permanently in charge of definite sectors of the battle zone.[19]

This was no easy matter to address. Both labour and materials were in short supply at this time. In January and February 1918, the British Army had submitted an order for 22,000 tons of barbed wire, they received 7,000. The issue of labour would not be resolved until March at the earliest, so the only labour available was the soldiers themselves when they were not in the line.

The period of the relief had seen heavy snow and a thaw was now underway. The ground that the Ulster Division held was reasonable for defence but as Falls (1922) points out, had at least one major failing:

> The front held by the 36th Division was in its natural features not ill-adapted for defence. It was crossed by a series of ridges and valleys running east and west, parallel to the front line. Behind the frontline system, which was on the same ridge as the German outposts and on its reverse slope, was a deep valley known as Grugies valley, from Grugies to the St Quentin – La-Fere Road, north of Urvillers, thence curving northwards into 'no man's land' towards Neuville-St Amand. Grugies valley therefore had its advantages and its dangers. On the one hand it afforded good masked positions for machine guns, on the other, it was a conduit, from the north -eastern end of which attack might flow down behind the line of resistance of the Forward Zone. Behind it was another ridge, upon which was a line of redoubts. Behind this again the ground sloped away gradually, rising to a slighter ridge, along which ran the Essigny – Contescourt Road. Upon the forward and reverse slopes of this last ridge were the positions of the two southern sectors of the Battle Zone, four thousand five hundred yards behind the front line. The northern sector as has been explained, was north of the St Quentin Canal.

---

18   IWM Doc. 4118 Captain Charles C Miller papers.
19   Edmonds, *Military Operations France and Belgium 1918*, Appendix 6.

These positions were good, but they had one great failing. The front line of the 36th Division ran roughly from West to East to Sphinx Wood, while thence the line of 14th Division ran more nearly north to south. The right flank was therefore very insecure. Should Urvillers fall, the right of the 36th Division's forward system would undoubtedly crumple, while should such a calamity as the capture of Essigny occur, the defences of the Battle Zone would be turned.[20]

If the British had identified a flaw in the defences, surely the Germans who had previously held the ground and were able to observe the British defences from their vantage point in St Quentin town would have identified this also?

As on all occasions when a new unit took over the line, it was incumbent on the opposing forces to gain intelligence on their new adversaries. Thus, it was no surprise that the Ulster Division was subjected to several German raids shortly after taking over the line. On the night of 21-22 January, a patrol of 10th Royal Irish Rifles was waylaid, and a subaltern and a serjeant captured. The battalion war diary recorded:

2nd Lt JF Scilley and Sergt C Townsend taken prisoner whilst on patrol, two OR wounded.[21]

Second Lieutenant Scilley was in fact killed in the raid and has no known grave, being commemorated on the Thiepval Memorial to the Missing. Serjeant Christopher Townsend 7/4399, aged 19, was from Vanderbilt Road, Earlsfield, London. Captured unwounded, he spent the rest of the war at Dulmen Prisoner of War Camp, Westphalia. On the same night, the war diary of 15th Royal Irish Rifles recorded:

21 January. Enemy patrol entered our trenches midnight night of 21-22 and captured one man – seriously wounded and wounded one NCO and three men.[22]

The man captured was 31 years old Private Andrew Anderson, 47208 from Reilly Street, Banbridge who had previous service in the Army Service Corps. Unfortunately, he died of his wounds and having no known grave is commemorated on the Thiepval Memorial to the Missing.

Private Andrew Anderson
15th Battalion Royal Irish
Rifles. (Great War Ulster
Newspaper Archive)

20   Falls, *The History of the 36th (Ulster) Division*, p. 188.
21   TNA: WO 95/2503/4: 10th Battalion Royal Irish Rifles war diary.
22   TNA: WO 95/2503/5: 15th Battalion Royal Irish Rifles war diary.

Whilst holding what was at that time a quiet part of the line, the French Army had had a laissez-faire attitude to the construction of defences, which meant that when the Ulster Division took over, they had basically to start from scratch. Even as a non-combatant, Father Gill in the sector with the 2nd Royal Irish Rifles, recognised the deficiencies:

> Whatever may be the merits of the French methods of defence, the fact remains that when we took over the sector, practically nothing had been done to prepare defensive positions. The front-line positions were very deficient. There was little or no barbed wire. There were no reserve trenches behind the forward system, thus the amount of work to be done was enormous. On arrival, our first work was the digging of reserve trenches. These trenches were not complete, they are only a foot or 18 inches deep. Whether they were intended to deceive the aerial photographers of the enemy or to be embryonic trenches to be completed later on was not clear. In any case several lines of trenches of this description were prepared. In the front line, the position was held by a series of advance posts, each separated from the others. These posts were reorganised and had to be wired and strengthened…The trench work was on the whole easy. The Germans calmly watched the digging operations and no doubt made their plans accordingly.[23]

Also a member of the 2nd Rifles, Lieutenant Thomas Witherow thought the system of defence strange and certainly not something the battalion had been used to, which provided added dangers:

> The line was rather peculiar in some ways. The front line was a long distance away from the Reserve line where HQ was located, the means of communication being a long winding trench, very muddy with the result that it took ages to reach the front line…Like the sector on the other side of the canal, the whole country was dominated by the ruins of the Cathedral of St Quentin so that the enemy were able to see every movement. In the neighbourhood of Company HQ which was on the top of a rise and therefore in full view of the enemy, there were many trenches which were only half dug and when we proceeded to use them to move about, the enemy snipers immediately became active and shots came unpleasantly near. This was the worst sector that I had been in for sniping.[24]

As the scheme of defence was a novelty, those in command decided to become involved to ensure that the *Memorandum on Defensive Measures* was adhered to, much to the exasperation of Captain Miller of the 2nd Inniskillings:

23   IJA/CHP1/27 p. 154.
24   Taylor, *The 2nd Royal Irish Rifles in the Great War*, p. 112.

St Quentin Basilica 1918 and St
Quentin Basilica interior 1918.
(Bundesarchiv. N1645 Bild 00217
& 00231/Heinrik Schmeck,
March 1918)

St Quentin Basilica exterior 2017
and St Quentin Basilica interior
2017. (Author's collection)

It remained to select the sites for the strongpoints, to consider best how they could be incorporated into the trench line at irregular intervals, and to get them dug, well wired, and as strong as possible in every conceivable way. In discussing the thing with Farnham,[25] I remember emphasising the vital necessity of pushing on as fast as possible. The strategic question of the actual location of the strongpoints seemed to me of minor importance. What was vitally necessary was that we should have the time to make them as strong as possible, and also time to accustom the men by practice on the spot, so that when the time came everyone should know the ropes and the strong points should be occupied with the minimum of delay… Of course, this was tremendously hard work. What it meant was that my battalion would hold the line for four days, but every night of the four days in reserve we had to march to the trenches and work. At the beginning the men stuck this well and cheerfully. I remember giving a lecture to my Company on the subject of this new idea in defence and noticing their interest. Everyone knew by then that in all probability we were in for a very bad time, but at least this much more elastic type of defence did give us a better chance of holding on and fighting back. Unfortunately, from this promising start ensued the worst and the last muddle which I ever experienced in the British Army. Once again, the Higher Command could not let things alone. We had already started to dig the strongpoints in the sites selected by the Colonels when the Brigadier chose to inspect them, and of course decided to alter the positions. We started all over again, but there were lots of brass hats who had to have their say in the matter and time and time again the position of the strongpoints was changed. The result was chaotic. In the first place the men were tired to death, in the second place since the position of the strongpoints was constantly being changed it was impossible to organise a regular drill by which every man knew his strong point and got there in the quickest possible time when ordered to do so. Lastly, instead of being deeply dug and strongly revetted and wired it was quite obvious that when the moment came to use them the strong points would hardly be strong enough to keep out a well-aimed snowball. The appalling and crass stupidity of it all. Putting up barbed wire entanglements at night time is a hard-enough job in itself, but we reached the point where we had to uproot the entanglements that we had previously erected on abandoned sites, cart them off and erect them on new sites, which is simply herculean labour. And all this was done on the nights when we were supposed to be resting against our next spell in the trenches.[26]

25   Arthur Kenlis Maxwell, Lieutenant Colonel Lord Farnham, officer commanding 2nd Battalion Royal Inniskilling Fusiliers.
26   IWM Doc. 4118 Captain Charles C Miller papers.

Had they been allowed to remain with the Division, the Entrenching battalions would have been a valuable resource which would have alleviated the pressure on the battalions in the line. However, the three battalions formed from the reorganisation of the Division were engaged in apparently non-essential tasks elsewhere. The war diaries record that in February 1918, 21st Entrenching battalion were working on an aerodrome whilst both 22nd and 23rd Entrenching battalions were involved in railway construction work.[27]

Some assistance in the construction of the strongpoints was provided to the battalions in the line by the Royal Engineer companies attached to the Division. One man engaged on this work was Sapper Alfred Henderson of 122nd Field Company Royal Engineers. Sapper Henderson was from Camberwell, London and had spent seven months in France earlier in the war with 152nd Field Company RE before being evacuated with peritonitis. Whilst engaged on the system of strongpoints as an engineer, he recognised the deficiencies in the scheme, but also the historical significance of the location:

> Here was a system, if it could be called a system of strongpoints. The front line was covered by three redoubts named left to right, Boadicea, Racecourse and Jeanne D'Arc Redoubts. These, more than 1,000 yards apart were on high ground rising from a long valley behind and were covering a loosely held system of trenches facing the German line about 1,600 yards ahead of them. The whole front about three and a half miles in length, far too much for our under-strength battalions. Although I was not aware of it at the time, this valley had been the scene of a remarkable exploit of the Cavalry of the 3rd and 5th Cavalry Brigades of the BEF on 28 September 1914 when the 12th Lancers, 20th Hussars and Scots Greys made a series of fine charges against a German Regiment of Uhlans and drove them back nearly to St Quentin. About a mile behind these forward redoubts were three similar redoubts – Ricardo, Quarry and Station Redoubts which were in fact, the designated Battle Zones for determined defence in the event of a front-line breakthrough by the enemy.[28]

Whilst the men of the Ulster Division were beginning to construct their defences, for the German forces, planning for their offensive was well under way. As mentioned in an earlier chapter, time was critical for the German Army. Commanded by General Erich Ludendorff as Quartermaster General and Field Marshal Paul von Hindenburg as Chief of the General Staff, both men were out and out militarists who crucially enjoyed the support of Kaiser Wilhelm. The events in Russia where shortages had fuelled revolutionary aspirations, were beginning to have a parallel in Germany at the end of 1917, where the populace were beginning to protest over shortages of food and other necessities

---

27   TNA: WO 95/828/10: 21st Entrenching battalion war diary, WO 95/957/4: 22nd Entrenching battalion war diary, WO 95/664/7: 23rd Entrenching battalion war diary.
28   IWM Doc. 11045 Sapper Alfred E Henderson papers.

partly enforced on them by the blockade of German ports by the Royal Navy. Both men realised that a decisive military offensive would have to take place before public opinion in Germany caused the Kaiser to revisit his unwavering support. The other factor was the realisation that America with its vast resources would soon be taking the field on the allied side which would undoubtedly eventually signal a German defeat. A successful offensive before American involvement would therefore placate a disgruntled public and establish Germany in a position of strength should they be forced to sue for peace.

The decision to proceed with the offensive was made in November 1917. It was a purely military decision, the German commanders unencumbered by the sort of political interference endured by Field Marshal Haig. The German commanders were aware that for any sort of success, the British Army had to be comprehensively dealt with. To achieve this objective there were three plans for attack on the table. One named *Operation George* – later changed to *Operation Georgette*, was in the Ypres area of Belgium. The second, named *Operation Mars* was against British Forces at Arras and the third, *Operation Michael* against British Forces near St Quentin. In essence, the decision of where to attack was made much simpler by the reorganisation of the British Army and by the extension of the British front line. This made the stretch of front line opposite St Quentin more weakly held, as General Gough had identified and crucially provided a junction between the British and French Armies in the area which could be exploited. The ground in this area was also relatively dry, in contrast with that further to the north which was bound to assist with the massive numbers of troops on the move.

The German plan was relatively simple. They intended a massive attack to drive a wedge between the British and French Armies. Once this wedge had been made the German Army intended to turn right and drive the British right back to the channel coast. It was a risky venture, as once the German Army turned right they would have had the French in a position to attack their flank, but Ludendorff and von Hindenburg considered this a risk worth taking. In addition to *Operation Michael*, once this was under way, versions of *Operations George* and *Mars* would be instigated to tie up British forces farther north and prevent them from assisting the troops subject to the initial attack. In respect to the German Emperor, Ludendorff named the entirety of the spring offensive, *Die Kaiserschlacht* – the Kaiser's Battle.

Once the decision of where to attack was made, planning on how and when, were the next important considerations. Acutely aware through intelligence that American forces would be ready to join the front line around April, pressure was on to be able to strike before that. Initial aspirations were for the end of February or the beginning of March, but this was always likely to involve some slippage. The transfer of Divisions from the Eastern Front increased rapidly over the winter and by the middle of February 1918, records indicate that there were 177 German Divisions on the Western Front. By 2 March, there were 181 and by 10 March, 185.[29] At full strength, this gave a total of infantry personnel alone of 2,775,000 men.

---

29   Edmonds, *Military Operations France and Belgium 1918*, p. 105.

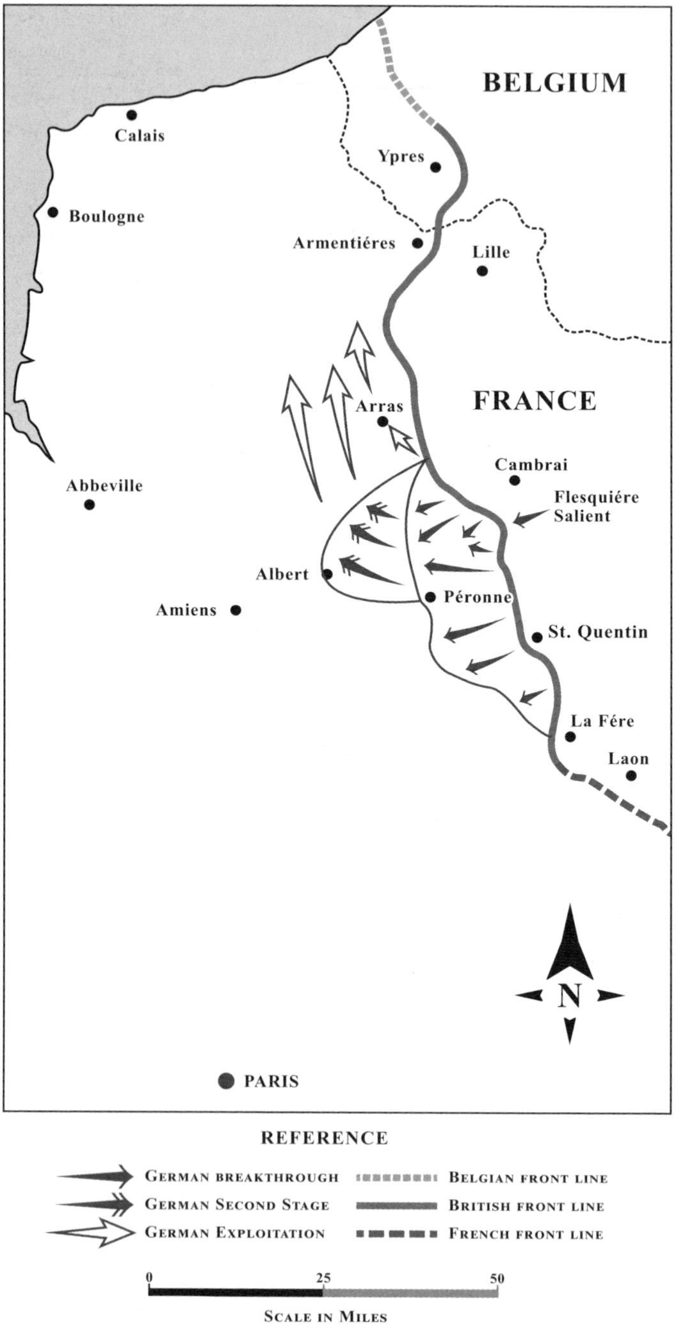

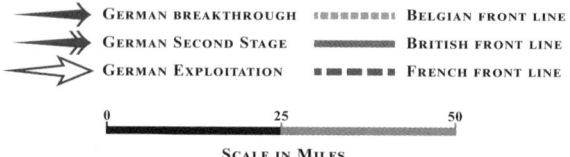

Map 5 The German Spring Offensive Plan

At the end of January, the commander of the British Fifth Army, General Gough became aware of the presence of the German 18th Army under the command of General von Hutier opposite his army at St Quentin. He was aware of von Hutier's reputation and of his resounding success the previous year at Riga. A mixture of intelligence, intuition and common sense told Gough that the attack was likely to fall in his sector of the front line. Alarmed at the resources allocated to him to defend the largest stretch of the British front line, he penned a letter to General Headquarters at St Omer on 1 February 1918, outlining the situation and requesting assistance. Highlighting the lack of reserves available to him, he continued in a prophetic manner:

> The more recent German attacks (i.e. Verdun February 1916, Riga, the attack on Italy) have been characterised by a short bombardment up to about six hours and the most strenuous efforts to obtain surprise. These efforts I cannot be sure of defeating; consequently, in his initial attack the enemy might find me disposed as at present, with the equivalent of eight Divisions in line on a 40 mile front; this would naturally go far towards ensuring him success, especially in view of the state of my defences.[30]

The letter also optimistically highlighted that given extra resources, the Battle Zone and Rearward Zone could be made into well defended areas by 15 March. Gough received a sympathetic hearing to his request. Between 2 February and 16 March, the effective strength of men involved in labour with 5th Army rose from 24,217 to 48,154.[31] Whilst this looks fine on paper, it is how these resources were deployed which should have given cause for concern. The Labourers worked six out of seven days, so around 15 percent of this total was resting each day. The majority were, in common with the recently raised Entrenching battalions, involved in the constructions of roads, railways, casualty clearing stations, ammunition dumps and on water supply projects. A minority was involved in improving defences – at best no more than 20 percent.[32] The apparent lack of reserves was an issue identified by the perceptive Father Gill:

> As far as my personal observations went during the excursions to Divisional and Corps HQ which were often necessary, there were practically no British troops in close reserve. Thus the main shock would have to be met by the Divisions actually holding the line.[33]

---

30   Ibid, Appendix. 11.
31   Ibid, p. 147.
32   Edmonds, *Military Operations France and Belgium 1918*, p. 147.
33   IJA/CHP1/27 p. 156.

General Gough was fairly close to the mark when he highlighted that any attack would be initiated by a short sharp Artillery bombardment. Having had resounding success with these tactics at Riga and Caporetto, the German commanders decided to continue with similar plans except on a much larger scale. In doing so they turned to the architect of the previous successes, Oberst Georg Bruchmuller. Nicknamed *Durchbruchmuller*, (literally 'Breakthrough Muller') by his contemporaries, he had been an officer in the Reserve at the outbreak of war and was 54 years old by the time of the offensive. He was discovered to have a unique skill in identifying just how much of a bombardment was necessary to soften up defences before Infantry were committed. His *modus operandi* was also to target artillery across the breadth of the enemy defences, not just concentrating on the front and reserve lines which had previously been the case. A mixture of high explosive, gas and

Oberst Georg Bruchmuller.
(Open source)

smoke shells were also to be utilised, calculated to sow confusion in the enemy ranks and cause gas masks to be worn which greatly hindered the movement and vision of defenders.

Bruchmuller's audacious plan was to bring the thousands of Artillery pieces required into the line at the last possible minute to gain the maximum element of surprise. This meant that these Artillery pieces would have no time to register[34] and would be firing from the map. Ordinarily, this may have presented a problem. However, as previously noted, the Germans had the coordinates of every location where the British were likely to station troops or artillery pieces and roads which would be used to bring up reserves and supplies, so from the outset they had a distinct advantage.

To carry out the artillery bombardment, the Germans assembled the largest concentration of Artillery yet seen in the war. In all 6,473 guns of all calibres, complemented with 3,532 trench mortars were to be involved.[35, 36] The bombardment was planned to last five hours and have seven distinct phases.[37] In all it was estimated that 1,160,000

---

34   Accepted practice at the time was to bring Artillery pieces into position and fire a number of rounds to register the guns. The fall of rounds would be mapped by an Artillery Observer who would communicate any adjustments required to the gun team.

35   General Sir Martin Farndale *History of the Royal Regiment of Artillery, Western Front. 1914-18* (Woolwich: The Royal Artillery Institution, 1986) p. 262.

36   Of this total, von Hutier's Army had the largest proportion, 2,448 Artillery pieces and 1,226 Trench Mortars.

37   See note entitled 'German Artillery Time Programme.'

rounds were to be fired in the five-hour bombardment, equating to 65 rounds fired <u>per</u> <u>second</u>. By contrast, the British bombardment before the opening day of the Battle of the Somme fired 1,500,000 rounds in seven days, equating to less than three rounds per second.

Following the massive bombardment calculated to soften up the defences, the infantry were to be deployed in an innovative manner. The usual manner was for a frontal infantry advance with the intention of overwhelming the oppositions defences. The problem with this was that when a particular defensive strongpoint provided resolute resistance, it tended to slow or even halt the entire offensive. To counter this, tactics successfully employed by General von Hutier at the Battles of Riga and Caporetto were introduced. This involved small, highly trained and lightly armed groups of soldiers whose instructions were to advance as far and as fast as they could. They were to flow like a river, If they encountered strong resistance, they were simply to bypass it and leave it for more conventional units following behind to deal with. These units were known as *Sturmtruppen* or Stormtroopers.

A German Medical Officer, Stefan Westmann[38] was attached to one such unit which he described in glowing terms:

> The new battalion to which I had been attached consisted of hand – picked young soldiers, fully trained in swift movements, everyone a first-class athlete, a champion thrower of hand grenades, which he carried in two bags in front of him. They did not have rifles, but twelve shot automatic pistols in wooden holders, and by a clever device the handle of the automatic could be fixed to the end of the holder, thus making a deadly little firing rifle. The side arms were spades with sharp edges which inflicted terrible wounds. The only thing which the ordinary French or British infantryman could do when attacked by these devils, was to throw his rifle away and put up his hands as quickly as he could. He had come up against the First XI of the Kaiser's Army.[39]

Whilst the elite of the German infantry were the Stormtroopers, all of the attacking infantry received three weeks intensive training during the winter of 1917-18. This training emphasized speed of movement and mastery of close quarter weapon skills with the grenade and light machine-gun. Lengthy route marches were also carried out to enhance fitness.

One such unit which was to become closely acquainted with the 36th (Ulster) Division was *Regiment der Infanterie Nr. 463* or IR 463 as it will be referred to from here on. Whilst we are aware of the composition of the 36th (Ulster) Division from its inception and subsequent reorganisation, it is of interest to learn something of the

---

38   He later anglicised his name to Stephen Westman, becoming a successful surgeon at Harley Street, London.

39   Stephen Westman, *Surgeon with the Kaiser's Army* (London: Kimber 1968) pp. 156-7.

background and composition of IR 463, who were initially to be in direct opposition to the Ulstermen.

IR 463 along with its sister battalions IR 464 and IR 465 comprised 238th Infantry Division which was commanded by Lieutenant General Hans von Below. The regiment was raised in January 1917 at Lockstedt Army Base near Itzehoe, north-east of Hamburg in the province of Schleswig-Holstein. A quarter of the regiment's men were transferred directly from the front, a quarter had been recovering in Germany due to sickness or injury, and the other half were recruits born in the years 1898 and 1899 and drafted on 21 November 1916.[40] The living conditions in Lockstedt base were, given the extremely long and harsh winter, by no means favourable. The tough field work in snow and ice took its toll on the bodies of the young troops. The rations did not suffice to quell their hunger by a long stretch, many being growing adolescents. It was unfortunately impossible, considering the strict rationing of supplies in Germany and immense demands of the million strong armies on the front, to grant any greater rations.

Initial training completed, the regiment first saw action in the retreat to the Hindenburg Line in April 1917, being involved in fighting near Le Catelet, west of St Quentin against the 48th (South Midland) Division. Later in 1917 they were to be involved in the Third Battle of Ypres, being specifically involved in the first and second Battles of Passchendaele between 13 October and 9 November during which they sustained 257 fatalities and a further 299 wounded.[41] IR 463 arrived at St Quentin on 10 November 1917 and remained there over the winter before being sent to Origny-Sainte-Benoite, east of the town for intensive training in February 1918. In common with the Ulster Division, the men of IR 463 had been through a lot from their formation, their original ranks having been decimated with casualties. Even though the Regiment had only been in existence for a year, it was battle hardened. However, having fought mainly defensive actions, their role was about to change.

Throughout February, the intelligence picture developed, and all indications were that an attack was in the final stages of planning. As early as 3 February, General Gough had briefed his commanders that an attack on their sector of the front was imminent. He emphasised that:

> Amiens was the objective based on, 1. Presence of von Hutier, 2. Evident preparation in hand, 3. Good German Divisions being withdrawn from the front for training (as had happened at Riga) and replaced by passive ones. This accounted for the front being unusually quiet. He highlighted the need for defence in depth

---

40   Rudolf Hoffmann, *Infanterie-Regiment 463. 7000 Niedersachsen im Grosskampfe der Westfront* (Bremen: von HM Hauschild, 1930) p. 8.
41   Hoffmann, *Infanterie-Regiment 463. 7000 Niedersachsen im Grosskampfe der Westfront*, p. 140.

to be completed, frequent raids, great alertness and every measure to prevent surprise.[42]

The focus on building defences fell on the infantry battalions of the Ulster Division. The battalion war diaries of each for the month of February tell the same story:

1st Battalion Royal Irish Rifles – 16th February in Div. Reserve. Worked on Battle Zone at Essigny. 22nd to Quarries at Grand Seraucourt. Work on Battle Zone continued until 28 Feb when went into line relieving 15th Royal Irish Rifles.[43]

12th Battalion Royal Irish Rifles – 17th-22nd February. Working parties were supplied day and night. 22nd To Essigny Station. Work on Battle Zone.[44]

1st Battalion Royal Inniskilling Fusiliers – 5-6 Feb moved to 36th Div from 29th. Villeselve 7 Feb. 150 OR from 10th Innis joined. 9th-14th February at Artemps. Whole of Battalion employed as working parties under RE Supervision. 23rd-28th, Working parties of 200 men at a time under RE Supervision in the Battle Zone.[45]

The issue was as had been highlighted by Captain Miller. The men were exhausted by the programme of manning the front line and then being used for labouring tasks. Priorities were not wholly on constructing defences though. Some of those who would have been expected to be at the forefront of defensive construction were diverted to other tasks which were deemed 'essential' to some, as was highlighted in the war diary of one of the Royal Engineer companies:

150 Field Coy Royal Engineers – Beginning of February saw the Company engaged in diverse tasks – working on constructing the Divisional Officers Hairdressing Room and an instrument room at the Brigade theatre at Grand Seraucourt, as well as repairing wire and dugouts in the front line.[46]

Sapper Alfred Henderson of 122 Field Company Royal Engineers was also having an altogether easier time:

42   Edmonds, *Military Operations France and Belgium 1918,* p. 144.
43   TNA: WO 95/2502/3: 1st Royal Irish Rifles war diary.
44   TNA: WO 95/2506/2: 12th Royal Irish Rifles war diary.
45   TNA: WO 95/2510/1: 1st Royal Inniskilling Fusiliers war diary.
46   TNA: WO 95/2497/3: 150th Field Company Royal Engineers war diary.

Attached to Colonel RE HQ at Ollezy. The village was intact. My job was to supervise the building of a dugout opposite the General's sleeping quarters. We had been working for about 10 days when we struck water, which was not surprising seeing that it was quite near a stream, a tributary of the River Somme. Since the cover was only about seven feet this was judged insufficient, so we began another one on higher ground. One day the General himself visited the site and asked me about our rate of progress. He seemed quite surprised when I told him that our rate was only about three feet per day. Life was very comfortable here at Divisional HQ nine miles from the front line. Just down the road in a field was a large marquee where the Divisional Concert Troupe entertained the troops that were fortunate enough to be able to visit them. The only turn I remember was a female impersonator on a swing who was singing a popular song of the time, 'Swing me over the garden wall just a little bit higher Obadiah do.' This was the first time that I had seen a female impersonator. I was not impressed.[47]

The night of 22 February saw the new system of defence implemented. All three Brigades took over the front line, 108th on the right, 107th in the centre and 109th on the left. Each had one battalion in the Forward Zone, one in the Battle Zone and one in reserve. Each battalion in the Forward Zone had two companies in the front line, or line of resistance, one for counter attack and one in reserve. This reserve company was based with Battalion Headquarters in the line of redoubts. From right to left the redoubts were known as Jeanne D'Arc, Racecourse, and Boadicea.

In his account, written after the publication of Falls, *The History of the 36th (Ulster) Division*, Sapper Alfred Henderson, 122 Field Company Royal Engineers, takes issue with Fall's sketch of defensive measures (reproduced as Map 2, Page 51) claiming that it paints a misleading picture of the true state of the defences:

> The view might give the impression that there was a reasonable network of trenches, but this was not so. In the main these were shallow and not to be passed through in daylight hours. All my work during the two weeks prior was done at night time around the Racecourse Redoubt and beyond Grugies. The whole defence system depended on the six so-called redoubts. The ground between the three forward positions and the three at the rear was very open country, exposed and no cover of trees.[48]

If Sapper Henderson's view is correct, and work could only be carried out on the defences at night, this limited still further the opportunity to construct adequate

47   IWM Doc. 11045 Sapper Alfred E Henderson papers.
48   Ibid.

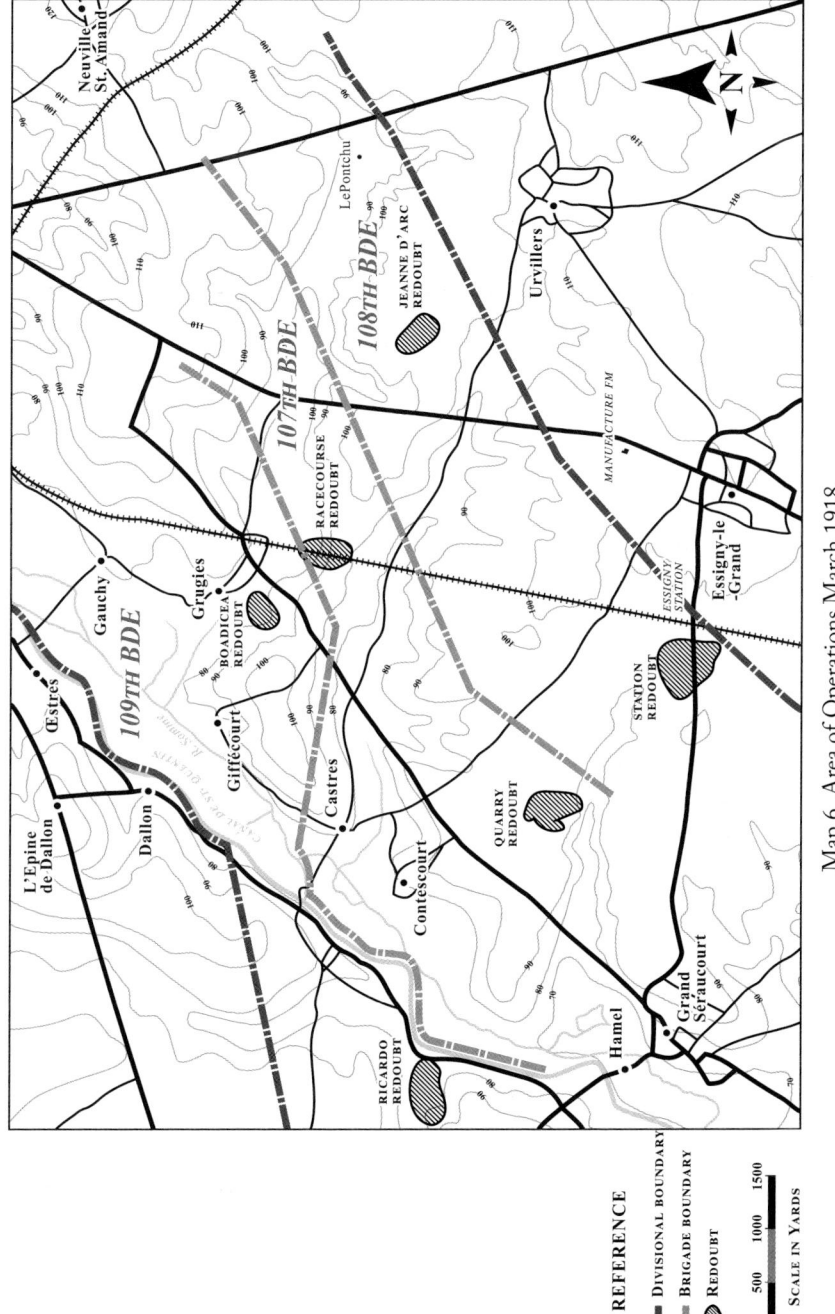

Map 6 Area of Operations March 1918.

REFERENCE

DIVISIONAL BOUNDARY

BRIGADE BOUNDARY

REDOUBT

0   500   1000   1500

SCALE IN YARDS

defences and threw into question whether as General Gough claimed, that the defences would be completed by 15 March.

On 23 February, the interest being shown in the construction of the new defensive system very nearly spelt the end for both the Corps and Divisional Commander and corroborates Sapper Henderson's view of unnecessary movement during daylight hours. It also gives some indication of the keen observation skills of the German Artillery observers. Major General Nugent described the incident in a letter to his wife:

> We had a narrow squeak yesterday. I had met the Corps Commander at a village in the forward area to ride over some new lines we were digging. There were about 12 of us all in a cluster on our horses when we heard a shell coming. We could hear it coming for so long getting louder and louder and suddenly it fell almost in the middle of us in the midst of a pile of bricks where there had been a house. It was a dud! If it had burst there would have been vacancies as we were all round within a few yards of it.[49]

Although he escaped unscathed, this was a healthy dose of reality for the Divisional Commander and an acute reminder of the hazards faced daily by the officers and men on the front line.

49   PRONI: D3835/E/2/16/24.

4

The Lull before the Storm

Adopting the attitude of prize-fighters, we hurled defiance at the enemy. Typewritten notices were circulated and ordered to be placed by patrols on the barbed wire in front of the German trenches. These notices invited the Germans to 'come on', warning them that if they did so they would learn to their cost the reason why. I do not know which of the authorities was responsible for this childish device. [1]

Fr. Henry Gill, Chaplain attached to 2nd Battalion Royal Irish Rifles,
107th Infantry Brigade 18 March 1918.

At the beginning of March, the final piece of the re-organisational jigsaw was put in place with the establishment of the 36th Machine Gun Battalion. Prior to this, there had been a Machine Gun Company attached to each of the three brigades. The battalion was under the command of Lieutenant Colonel Guy de Hoghton MC, formerly King's Own Yorkshire Light Infantry. The battalion war diary describes its composition and disposition:

> The formation of the battalion coincides with the reorganisation of the Division and the extra personnel to complete establishment is drawn from the disbanded battalions. A, B and C Coys in the line having a total of 30 guns in the Forward Zone and 20 Guns in the Battle Zone. D Coy in Divisional Reserve at Happencourt. [2]

The 50 machine guns of the battalion provided a fearsome defensive capability. Each machine gun team was armed with the Vickers Machine Gun which had been in service with the British Army since 1912. It was exceedingly reliable, firing .303 ammunition contained in 250 round canvas belts to an effective range of just over 2,000 yards, with a maximum rate of fire approaching 500 rounds per minute. A

---

1   IJA/CHP1/27 p.158.
2   TNA: WO 95/2498/3: 36th Battalion Machine Gun Corps war diary.

Vickers Machine Gun Team in action. (Open source)

crew of six manned each gun which was mounted on a tripod and with all equipment weighed close to 50 lbs.[3]

The officers of the machine gun battalion liaised with the battalion commanders holding the Battle and Forward Zone positions over the best place to situate the machine-gun teams to obtain maximum defensive effect and where necessary, Royal Engineers were brought in to construct machine gun posts as alluded to in his memoirs by Sapper Alfred Henderson:

> My work for the first 10 days of March was mostly concerned with the construction of a machine – gun post near Racecourse Redoubt. One in particular was under the railway which was elevated across the valley at this point. The post covered the villages of Castres and Urvillers but mainly directed along the valley eastwards.[4]

Also, as the month began, both sides stepped up their efforts to discover the location and strength of the other's defences and to gain some intelligence on those defences. This manifested itself in a number of raids carried out by either side which were short, vicious exchanges and invariably resulted in casualties. On 1 March, a raid took place

---

3   Vickers Machine Gun <http://www.vickersmachinegun.org.uk> (Accessed 3 November 2017).
4   IWM Doc. 11045 Sapper Alfred E Henderson papers.

near the village of Essigny on the right of the Ulster Division sector. The position was held by the 1st Battalion Royal Irish Rifles and their war diary gives a detailed account of what ensued:

> At 8:20 p.m. on 1 March a heavy trench mortar and artillery bombardment lasting about 20 minutes preceded a raid by a party numbering about 80. Our sentries in St Bruno trench saw a large body of the enemy crawling under and in some cases lifting and cutting our wire. They were able to enter the front-line trenches by bombing and continued to bomb the trench and dugouts. They severely wounded an officer, Lt HD Sinclair and killed one man and wounded seven others. One man was taken prisoner. The enemy left no dead or wounded, but it is certain that he suffered heavy casualties.[5]

The wounded officer was 23 years old Lieutenant Herbert Darbishire Sinclair from Adelaide Park, Belfast. The son of a Yarn and Cloth Merchant, he was educated at the Royal Belfast Academical Institution. He was seriously wounded in the head and right forearm by a grenade thrown by the attackers. The injuries he sustained ended his war and after lengthy treatment, he relinquished his commission in January 1919.[6] The man killed was Lance Corporal James Clegg from Birkenhead, Cheshire. He had previous service with the Army Service Corps and had been in France from October 1914. He was transferred to the Royal Irish Rifles in September 1917 as part of a draft from the ASC.[7]

On the same night, the Germans attacked the positions held by the 2nd Battalion Royal Inniskilling Fusiliers, killing an officer and wounding two soldiers. The officer who died was 22 years old Second Lieutenant William Brown from Cootehill, Co Cavan. A Bank Official with the Provincial Bank before the war, he had been educated at the Royal School, Dungannon. He had enlisted in 1915 as a private soldier in the Royal Irish Fusiliers and was commissioned into the Royal Munster Fusiliers, joining the 2nd Inniskillings on attachment in May 1917. His commanding officer Lieutenant Colonel Lord Farnham wrote, 'On the night before his death, he led a raid in a most gallant manner over the enemy lines. He was a most popular and promising officer.'[8]

With the battalions holding the front line on the alert, German raids did not always go to plan. On 4 March the war diary of the 1st Battalion Royal Irish Fusiliers describes a major miscalculation by the Germans:

---

5   TNA: WO 95/2502/3: 1st Royal Irish Rifles war diary.
6   Lieutenant Sinclair's younger brother, 20 years old 2nd Lieutenant George Stanley Sinclair also attached to 1st Battalion Royal Irish Rifles was accidentally killed whilst supervising bombing practice on 28 May 1917.
7   L/Cpl Clegg is buried at Grand Seraucourt British Cemetery, grave II.B.3.
8   Jim Condon *Officers of the Royal Inniskilling Fusiliers in World War 1* (Enniskillen: Royal Inniskilling Fusiliers Museum, 2003), p. 35. Second Lieutenant Brown is buried at Grand Seraucourt British Cemetery, grave II.B.2

4 March 1:50 p.m. The enemy being of the impression that our front trenches were not held during the day and that we had taken up a position in the rear, sent out two strong patrols of 20-30 men each and attempted to enter our lines at Ruined House and Sphinx Wood. Both parties on approaching our lines came under heavy Lewis Gun fire also a barrage of rifle grenades was fired at them, some of these parties retired and others took cover in shell holes. We organised bombing parties who rushed the enemy and captured one officer and seven men. Heavy casualties must have been inflicted on the enemy. We had one OR wounded.[9]

On the same day, another German raiding party approached the positions held by the 1st Inniskillings:

4 March. A raid comprised of about 20 Boche was observed approaching our lines at about 11:30 a.m. It was engaged with Lewis Gun and Rifle Fire and was hotly pursued by a party under Lord Farnham who was taking our own commanding officer round the front line. As a result, the enemy was dispersed leaving two dead, two wounded and one unwounded prisoner.[10]

The interesting thing about both of these German raids is that the Germans felt confident enough to approach the British lines in daylight, a practice usually confined to the hours of darkness. The rarity of the situation was highlighted by the Divisional Commander in his daily letter to his wife:

The Germans did a very extraordinary thing today. They came over in parties in broad daylight and naturally got severely biffed. We took one officer and several men prisoners.[11]

Numerous reports are also contained in war diaries up to Divisional level of German officers being seen during the day observing the Ulster Division positions through field glasses from St Quentin, no doubt fine tuning their attack preparations.

More innovative forms of propaganda were also initiated as an early form of psychological warfare. As Father Gill mentioned, British patrols left notices on the German wire showing that they knew reinforcements had recently arrived from Russia. The 36th Division War Diary recorded with bravado:

9   TNA: WO 95/2504/3: 1st Battalion Royal Irish Fusiliers war diary.
10   TNA: WO 95/2510/1: 1st Battalion Royal Inniskilling Fusiliers war diary.
11   PRONI: D3835/E/2/17/1 Farren Connell papers.

13 Mar. We have been distributing propaganda on the enemy wire, telling him what he is going to get when he comes and how great the difference is between East and West.[12]

On their side, the Germans retaliated somewhat ingeniously by sending copies of the *Gazette des Ardennnes*[13] across the British lines attached to paper balloons. More conventional means were also employed to try and get further information. On the British side the Royal Flying Corps was flying daily missions over the German lines to glean up to date information. As Jones (1934) observed:

Each day the reconnaissance reports and air photographs added something. Particularly noticeable was a daily extension of the network of light railways behind the German lines, a growing concentration of German air units and an abnormal number of lights in enemy back areas reported by night flying pilots.[14]

This information was quickly analysed and disseminated, particularly to Artillery units who targeted suspected concentrations of German activity. What increased British suspicions was that the Germans unusually failed to reply to the British Artillery fire. What also irked Captain Frank Broome of 173rd Brigade Royal Field Artillery, part of the 36th Division's Artillery, was the refusal of the French to allow the Artillery to target the historic basilica in St Quentin which dated from the sixteenth century:

Knowing the German's intentions, we carried out an active programme of harassing fire which must have caused them heavy losses but to which they did not reply. Their silence became quite uncanny. They held the town of St Quentin on which we were forbidden to fire out of French sentiment and unsurprisingly the Germans made use of as an observation post. Occasionally we would send over a few shells into the town on the quiet and our frustration must have been most welcome to the Germans.[15]

Whilst not actively retaliating, the Germans worked out deception plans as described by the German Medical Officer Stefan Westmann, to fool the Royal Flying Corps pilots, the Artillery and raiding parties of the Infantry:

---

12   TNA: WO 95/2492/2: 36th (Ulster) Division War Diary.
13   The *Gazette des Ardennes* was a German propaganda paper published in occupied France and Belgium between November 1914 and November 1918.
14   Henry Albert Jones, *The War in the Air: Being the story of the part played in the Great War by the Royal Air Force. Volume IV* (Uckfield: Naval & Military Press reprint of 1934 edition), p. 268.
15   Frank Napier Broome, *Not the Whole Truth* (Johannesburg: University of Natal Press, 1962), p. 89.

The deception practised on the enemy artillery observers as to the appearance of new German batteries of large or small calibre was worked out to perfection. Our batteries had half their guns constantly on the move, appearing here, there and everywhere, firing at night a few shots into enemy territory, and when next morning British or French reconnaissance aircraft flew over to take pictures of the new battery position, there it apparently was but actually consisted of wheels of farm carts with a wooden beam, all scarcely camouflaged. The British Artillery fired fiercely on these dummies and the next night, a few hundred yards away, a new battery 'popped up'. This intended deception manoeuvre went on for weeks from north to south and especially on those parts of the front where no attack was intended to take place. The enemy got restless and wanted to find out what troops occupied the sector opposite, so the Germans did not exchange the old troops for new ones who might, when taken prisoner, have given away the game.[16]

There was now no doubt that the German attack was looming, and the unusual behaviour of the Germans should have given some indication that one possible area for attack was on the Ulster Division front. As the month progressed, intelligence from the Royal Flying Corps added to the suspicion that an attack was coming sooner rather than later as the Divisional war diary recorded:

> Photographs show that the enemy has done a great deal of new work opposite our sector and in particular dug a small new salient opposite our left Brigade apparently with the object of improving his view of our lines.[17]

The battalions continued their programme of exhausting work to prepare defences and the Royal Engineers continued with a preparatory programme of preparing all the bridges across the Somme and St Quentin Canal for demolition should the need arise. On 8 March, Major General Nugent wrote to his wife, voicing his concerns:

> The indications and the reports of prisoners look like an imminent German attack somewhere on this particular front, but the exact place we cannot tell.[18]

Ironically, on the same date, *The Daily Mirror* published the following on its front page under the headline: 'Where foe may launch his big offensive – Junction of Franco-British lines near St Quentin likely spot.' The article continued:

16   Stephen Westman, *Surgeon with the Kaiser's Army* (London: Kimber 1968), p. 154.
17   TNA: WO 95/2492/2: 36th (Ulster) Division War Diary.
18   Nicholas Perry (ed.) *Major-General Oliver Nugent and the Ulster Division* 1915-1918 (Stroud: Sutton Publishing, 2007), p. 208.

At the junction of the Franco-British lines near St Quentin the enemy has conceived the plan of operating on a big scale on the extreme British right wing with a view to breaking its contact with the French left wing.[19]

Two days after this article appeared, the Germans made their final decision and an Operational Order for the offensive was issued by Field Marshal von Hindenburg:

The Michael attack will take place on 21st March. Break into the first hostile position at 9:40 a.m.[20]

Final preparations began to get underway far behind the German lines and a massive mobilisation commenced to get the hundreds of thousands of troops and thousands of artillery pieces and trench mortars moving towards their allotted positions. Amongst them were the men of IR 463:

On the 14th of March the regiment orders six officers and 500 men to transfer mines onto lorries for their transportation to St. Quentin where they will be housed. On the 16th, English pilots release flyers over Origny with the captions, 'Welcome on the 20th March!' You have nearly got wind of our plans my dear Tommies, yet not quite. Fritz will come, don't worry! With music! You will be amazed. The time has come to take their leave from Origny and Thenelles. They are admittedly, not the homeliest of villages, yet they have for weeks provided accommodation for the regiments, every soldier has grown close to this place, knowing every house, tree and pathway. This is why even this farewell will be hard. Who will return from battle?[21]

With the news of the likely attack available for public consumption and the battalions in a desperate race to complete barely adequate defences, what happened next within the Ulster Division in particular, is quite simply hard to comprehend.

On 5 March, the 1st Battalion Royal Irish Fusiliers were holding a position in the front line. The day was an auspicious one for the Regiment, being the anniversary of the Battle of Barossa on 5 March 1811 when the battalion, as the 87th Regiment of Foot, seized the French Eagle standard during the siege of Cadiz, Spain. The day could obviously not be celebrated on the exact date. However, when relieved from the front line and in billets at Grand Seraucourt, 11 March was declared a holiday for the battalion. No work was done by the men and a special dinner was had by the officers attended by distinguished guests including the Brigade Commander, General

19   *The Daily Mirror*, Friday 8 March 1918, p. 1.
20   Edmonds, *Military Operations France and Belgium 1918*, p. 147.
21   Hoffmann, *Infanterie-Regiment 463: 7000 Niedersachsen im Grosskampfe der Westfront*, p. 183.

Withycombe. It could be said that having been engaged in hard labour and holding the front line, this was a morale booster and an exercise in excellent man management which was greatly appreciated by the men. Six days later however, was St Patrick's Day, a day traditionally marked in the military by the distribution of shamrock, church services and some entertainment for the troops.

With the German Offensive a matter of days away, St Patrick's Day, 17 March was bizarrely designated as a holiday for the entire Division and not only the 36th, who had after all no better claim to the day, but other Divisions in the Fifth Army availed of the holiday. Even General Gough, the Fifth Army Commander entered into the spirit of things and gave his rationale for doing so, as he later recalled:

> On Sunday 17th – St Patricks Day – the 20th Division had some sports and an Officer's Jumping Competition, for which I entered both my chargers. In the afternoon, I went down to have a chat with the Officers of the Division and rode my two horses, one of them being 4th out of a total of 120 entries. I did this not only for the sake of a ride round the jumping course, which I enjoyed, but because I thought it was good to meet the 20th Division and see its members under friendly conditions and also to show some calm confidence in the outcome of the great events before us. I remember that the Duke of Wellington attended the Duchess of Richmond's Ball in Brussels just before Waterloo. And that one of his principal reasons was the same. I felt I had a good precedent for thus spending my Sunday afternoon.[22]

The interesting fact about this is that the 20th (Light) Division, who were one of the Fifth Army Reserve Divisions, had no Irish units attached to them whatsoever.

Perhaps the feeling of calm confidence alluded to by General Gough was also ordered to be displayed by his Divisional Commanders. Certainly, in the Ulster Division no efforts were spared to enjoy the day. Every unit war diary of the Division comments that a holiday was ordered on the day, some go into much more detail than others. The 2nd Inniskillings got things off to an early start:

> A Boxing tournament was held on the evening of 16th inst. when some very good amateur talent displayed. Four weights being displayed, Heavy, Welter, Middle and Lightweight. Lieutenant Colonel Lord Farnham was Referee, Lieutenant Cox MC and Private Quinn – Judges, Captain Burke – Timekeeper. Prizes were distributed at the sports the following day (St Patrick's Day.)[23]

Much was made within the Division of the fact that both the regular battalions of the Royal Irish Rifles and the Royal Inniskilling Fusiliers were based together for the first time on St Patrick's Day. The Inniskillings took the opportunity to have inter

---

22   Gough, *The March Retreat*, p. 63.
23   TNA: WO 95/2510/2: 2nd Battalion Royal Inniskilling Fusiliers war diary.

– battalion sports, as the war diary of 2nd battalion relates with no small degree of satisfaction:

> St Patrick's Day. Shamrock was distributed to all ranks in the Battalion. The day was observed as a holiday and combined sports (1st and 2nd Battalions) were held. The officers were at home to their friends as were the Sergeants. The principal events of the day were: Tug of War, catchweights, inter battalion – won by 2nd battalion. Cross Country run – won by 2nd battalion, Football match – won by 2nd battalion, one mile race – won by 2nd battalion, Hidden Treasure Race – won by 2nd battalion. A most successful and enjoyable day concluded at about 6.30 pm when prizes were distributed by Brigadier General WF Hessey DSO. [Brigade Commander 109th Brigade][24]

Lieutenant Colonel Lord Farnham commanding 2nd Inniskillings, thoroughly enjoyed the sports and in a letter to his wife that day, hinted that the evening's entertainment was likely to be as good, if not better:

> A line to say we had a very successful day in our sports. A lovely day and an ideal spot and the Bosch [sic] did not intervene. We are having a Battalion Mess tonight to celebrate the occasion. In fact it may be rather lively, I hope not too much so.[25]

Festivities and a heightened sense of occasion were no less evident within the Royal Irish Rifles:

> St Patrick's Day. Observed as a holiday. 1st and 2nd battalions united at Mass by Reverend Father Gill DSO MC. The first time both battalions had celebrated Mass together since 1854. A football match was then held between the battalions which the 1st Battalion won 2-1. Battalion sports were held in the afternoon. The battalion also won the 'Open Cookers' event in a competition open to the whole of the 5th Army near Ham.[26]

Acknowledging the significance of the circumstances, Father Gill was nonetheless restless:

> We spent St Patrick's Day in the traditional manner. As it fell on a Sunday, the religious celebrations presented no difficulty...We had our sports on high ground

24   TNA: WO 95/2510/2: 2nd Battalion Royal Inniskilling Fusiliers war diary.
25   PRONI: D3975/E/8/29/8 Farnham papers.
26   TNA: WO 95/2502/3: 1st Battalion Royal Irish Rifles war diary.

from which St Quentin could be seen. No doubt the Germans could also see us and allowed us to play.[27]

Sapper Alfred Henderson, a Londoner, entered into the spirit of things with Irishmen of divergent political leanings within 122nd Field Company, Royal Engineers:

> Three days before was the 17th March, and St Patrick's Day had been celebrated in a mild manner for Ulstermen by a sing-song in our dugout. Of course, being in the line, no strong drink was available, not even a ration of rum since it was officially recorded that the general conditions did not merit it. I had been called upon to sing my usual songs, 'Just kiss yourself goodbye' and its sequel, 'Won't you come home Bill Bailey.' I think that they liked to hear my cockney accent. Then we had from a Welshman, 'When I dream of old Ireland I am dreaming of you.' This was followed by 'The Mountains of Mourne' and others not so well known to some of us. Most of the Ulstermen were sporting bits of shamrock that had come from home. My mother had sent me a St Patrick's card to which was attached a small sachet containing 'true shamrock seed' which I duly planted with ceremony in the Cutting. For a few of my comrades this was a first experience of action and less than half were Irishmen, or Orangemen. Many had been recruited from the shipyards of Belfast. However, we all got on well with one another and I remember that two of the Company were avowed Sinn Feiners but that meant nothing at this time. This was a free for all, very much in the tradition of the 'Fighting Irish.'[28]

Whilst the sentiments of Gough regarding the celebration of St Patrick's Day are laudable, the circumstances facing his army were vastly different than those facing the Duke of Wellington at Waterloo. In that battle, the opposing French and British armies had a similar strength, around 69,000 men each. The Duke of Wellington though had an advantage, in that he had another 37,000 troops as allies from various European states and principalities.[29] From his own account, General Gough states that in 1918, General von Hutier had 13 Divisions in the front line and eight in the second line.[30] The British forces were therefore heavily outnumbered:

> To meet him stood four Divisions and two Brigades of the II and XVIII Corps, with the equivalent of another Brigade in the form of the 2nd Cavalry Division. It might be fair also to count the 20th Division in GHQ reserve, though it was 15

---

27   IJA/CHP1/27 p158.
28   IWM Doc. 11045 Sapper Alfred E Henderson papers.
29   Battle of Waterloo <http://www.battleofwaterloo.org> (Accessed 15 September 2017).
30   Edmonds, *Military Operations France and Belgium 1918.* Edmonds claims that opposite Lieutenant-General Maxse's XVIII Corps (36th, 30th and 61st Divisions) were 14 German Divisions, p. 175.

miles from the front and could not get into the fight on March 21. The strength of the Fifth Army allowed one man per yard of its far-flung line. The actual odds against my Army on the opening of the battle were four to one. It is interesting to note that in no previous assault during the whole of the war had the ratio of attackers to defenders exceeded two to one.[31]

Facing the 36th (Ulster) Division alone were three German Divisions, 238th Infantry Division, 36th Infantry Division and 1st Bavarian Infantry Division. With the introduction of the new defensive scheme, the Ulster Division would have three battalions in the forward zone, totalling around 2,500 men. The three German Divisions facing them numbered around 45,000. General Gough's decision to grant a holiday four days prior to the opening of the offensive, must therefore be looked at as an act of bravado bordering on the reckless. It was obviously a popular decision, but one which ignored the gravity of the situation. In the circumstances, the holiday could have been rescheduled, as in the case of the Barossa Day celebrations. An extra day's work on the defences may have made some appreciable difference and may have saved some lives. However, we will never know.

Following the holiday, it was back to the grindstone on 18 March. The 1st Royal Irish Rifles and 1st and 2nd Inniskillings spent that day and the next improving defences in the Battle Zone. Other battalions not in the front line carried out intensive training. Further pieces of the intelligence picture began to fall into place. The war diary of 173rd Brigade Royal Field Artillery noted:

> 18 March. At about this time, aeroplane photos coupled with information from deserters revealed the presence of large numbers of new Trench Mortar emplacements in the enemy's line. These were made to resemble shell craters from which they were hardly distinguishable. The great number of these gave rise to the supposition that the enemy would rely on gaining a footing in the Forward Zone by this means rather than by the use of tanks. These positions and the locations in which they were present in the largest number were heavily dealt with by artillery.[32]

On 19 March, concrete information of the timing of the offensive was obtained by a patrol of 15th Royal Irish Rifles. The war diary of this battalion from 1-20 March 1918 is missing, but Serjeant William Finlay MM,[33] who was subsequently taken prisoner, described what happened:

---

31   Gough, *The March Retreat*, p. 66.
32   TNA: WO 95/2496/6: 173rd Brigade Royal Field Artillery war diary.
33   Serjeant William Finlay MM, 15/11664 15th Royal Irish Rifles was a regimental medical NCO. Prior to the war he was a Joiner and resided with his wife, Abigail at 15 Dandy Street, Whitehouse, Co. Antrim.

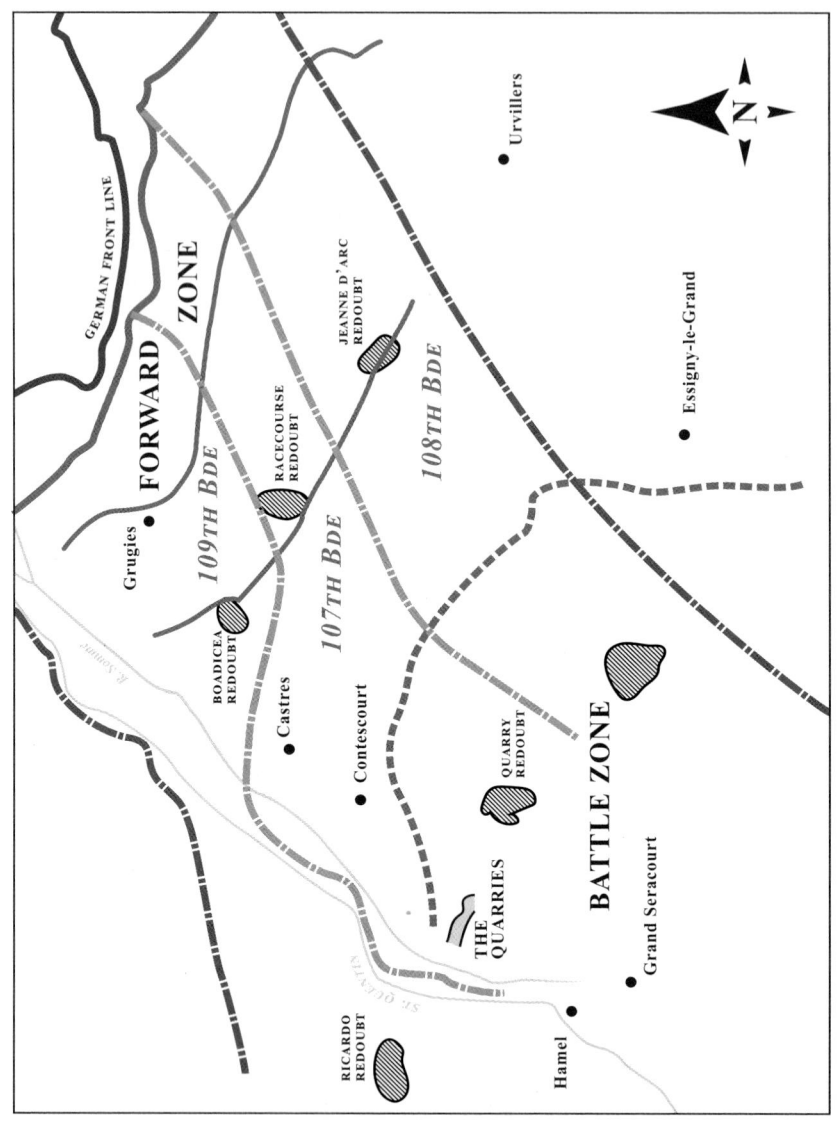

Map 7 Forward and Battle Zone.

Two days before the offensive we captured two Germans in no man's land and they told our officers about the coming German attack on 21st, well that put everyone on the alert and arrangements were made to counteract it.[34]

The two captured Germans were from the contested region of Alsace on the border between France and Germany and were attached to the 414th Trench Mortar Company. They confirmed that shell holes which from aerial photographs appeared to have been modified, were in fact Trench Mortar emplacements. They also confirmed that St Quentin itself was packed full of German troops. Their information appears from various accounts, to have been taken at face value. Writing to his wife on 20 March, Major General Nugent commented:

Two Alsatian deserters came in last night and from their statements which are confirmed from other sources there seems no doubt that the day is very near. We expect to be attacked tonight or tomorrow and it is going to be a very big attack and will last for weeks.[35]

More than any other piece of information, the details provided by the deserters appears to have galvanised the Division into action and the information provided was quickly disseminated to all units. The war diary of 173rd Artillery Brigade recorded that they stepped up their firing rate from 19 March:

19 March. Definite information was obtained from enemy deserters that the enemy attack would take place on the morning of 21st. These deserters testified to the enormous concentration of troops behind the enemy lines, large numbers of which had actually taken up their positions in dugouts in the enemy front line. Harassing fire was therefore prosecuted more vigorously than ever.[36]

Following the harassing fire bombardment, which spectacularly scored a direct hit on an ammunition dump on the outskirts of St Quentin, there was surprisingly no retaliation from enemy artillery which was completely out of the ordinary. The Ulster Division Artillery were then ordered to complete the relocation of all their Batteries from the Forward Zone to a point behind the Battle Zone. This order ensured that Captain Broome of 173rd Brigade RFA became a very busy man:

When it was known for certain that the attack would come early on 21st March we were ordered to carry out a heavy counter-preparation from our forward battery positions throughout the preceding night but leaving enough time for

34   PRONI: D4101/1 Serjeant William Finlay papers.
35   PRONI: D3835/E/2/17/11 Farren Connell papers.
36   TNA: WO 95/2496/6: 173rd Brigade Royal Field Artillery war diary.

the batteries after firing all their ammunition to withdraw to their prepared positions covering the Battle Zone. This meant that the whole of my daylight hours of the 20th had to be spent in organising the transportation of the ammunition to the forward batteries. The work could never have been done in the time with our own horse transport and our own loading manpower, but I was lucky to get the use of a trench railway and tractor and a party of loaders and finished the job before sunset.[37]

The order for the Artillery to be relocated was a controversial one which did not inspire much confidence in those who were manning the Forward Zone and increased the feelings of isolation and was a confirmation, if any was needed, that the battalions in the Forward Zone were expendable. In essence, this assumption was correct. In an after-action report, the war diary of Captain Broome's Brigade recorded the reasoning:

> Between 10:30 p.m. and 12 midnight all remaining batteries were withdrawn to positions behind the Battle Zone. Practically all ammunition was removed from the forward positions or fired before they were evacuated. From information received later through Forward Observers it is certain that had Batteries remained in forward positions they would have been annihilated without having been able to take any active part in the battle.[38]

This was scant consolation to the battalions in the Forward Zone. Following the St Patrick's Day festivities some reliefs had taken place and the disposition of the 36th (Ulster) Division on the eve of the battle was, from right to left:, as follows:

108th Brigade
Forward Zone – 12th Battalion Royal Irish Rifles. Battalion HQ was at Jeanne D'Arc Redoubt
Battle Zone – 1st Battalion Royal Irish Fusiliers. Battalion HQ was at Station Redoubt
Rear Zone – 9th Battalion Royal Irish Fusiliers at Grand Seraucourt

107th Brigade
Forward Zone – 15th Battalion Royal Irish Rifles. Battalion HQ was at Racecourse Redoubt
Battle Zone – 1st Battalion Royal Irish Rifles. Battalion HQ was at Quarry Redoubt
Rear Zone – 2nd Battalion Royal Irish Rifles at Grand Seraucourt

37   Broome, *Not the Whole Truth*, p. 89.
38   Ibid.

109th Brigade

Forward Zone – 2nd Battalion Royal Inniskilling Fusiliers. Battalion HQ was at Boadicea Redoubt

Battle Zone – 1st Battalion Royal Inniskilling Fusiliers. Battalion HQ was at Ricardo Redoubt

Rear Zone – 9th Battalion Royal Inniskilling Fusiliers at Artemps.

The Division's Pioneer Battalion, 16th Royal Irish Rifles had its Headquarters at Grand Seraucourt. Companies of the battalion were working flat out, principally at the Forward Zone Redoubts in an attempt, even at this late stage to improve the defences. On receipt of information of the imminence of the attack, the Division's Field Ambulance deployed extra Stretcher Bearers and medical personnel to the Forward Zone Redoubts.

Despite the best efforts of the working parties of the battalions and the Royal Engineers, the Forward Zone defences were wholly inadequate. Captain Miller, 2nd Inniskillings was certainly apprehensive:

> We went into trenches as I remember it on the night of March 19th 1918. Somewhere about midnight on March 20th I got a chit from Farnham to the effect that it was a certainty that the attack would come on the 21st or 22nd, that there was to be no question of retreat and that the main battle would be fought some three miles behind us. He wished me good luck and I returned his wishes as I liked Farnham very much and it seemed to me that this was likely to be the end of our acquaintance. I then got my four platoons into their strongpoints taking all my men out of the front line. It was a dead still and rather chilly night and this was accomplished easily and successfully. I myself was in the strong-point allocated to Company HQ, and having got in there I had time to make a visit to one of the points occupied by my platoons. I hated the look of it, a couple of dugouts hastily made and inadequately wired and I wished that I had disobeyed orders, and put them into one of the previously discarded strongpoints.[39]

The Forward Zone redoubts really were in an isolated position. They were unable to mutually support each other, and they had no connection with the Battle Zone to the rear. The gaps within them were ripe for exploitation by fast moving infantry, especially the German stormtroopers whose instructions were to advance at speed and if they met an obstacle to move round and past it.

Whilst Captain Millar was apprehensive, there was no less apprehension on the German side. Leutnant Hoffmann of IR 463 knew that this was the last throw of the dice for the German Army:

39   IWM Doc. 4118 Captain Charles Miller papers.

It was obvious to all what was coming, and we were glad that the monotonous life in the trenches was over. Most of us were 19 or 20 years old and we longed for victory and peace. We didn't hate the English and French, especially the English for whom we had some understanding, being of the same stock. Had they not come from Schleswig-Holstein near where I lived in Hamburg some 1400 years earlier? This was the last desperate attempt to bring about a change in our fortunes. Maybe 20-30 percent of our unit were keen because they hoped to find plenty of food and alcohol, they were mostly the young ones. But the rest of us weren't at all enthusiastic, we just wanted to get the war over with and get home alive.[40]

The advance of IR 463 to their front-line positions was impeded however, by the attentions of the night-flying Squadrons of the Royal Flying Corps:

During the night of the 20th of March, the regiment moves into its marshalling area. The 1st Battalion into the front trenches the 3rd to the right of them and 2nd positioned behind them both. The combat supplies are located on the road Homblières – Marcy. Every man has meals for two days and also two reserve portions, in addition to this they have four grenades and 150 cartridges of ammunition. The regiment's advance march is held up by lively armed attack, however only a low number of losses are incurred. Brave Lt. Bruhns falls victim to an aircraft bomb.[41]

Despite the intensive preparations of both attackers and defenders, there was one factor over which neither had control – the weather. In the week leading up to 20 March, the weather had been typical of early Spring. Mists in the morning giving way to reasonable weather with showers and longer spells of rain. On five days of the week 13-20 March, there had been fog in the morning with visibility described by the meteorologists as poor or indifferent.[42] (See footnote for full description of visibility grades). On 20 March, the weather forecast issued by the Meteorological Office at British GHQ described the day starting off as fair, becoming bright and sunny and that mist would develop around 5:00 p.m. and would become ground fog by 9:00 p.m. On no day in the previous week had there been mist or fog in the evenings. It is probably for this reason that no special instructions were issued as to special actions to be taken in the event of an attack in fog. It was possibly an assumption that the Germans

---

40   Middlebrook, *The Kaiser's Battle*, p. 63.
41   Hoffmann, *Infanterie – Regiment 463. 7000 Niedersachsen im Grosskampfe der Westfront*, p. 183.
42   Edmonds, *Military Operations France and Belgium 1918*, p. 111. The varying degrees of visibility were graded by the meteorologists as:

would not risk an attack in the fog due to the dangers of their troops becoming disorientated and isolated.

The Germans however, had gone too far in their preparations to stop now. They were concerned by meteorological reports of fog, especially as they were to deploy large amounts of gas shells. As Leutnant Hoffmann of IR 463 noted:

> On the 20th March the weather conditions, in particular the wind strength, were by no means very advantageous. The Army Supreme Command had concerns as the building of the artillery offensive would be based upon the use of gas. The latest reports were not especially favourable, yet the attack still seemed possible. An order was therefore sent to the army groups at 12 Midday that the attack would take place, as planned, on the 21st March.[43]

In the evening of 20 March as the mist developed into a creeping fog, on the British side Father Gill was uneasy as he prepared for bed:

> That night we retired to sleep with a most complete uncertainty as to what the morrow was to bring. Everything had hitherto been quiet at night with few exceptions. Certainly, no shell had fallen in the village since our arrival.[44]

One man who was luckier than most was Gunner William Grant, of the Division's 173rd Brigade Royal Field Artillery. At 6:00 p.m. on 20 March, his warrant for long awaited leave came through and he made his way to Ham railway station where he departed for Le Havre at 3:00 a.m. on 21 March. As he left Ham he described how British Artillery was still firing, 'as hard as it could'.[45]

Indifferent – objects cannot be seen beyond a distance of		5,000 metres
Poor	— " —	3,500 metres
Very Poor	— " —	1,000 metres
Bad	— " —	500 metres
Very Bad	— " —	120 metres

43 Hoffmann, *Infanterie – Regiment 463. 7000 Niedersachsen im Grosskampfe der Westfront*, p. 181.

44 IJA/CHP1/27, p. 160.

45 IWM Doc. 6477. Gunner Grant was held at Le Havre until 24 March and then ordered to re-join his unit. It took him three days to reach 36th Division, and he remained with them in an infantry capacity until he reached Gamaches with the other remnants of the division on 31 March.

5

The Hammer Falls – 21 March 1918

The long expected has come at last. The German bombardment began at a quarter to five this morning and is still going on. In all my experience out here, I have never known anything more terrific. It isn't a series of reports, but it is just one long roar.[1]

Major General Sir Oliver Nugent's description of the opening
of the battle in a letter to his wife written on 21 March 1918
from his Headquarters at Ollezy.

When trying to piece together accurate accounts of any engagement during the Great War, the war diaries of the battalions involved are usually the best start point and by examining accounts of neighbouring battalions and units, a more or less complete picture can be built up. For the German Offensive of March 1918 however, this has proved much more difficult. This is primarily due to the nature of the action. For some units, no war diary exists for a period of weeks, others are scant in detail and some others were clearly written well after the event. Certainly, no blame could be attached in relation to this, as those charged with annotating the daily course of events had more important distractions to deal with! However, within the war diaries which exist, are a number of detailed after-action reports which enable the researcher to interpret how events unfolded. Official and unit histories also provide important detail, although in some, it is evident that a 'direct lift' has taken place from the war diaries and after-action reports. In the 36th (Ulster) Division however, this process is hampered by the fact that there are no unit histories for both 12th and 15th Battalions Royal Irish Rifles, both of whom had crucial roles on 21 March.

Research within local and national archives has uncovered a number of contemporaneous accounts from servicemen who were actually involved which, when read with official material, assist greatly in building the picture and in explaining events. Chief among these accounts are reports within officer's personal files which were completed after capture. The Army Act 1907 consolidated the Army Discipline and Regulation

---

1   PRONI: D3835/E/2/17/11 Farren Connell papers.

94

Act 1879, the first part of which covers the area of discipline and provided that a Board of Enquiry had to be established to investigate each instance of surrender. Surrender without good cause was a serious breach of military law, as the Act states:

Part 1 – Offences in respect of Military Service

4. Every person subject to military law who commits any of the following offences, that is to say, 1. Shamefully abandons or delivers up any garrison, place, post or guard, or uses any means to compel or induce any governor, commanding officer or other person shamefully to abandon or deliver up any garrison, place, post or guard which it was the duty of such governor, officer or person to defend or, 2. Shamefully casts away his arms, or tools in the presence of the enemy or, 3. Treacherously holds correspondence with or gives intelligence to the enemy; or, treacherously or through cowardice sends a flag of truce to the enemy or; 4. Assists the enemy with arms, ammunition or supplies, or knowingly harbours an enemy not being a prisoner, or 5. Having been made a prisoner of war, voluntarily serves with or aids the enemy, or 6. Knowingly does when on active service any act calculated any act calculated to imperil the success of His Majesty's Forces or any part thereof or 7. Misbehaves or induces others to misbehave before the enemy in such manner as to show cowardice, shall on conviction by court martial be liable to suffer death, or such less punishment as in this Act mentioned.[2]

Each and every officer captured in the offensive had to give a detailed account of their capture, which was considered by a Board of Enquiry comprising a Major General, Brigadier General and Lieutenant Colonel. On consideration of the evidence, a letter was forwarded stating whether or not blame was to be attached. Now, no-one with any sense was going to submit an account which stated that they were negligent, and I have yet to see an account where blame was attached. However, this was not a rubber-stamping exercise and I have seen many occasions where clarification was sought, naming other officers who had given slightly different versions. It appears therefore, that efforts were made to examine the veracity of accounts. For these reasons, it should be taken that the accounts may be slightly embellished in favour of the respondent. However, when examined against existing material, in many cases they are exceedingly accurate and greatly assist in explaining the course of events. For that reason, I have incorporated many of them within the narrative, firstly to assist in explaining how a particular unit fared, and secondly to personalise what can be sometimes, 'dry' accounts.

In the accounts of the units of the 36th (Ulster) Division, there are various times given for the opening of the bombardment. These vary from 4:15 a.m. to 'around 5 o'clock'. Given the chaos that existed within British lines at the opening of the battle it is reasonable to assume that, with typical Teutonic efficiency, the bombardment commenced at 4:40 a.m. as directed in the German operational plan.

2   The War Office *Manual of Military Law* (London: War Office, 1907) pp. 267-8.

The question that had plagued British Commanders as to where exactly the German offensive would fall was answered in the early hours of 21 March. The main thrust of the attack targeted the area where the right flank of 36th Division and the left flank of the 14th (Light) Division met.

Before turning to the experiences of the Ulstermen, it is of interest to see how the Fifth Army Commander dealt with the opening of the offensive:

> At 10 minutes past five I was awakened by the roar of a bombardment, which, though it sounded dully in my room in Nesle [25 miles SW of St Quentin] was so sustained and steady that it gave me the impression of some crushing smashing power. I jumped out of bed and walked across the passage to the telephone in my office and called up the General Staff. On what part of our front was the bombardment falling? The answer came back almost immediately, 'All four Corps report heavy bombardment along their front... no sign of any Infantry advance as yet.' This at once opened my eyes to the magnitude of the attack on the Fifth Army...We issued a few orders and warned all concerned... I looked out of my window and in the morning light I could see that there was a thick fog, such as we had not yet experienced in the whole of the winter. We were getting into Spring and it was extraordinary to have so dense a fog at this date... I threw myself back on my bed and went to sleep for an hour. By 8:30 a.m., shaved, bathed and fed, I was back at the telephone, but no reports of the German advance had yet reached us.[3]

In being able to return to sleep it could be argued that General Gough must have been supremely confident in the plans put in place and in the state of the defences. Both however, were about to be tried in the sternest test possible.

In adequately explaining what happened to the troops of the Division on 21 March, I intend to deal with the experiences of each battalion, starting with those in 108th Brigade and working from the right of the line held by the Division to the left.

108th Brigade

The battalion holding the Forward Zone and who therefore met the full force of the initial German attack, was the 12th (Service) Battalion Royal Irish Rifles (Central Antrim Volunteers). The battalion had held the front line since 16 March when they had relieved the 9th Royal Irish Fusiliers. The position held by the battalion straddled the St Quentin-La Fere Road, with the most forward positions at Sphinx Wood, some five hundred yards to the east of this road. The Battalion HQ was at Jeanne D'Arc Redoubt, with a forward position at Le Pontchu quarry which was a mile in front of the Redoubt. Forward of the Le Pontchu position were two trenches named

---

3   Gough, *The March Retreat* p. 73.

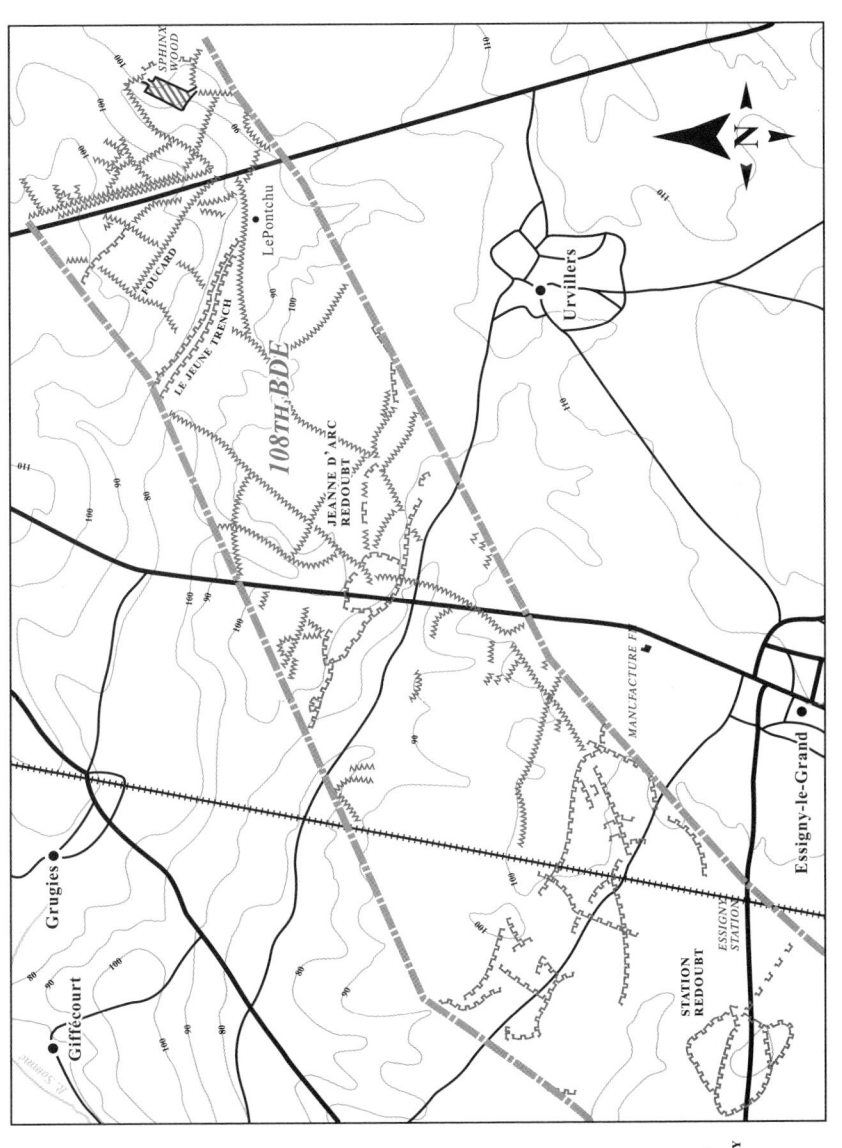

Map 8 108th Brigade Defensive Zone.

Lejeune and Foucard which held a view of the road. Present with the Battalion HQ at Jeanne D'Arc were 160 officers and men of No. 1 Company, 16th Battalion Royal Irish Rifles, the Divisional Pioneer battalion who were still working on the defensive scheme.

The battalion holding the Battle Zone, the 1st Battalion Royal Irish Fusiliers was just over two miles to the rear at Station Redoubt. Whilst this battalion had some trenches forward of this position, there were large swathes of open ground between the battalions which had no defensive workings at all.

Just prior to going into the line, on 10 March the 12th Royal Irish Rifles had lost its commanding officer, Lieutenant Colonel William Richard Goodwin DSO, who was taken to hospital through illness. This was a blow as Lieutenant Colonel Goodwin was an experienced soldier, having commanded the battalion since 1916 and had led the battalion with great gallantry during the Battle of Cambrai in November 1917. He was replaced by another experienced officer who had been with the battalion since St Patrick's Day 1915, 26-year-old Acting Major Augustus Henry Hall. Major Hall had been born in Oxfordshire in 1892 and before the war had worked as a Tea Planter in Ceylon (now Sri Lanka). He had enlisted in the 16th (Service) Battalion Royal Irish Rifles (Pioneers) at Lurgan, County Armagh on 28 January 1915. Serving as a Rifleman, he applied for a commission almost immediately and was appointed as 2nd Lieutenant in the 12th Royal Irish Rifles on St Patrick's Day, 1915. He had fought with the battalion in all the major engagements since their arrival in France. Major Hall was in charge of Battalion Headquarters at Jeanne D'Arc Redoubt. At the forward position at Le Pontchu, the Acting Battalion 2i/c, Captain Thomas Shannon Adamson was in charge. Somewhat older than most in the battalion, Captain Adamson aged 42, was from Whitehead, County Antrim and had been a Company Commander in the Ulster Volunteer Force prior to obtaining his commission in September 1914.

Captain Thomas Shannon Adamson 12th Royal Irish Rifles. (Great War Ulster Newspaper Archive)

The accounts of the officers of the battalion vary in the time that they believed that the German bombardment commenced, with times between 4:00 a.m. and 4:30 a.m. being quoted, giving some idea of the confusion that reigned. The order to man battle stations was issued to all companies at 4:45 a.m. but immediately after this all telephone communications were cut. This was primarily due to the knowledge and keen observation work of the Germans who specifically targeted lines of communication, even though the telephone cables had been buried to a depth of six feet. The Battalion

HQ from the start was effectively blind and cut off from its forward companies. The fog which had begun to form the previous night was now so thick that visual communication was also impossible. Captain Adamson at Le Pontchu quarry observed:

> A heavy enemy bombardment was opened as anticipated from information received from Bde at 4.00 a.m. on 21st, continued with extreme violence until 9:15 a.m. when I noticed it lifted from front and support lines but continued with even greater violence around Forward Bn HQ, accompanied with smoke and gas shells. This with natural ground fog made observation for more than 10 yards impossible and gas masks had to be worn also.[4]

Captain Adamson's account highlights the effectiveness of the German Artillery programme which shifted to focus with unerring accuracy on defensive strongpoints. In the absence of any other means of communication, Major Hall sent out three runners into the fog to make contact with the forward companies. None were ever heard of again.

After five hours of bombardment the infantry assault began. Captain Adamson had deployed A Company to his right and D Company to his left at Le Pontchu. The first reports of an infantry attack came at 10:30 a.m. when a runner from D Company arrived and informed Captain Adamson that the enemy had broken through on the left of D Company and were attacking Company positions from the left and rear. This attack had taken place through lightly defended positions between 12th and 15th Royal Irish Rifles, the Germans being greatly assisted by the fog which rendered the defenders unsighted. At this early stage in reality, the die was cast for 12th Rifles. In a desperate attempt to shore up the D Company defences, Captain Adamson ordered C Company under the command of 21 years old Captain Leslie James Johnston forward. Leslie Johnston was born at Dublin but prior to the war was resident at Wellington Park, Belfast. He had attended Rosetta National School and Belfast Technical College and was employed by the Commercial Union Assurance Company at Donegall Square West Belfast. He had obtained his commission in October 1915. In his report made after capture, Captain Johnston stated:

> I was in command of the counter-attack Company which was in dugouts some 500 – 600 yards in rear of the front line. My instructions were that I was to remain in these dugouts until the SOS signal was seen to be fired from the outposts and until information had been received from the front line that the enemy had attacked. Owing to the intense natural fog and the mist caused by the severe gas shelling, the SOS signal was not seen, but at about 9:30 a.m. word came from the front line by the one remaining telephone wire, that the enemy had attacked. This information was late because as we advanced from our dugouts

---

4   TNA: WO 339/74778: Captain TS Adamson service record.

we encountered a small German party about 50 yards from us. So, before we could occupy the trench designated to us, we had to clear it of Germans. We did so and for four hours continued desultory fighting, taking a number of prisoners. We could not see for more than 30 yards with the result that large numbers of the enemy got past us.[5]

Not only were Germans streaming past on the left as D Company had originally reported, but also on the right, using the conveniently located St Quentin-La Fere Road. It soon became obvious to the defenders that a substantial gap had been forced between 12th Rifles and the 8th Battalion King's Royal Rifle Corps, 41st Brigade, on the left of the 14th Division line. Many accounts from units and individuals in the 36th Division place the blame for this breach entirely on 14th Division. In a letter to his wife, Major General Nugent stated:

> The fog lifted about 1:00 p.m. but it had done its foul work by hiding the Boches until they were up close to our main battle line. Then the Division on our right, I regret to say the 14th and my old Brigade the 41st too,[6] gave way and let the Germans in behind me.[7]

The 36th (Ulster) Division war diary account of operations stated:

> But at 1:15 p.m. while the enemy was attacking the Battle Zone positions all along the front of our sector, it was discovered that he had completely broken through on the Division on our right, was in the very important tactical point of Essigny village and advancing northwards towards Essigny station.[8]

The war diary of 108th Brigade stated:

> 1:10 p.m. The 14th Div. on our right were now retiring south of Essigny leaving our right flank in the air.[9]

The available evidence would indicate that these accounts are somewhat harsh on 14th Division. The war diary of 8th Battalion King's Royal Rifle Corps was destroyed, but accounts from officers indicate that A Company under the command of Major Norman Elsdale Barber held out in the Forward Zone until around 1:00 p.m. A letter

---

5   TNA: WO 339/47045: Captain LJ Johnston service record.
6   General Nugent had been Brigadier General commanding 41st Infantry Brigade from May to September 1915 prior to promotion.
7   PRONI: D3835/E/2/17/12A Farren Connell papers.
8   TNA: WO 95/2492/2: 36th (Ulster) Division war diary.
9   TNA: WO 95/2504/3: 108th Infantry Brigade war diary.

that he wrote from captivity is quoted along with others in the brigade war diary. He stated:

> We had a great fight on 21st and held out for four hours until all our ammunition had run out and we were surrounded on all sides. Finally, we decided to try and fight our way back again and did so for some distance but were finally overpowered. All our ammunition was gone so there was nothing else for it. The chief reason for the enemy's success was the thick fog which enabled him to get all around and we could not see to fire on him.[10]

The 8th Battalion King's Royal Rifle Corps sustained 52 fatalities on 21 March and of a battalion that had a strength of 42 officers and 950 other ranks before the battle commenced, only two made it back. The accounts of these two men are paraphrased in the brigade war diary which states:

> Their story is that owing to the thick mist the Boche was able to get right round them through a gap he had made in the 36th Div. on our left without being seen.[11]

It is only natural to protect your own and official accounts find it easy to blame someone else. The truth appears to be that the German infantry advance occurred in such massive force that nothing was going to stop them. The extent and speed of the German infiltration is highlighted in the regimental history of the King's Royal Rifle Corps which states:

> In fact, the enemy had reached Brigade Headquarters before they had reached our front line.[12]

This is further evidenced by the experience of the 7th Rifle Brigade who were holding a position in the Battle Zone of 41st Brigade. This Battalion had 47 men killed and 545 officers and men reported missing, the majority of which were most likely taken prisoner.[13] Some may have retired expeditiously in the face of the overwhelming assault, but as with the Ulster Division, the German attackers moved with such speed aided by the poor visibility that gave the defenders little time to organise. The new defensive system had left lightly defended areas which were wholly inadequate defensively and were ruthlessly exploited by a highly motivated enemy. The experience of

---

10 TNA: WO 95/1894/5: 41st Infantry Brigade war diary.
11 TNA: WO 95/1894/5: 41st Infantry Brigade war diary.
12 Lieutenant General Hutton et al., *The King's Royal Rifle Corps Chronicle 1918* (Winchester: Warren & Son, 1919), p. 131.
13 TNA: WO 95/1896/1: 7th Rifle Brigade war diary.

those in command of 41st Brigade was exactly the same as that of the Brigades in the Ulster Division, they simply had no idea what was happening until it was too late. This issue is emphasised in the official history of the Rifle Brigade:

> Although the enemy's infantry assault appears to have been delivered about 9:00 a.m. it was not until 11:47 a.m. that the first definite news reached HQ 14th Division. At that time a message was received from 41st Brigade to say that a MGC Sergeant from 36th Division had arrived with a report that parts a mile NW of Urvillers were surrounded. From then on until noon, other messages were received to the effect that the enemy had broken through the forward defences on the Divisional front and also on that of 36th Division and at 12:20 p.m. the latter passed on a report that the enemy had been seen in the Grugies valley. By 1:22 p.m. it was evident that the enemy had reached the Battle Zone along the whole Divisional front.[14]

Captain Johnston of 12th Royal Irish Rifles meanwhile, had moved his men up to Foucard trench which ran nearly parallel with and was about 300 yards from the St Quentin-La Fere Road. At around 1:00 p.m. the fog began to lift and what this revealed astonished the troops:

> When the fog lifted about 1:00 p.m. we saw how the operation had progressed. German transport guns were about three to four hundred yards in front of us, his foot infantry were from one and a half to two miles behind us and the trench which I held was being attacked from the front and on both flanks.[15]

What Captain's Johnston and Adamson were unaware of until this point, is that the German troops who were one and half to two miles behind had already captured Jeanne D'Arc Redoubt. For Major Hall and his party, the end came relatively quickly at around 11:00 a.m.

> At 10:30 a.m. one of my outposts reported to me that the enemy had broken through the front of the 15th Royal Irish Rifles, the battalion on my left and was being engaged by my outposts. I went to my office and was writing a message to my Reserve Coy Commander warning him when a bomb burst at the door of my office which was off the main shaft to my HQ dugout. I ran to the top of the shaft and was seized by three Germans. The enemy had rushed me in the rear from the direction of Essigny while we were engaged with them on the front. I was taken from Jeanne D'Arc almost at once... Owing to dense fog and tear shells

---

14   Brigadier General William W Seymour, *The History of the Rifle Brigade in the War of 1914–1918 Vol II, January 1917–June 1919* (London: The Rifle Brigade Club, 1936), p. 233.
15   TNA: WO 339/47045: Captain LJ Johnston service record.

it was impossible to distinguish my own men from Germans at a distance of 15 yards. The enemy attacked Jeanne D'Arc when their barrage was actually on it.[16]

The Pioneer complement of 16th Rifles who were in Reserve dugouts behind Jeanne D'Arc were placed in something of a quandary as the German attack developed. Their instructions in the event of an attack were to make their way back to their Battalion Headquarters at Grand Seraucourt. As this entailed moving over open ground for around four miles in the midst of an artillery bombardment, this option was rapidly discounted. The Company Commander, Captain Hugh Montgomery Baillie and Lieutenant William Quinn Rea[17] made their way at around 11:00 a.m. towards the battalion HQ at Jeanne D'Arc to ascertain the situation. Unfortunately, this coincided with the arrival of the Germans and both were captured. Both men were taken by the Germans to the rear, but the battle was still raging and crossing open ground was exceptionally dangerous as Lieutenant Rea recorded:

> Captain Baillie and myself were at a road junction 1500 yards west of Urvillers on the Essigny-St Quentin Road. We had been taken prisoner together but were not out of danger when Captain Baillie was shot through the head by my side. I did not see him buried.[18]

Captain Hugh Baillie was 24 years old when he was killed. A Solicitor's Apprentice with the Belfast firm of Carson & McDowell, he resided at 'Ellerslie', Ravenhill Park, Belfast and was a member of the Ulster Volunteer Force. He had enlisted as a Private in the 16th Battalion Royal Irish Rifles in November 1914 and simultaneously applied for a commission. He was appointed 2nd Lieutenant in the Battalion in January 1915. The 16th Rifles at Grand Seraucourt had no idea as to the fate of the party at Jeanne D'Arc. The battalion war diary simply recorded:

> The entire of No 1 Company consisting of nine officers and 150 other ranks failed to appear at the rendezvous and having apparently been cut off at Jeanne D'Arc were subsequently posted as missing.[19]

Given that it was known that Jeanne D'Arc had fallen at a relatively early stage, it was assumed that everything to the front of this position was in German hands and so British Artillery commenced a barrage which unfortunately targeted the positions held by Captains Adamson and Johnston, causing many casualties. Despite this

---

16   TNA: WO 339/26870: Acting Major AH Hall service record.
17   Lieutenant William Quinn Rea was 24 when he was captured. From the Antrim Road, Belfast, he was repatriated in December 1918.
18   TNA; WO 339/22463: Captain Hugh Montgomery Baillie service record.
19   TNA: WO 95/2498/2: 16th (Service) Battalion Royal Irish Rifles (Pioneers) war diary.

'friendly fire' bombardment and being attacked on three sides by the Germans, Captain Johnston directed an attack of withering Lewis Gun and rifle fire against a German transport convoy on the road in front of his position. At such close quarters, the effect was devastating and the convoy was completely destroyed, with every man and horse killed or wounded. One of the men involved in this incident was 21 years old Rifleman Robert McGookin from Larne, who described the action in his memoirs:

> There was a road which ran between the quarry and the front line and down the road came six German transport wagons with a team of six horses and riders attached to each. With our Company we had a Lewis Gun and it was sickening to see the havoc it created amongst this transport. We got the order, 'Rapid Fire' and every bullet found a billet in a German; it was utterly impossible to miss because the Germans were so thick on the road. In about ten minutes there was not a horse or rider standing on the road.[20]

About 1:20 p.m. seeing that their position was fast becoming untenable due to the increasing intensity of German attacks, Captain Johnston withdrew the remnants of his Company to Lejeune trench, some 300 yards to the rear. This manoeuvre however only served to postpone the inevitable, as Captain Johnston recorded:

(Top) Captain Hugh Montgomery Baillie 16th Royal Irish Rifles and (Bottom) Lieutenant William Quinn Rea 16th Royal Irish Rifles. (Great War Ulster Newspaper Archive)

> The enemy pressed us closely and his MG fire was very severe. We were also being shelled by our own heavy artillery. Then what seemed to be a German support battalion accompanied by a tank attacked us. The tank caused us a number of casualties and the enemy infantry succeeded in getting past our flanks. I immediately consulted the

20   Catherine Minford et al., *It wasn't all Sunshine: An Ordinary Man's Account of the First World War* (Larne: Larne Borough Council, 2012), p. 112.

A German Convoy in March 1918 similar to the one decimated by 12th Royal Irish Rifles.
(Bundesarchiv. Bild 183 – R28716)

OC Forward Battn. HQ who decided that as retirement was impossible, to save further loss of life we would require to surrender, which I did.[21]

The account of Captain Adamson indicates that two tanks attacked the position, one being a captured British tank. The other was the A7V *Sturmpanzerwagen*, one of Imperial Germany's first tanks. An absolute monster of a weapon, the tank had a crew of 18 and was armed with a 57mm cannon and six Maxim machine guns.[22]

An example of German ingenuity which had initially puzzled Captain Adamson was explained after his capture, as he recalled:

During the attack, I continually heard bells sound but could not understand the reason. Afterwards I discovered that each enemy section had one, doubtless to help to keep direction in the fog and mitigate against the possibility of attacking each other in mistake for us.[23]

21 TNA: WO 339/47045: Captain L.J. Johnston service record.
22 A7V *Sturmpanzerwagen* <http://www.tanks-encyclopedia.com/ww1/germany/sturmpan zerwagen_A7V.php.> (Accessed 15 Jun 2017). Only 20 of these tanks were ever made as its low ground clearance – less than two inches, made it impractical for any off-road operational activity.
23 TNA: WO 339/74778: Captain TS Adamson service record.

A7V *Sturmpanzerwagen*. (Bundesarchiv. Bild 103 – 204017)

Due to the confusion of the battle, differing times are recorded as to when the 12th Rifles surrendered. These vary between 2:30 p.m. and 4:00 p.m. From the accounts of Captains Adamson and Johnston, it would appear that the end came sometime around 3:00 p.m. The 12th Rifles had 22 Officers and 566 other ranks in the front line at the commencement of the battle and all were reported missing. The Commonwealth War Graves Commission records that 36 men from the battalion were killed that day. Amongst this number was 38 years old 2nd Lieutenant William Douglas Magookin DCM, from Newport Street in the Oldpark area of Belfast. A Bricklayer by trade, 2nd Lieutenant Magookin had enlisted in the 15th (Service) Battalion Royal Irish Rifles (North Belfast Volunteers) and embarked for France with the battalion in October 1915. In November 1915, he was awarded the Distinguished Conduct Medal for rescuing a wounded man from in front of the German wire at Beaumont Hamel.[24] He was commissioned into the 12th Rifles in March 1917. An officer who was popular

---

24   The citation reads, 'For conspicuous gallantry on 21st November near Beaumont Hamel. Hearing that a wounded man was lying out near the enemy's lines, he went out with 2nd Lieutenant Harpur to his rescue. After proceeding some 350 yards they found the wounded man some 20 yards from a German listening post and carried him back under heavy machine-gun and rifle fire which the enemy opened on them.' (*The London Gazette*, 22 January 1916). The man rescued was Rifleman Thomas Williamson from 7 Hazelnut Street, Belfast who succumbed to his wounds shortly after being rescued. 2nd Lieutenant Magookin was survived by his widow Dorothea. His sacrifice is commemorated on the Roll of Honour at Cliftonville Presbyterian Church, Belfast.

with the men, his death was witnessed by Rifleman Robert McGookin, who was with him at the time:

> The Germans made an attack on the right communication trench and the party I was with under Lieutenant Magookin DCM was ordered to meet them with bombs. It was in this trench that the good officer met his death. He led us up the trench to meet the Germans and we ran slap bang into them before we knew where we were. Lieutenant Magookin fired into them with his revolver killing about half a dozen of them and all the while we threw bombs into the rear and middle of them. When this officer had used all his revolver ammunition he disfigured a German's face with the empty weapon and this was his last action for he received two bullets from an automatic pistol which went clean through his throat and he dropped with a groan.[25]

By contrast, three 19-year-olds, exactly half the age of Second Lieutenant Magookin, also fell:

- Rifleman James Johnston Davidson 355, son of Benjamin Adair Davidson and Elizabeth Johnston Davidson of Carnmoney, Belfast.[26]
- Rifleman James Watson 1425, brother of Agnes Black 11 Hemp St, Belfast.
- Rifleman Hugh Welsh 1613, son of William and Catherine Welsh of Conlig, Co. Down.

None of the four have a known grave and all are commemorated on the Pozieres Memorial to the Missing.

Second Lieutenant William Douglas Magookin DCM. (Great War Ulster Newspaper Archive)

The actions of 12th Rifles and particularly those of Captain Johnston and C Company were simply heroic. They had survived artillery bombardments from both German and British Artillery and massed infantry attacks using rifles, machine-guns and at least one attack using *flammenwerfer*, (flamethrowers). They had fought one German battalion to a standstill and were only forced to surrender when attacked by a fresh battalion supported by tanks. Their actions held up the German advance however,

---

25   Minford et al., *It wasn't all Sunshine*, p. 113.
26   Rifleman Davidson is commemorated on the family memorial at Carnmoney Old Graveyard, Newtownabbey.

due to the massive numbers of German infantry, it was a battle they were never going to win.

Due to the nature of the conflict and the fact that all the combatants had been taken prisoner, it was only on repatriation that the full facts of the actions of C Company, 12th Rifles became known. To mark their gallantry, Captain Johnston was awarded the Military Cross, Company Serjeant Major Clement Joseph Farrell[27] and Serjeant Robert Jackson MM,[28] were awarded the Distinguished Conduct Medal and four awards of the Military Medal were also made to members of the Company.

Whilst the 12th Rifles were fighting for their lives, the inadequacies of the defensive system were being cruelly exposed. Once the Artillery bombardment was opened, all communications that the 1st Royal Irish Fusiliers (holding the Battle Zone) had with the 12th Rifles in front of them were lost and the Rifles were basically on their own. The Brigade Headquarters at Grand Seraucourt was equally unsighted and had no communication with their Battle Zone or Forward Zone. It was not until 12:25 p.m. fully two and three-quarter hours after the German infantry assault began, that Brigade received a message from 1st Royal Irish Fusiliers informing them that a heavy barrage was under way on the Battle Zone and that the enemy had broken through in the Forward Zone. The 36th Divisional Headquarters at Ollezy knew no more. The first intimation that they had of an infantry attack was not from their own brigades but from 30th Division on their left, who reported at 11:45 a.m. that the enemy had attacked their Forward Zone. This meant that on the Ulster Division front, the Germans had a two hour head start before those charged with managing the defences realised that they were being attacked.

The 1st Battalion Royal Irish Fusiliers had their Battalion Headquarters at Station Redoubt in the 108th Brigade Battle Zone. Station Redoubt was positioned on the Essigny-le-Grand to Grand Seraucourt Road, roughly 800 yards west of Essigny Railway Station and around one and a half miles from the village itself. This was a strategically important position as it was quite clear that with the gap forced in the line between the 36th and 14th Divisions, that the Germans were making use of the main road from St Quentin to Essigny and then, on reaching Essigny intended to turn right towards Grand Seraucourt, thereby cutting off the 36th Division troops in the Forward and Battle Zones. To combat any German advance from this direction, teams from the 36th Machine Gun Battalion were in position at the railway cutting covering the railway station and the road from Essigny.

---

27   Company Serjeant Major Clement Joseph Farrell 8043 was from Palmerston Road, Dublin. He had enlisted in the Royal Irish Rifles in 1906, initially serving with 2nd Battalion. Following the Armistice, he remained in the Army serving with the Royal Ulster Rifles in Iraq.

28   Serjeant Robert Jackson was born at Dunadry, Co. Antrim in December 1896. He enlisted in the 12th Battalion Royal Irish Rifles at Ballyclare on 16 September 1914. He was awarded the Military Medal for gallantry at the Somme in 1916. Following repatriation, he emigrated to Canada.

Sapper Alfred Henderson, 122nd Field Company Royal Engineers was in a dugout near Station Redoubt and was rudely awakened by the initial bombardment:

> For myself, I was not awakened by the noise, perhaps I was more accustomed to this sort of disturbance by now... I have noted in my diary, the time was 5:30 a.m. Immediately I noticed the familiar 'pear drops' smell, and worse an irritation of the nose and my eyes began watering. So hurriedly donning my anti-gas mask and dressing I went out to find my officer. I was suffering some inconvenience due to the watering of eyes and nose – I must have taken in some gas in my sleep, but the irritation gradually abated. The Germans were using on this Battle Zone area what they named Green Cross and Blue Cross shells. Green Cross were filled with Diphosgene,[29] a liquid which gave off a very unpleasant smell. The Blue Cross shell was mostly High Explosive with a quantity of liquid Diphenyl-Chlorarsine[30] which gave off a gas which caused sneezing. It was very dark the air was heavy with smoke and fumes from the exploding shells. The crashing of the shells on the railway track was throwing up clouds of road metal. The earth shook with the concussions, the wind came in waves and one felt terribly confined, not to say trapped within the walls of the embankments. The general obscurity due to the darkness, fumes and smoke was added to by a natural mist which reduced visibility to a matter of feet.[31]

Having survived the initial bombardment and still enveloped in smoke, gas and the thick fog, the first notice 1st Royal Irish Fusiliers had of the German Infantry attack was at 12:47 p.m. when stormtroopers launched an attack on positions on the left of the battalion frontage. That the attack initially manifested itself on this position is proof that the German tactics of by-passing obstacles, in this case Jeanne D'Arc Redoubt, were working. Ten minutes later, the entire Battle Zone was being attacked and as the fog lifted around this time, those in Station Redoubt could clearly see that the Germans had forced 14th Division troops out of Essigny. It was only a matter of time before they advanced towards Grand Seraucourt and attempted to cut off the Fusiliers.

To assist 1st Battalion, their sister battalion, 9th Royal Irish Fusiliers under the command of Lieutenant Colonel Philip Edward Kelly, a native of Newport, County Mayo, were moved forward. Three companies of the Battalion, who had been in the Rear Zone at Grand Seraucourt, took up a position facing Essigny Station whilst D Company under the command of 21 years old Captain Herbert Shelton Dean from

29 Diphosgene was developed as a poison gas to attack the pulmonary system. Its vapour degraded filters used in gas masks at the time.
30 Diphenyl-Chlorarsine30 was a chemical used in High – Explosive shells. Its rapid dispersal caused violent sneezing.
31 IWM Doc.11045 Sapper Alfred E Henderson papers.

View from Station Redoubt towards Essigny-le-Grand. (Author's collection)

Kettering, Northamptonshire, were sent to Station Redoubt to reinforce the position there. In addition, two machine gun teams from the Machine Gun Corps HQ at Happencourt were sent to the area of the railway cutting and Essigny Station to provide fire support. The Machine Gun Battalion had had a particularly terrible start to the day. When the German bombardment started the first shell scored a direct hit on their headquarters, killing three and wounding 10.[32]

The machine gun detachment sent to support the Fusiliers was commanded by 21 years old Lieutenant Kenneth Joyce Nelson Hansell. Lieutenant Hansell had been born at Hyogo, Japan and was educated at Charterhouse School, Surrey. He had been commissioned as a 2nd Lieutenant in the Leinster Regiment in August 1915 and was attached to the Royal Irish Rifles. He had been appointed to 107th Machine Gun Company in July 1917. On arrival with the Royal Irish Fusiliers on the morning of 21 March he deployed his teams to the railway cutting overlooking Essigny Station. The Machine Gun Battalion war diary recorded the events of the morning:

> Two guns under Lt. K Hansell moved to Essigny-le-Grand Station. A dull misty morning. Unable to see more than 100 yards. MG posts appear to have been particularly targeted and at least 10 MG's destroyed in the initial attack. About 8:30 a.m. two guns of A Coy N. of the Railway cutting at Essigny Station saw the infantry of 14th Div. retiring and they stated that the enemy had taken Essigny

32   TNA: WO 95/2498/3: 36th Battalion Machine Gun Corps war diary.

village. About 9.00 a.m. enemy advanced from the village in the direction of the station and at the same time information was received that he was making his way down the railway cutting. One gun was mounted on the side of the railway cutting to stop this latter movement and half an hour later a large body of enemy approached. When it became certain that they were Germans, fire was opened on them and they dispersed. At the same time, several of the enemy entered a trench on the West side of the cutting and opened fire, killing the number one and two of the team. The remaining gun worked by Lt. KJN Hansell stopped the movement of the enemy towards Essigny Station and did great execution for three quarters of an hour when Lt Hansell was killed, and the gun destroyed.[33]

In common with many others, Lieutenant Hansell has no known grave and is commemorated on the Pozieres Memorial to the Missing and also in the War Memorial Chapel at Charterhouse School.

Slightly further to the north of Lieutenant Hansell and protecting the right flank of 1st Royal Irish Fusiliers were other machine gun teams under the command of 34 years old Lieutenant Arthur James Lamport. Lieutenant Lamport was from Southampton and was commissioned into the Welch Regiment in 1915 before transferring to the Machine Gun Corps. His account gives a valuable insight into the confusion which resulted from the fog:

On the 21st March 1918 from the commencement of the enemy bombardment at 4:30 a.m. until about 11:30 a.m. my gun positions were enveloped in a very thick fog. During that time, I received no information regarding the movements of the enemy. At 11:30 a.m. I was with my two forward guns which were at the left end of a long trench and had one Sergeant, one Corporal and 10 men with me. Shortly afterwards I heard a Vickers gun fire a burst of about five rounds in my rear and a German gun reply. I couldn't see anything because of the fog though the latter was now getting less dense. I sent a runner back, then one of my sentries pointed out some dim figures on my front. They were advancing in extended order. I immediately ordered all men up to man the guns. At the same time, I also saw groups of men advancing from a direction 1/4th right – some of the latter seemed to be wearing British Steel Helmets and some German ones and at first I thought it was some of our own men bringing back German prisoners, but on examining them through glasses I thought they were German and I ordered both guns to open fire. My Sergeant, who was also looking through glasses shouted out, 'They are our own men sir!' I ordered both guns to cease fire. This happened three or four times before we were finally certain they were Germans through our seeing that they wore German packs and Sergeant Findley being wounded by them.

33   TNA: WO 95/2498/3: 36th Battalion Machine Gun Corps war diary.

Essigny-le-Grand village 2017. (Author's Collection)

The enemy in front held up their hands as they advanced in token of surrender. We dispersed them.[34]

Two Batteries of the Royal Field Artillery, A and C Batteries 173rd Brigade RFA who had been repositioned the previous evening close to Lieutenant Lamport's position, were forced to move again as they came under attack from German machine-gunners and at 12:40 p.m. the Commander Royal Artillery ordered all Artillery units to withdraw into the Battle Zone. Unfortunately, the guns of the two batteries had to be abandoned as the German advance threatened to overtake them. In doing so, the gunners removed the breech blocks, rendering the artillery pieces useless.

Records indicate that the Germans of 1st Bavarian Division and 5th Grenadiers captured the ruins of the village of Essigny by 1:00 p.m. and then turned their attentions towards the railway station and Station Redoubt. The following account from Goes, (1933) indicates the ferocity of the fighting to which both battalions of the Royal Irish Fusiliers and the Machine Gun Corps teams were subjected:

Then the unnatural sea of fog moves, the thick clouds roll back and silvery streams of light shine through: sun and with her, victory! In the initial storming, the

34   TNA: WO 339/35055: Lieutenant Arthur James Lamport service record.

battalions, 'Matthaei', 'Ianssen' and 'Schweinichen', penetrate the allied position, moving against the second, battling through it and throwing themselves against the train station barracks at Essigny. Around the railway embankments and shell holes, all developed into secure footholds, a bloody and endless battle ensues, in which sections of the 11th Company and 5th Grenadiers also engage. A German light *Feldhaubitze*[35] fires with terrible accuracy into the ranks. English lead cuts down valiant front soldiers such as daredevil Leutnant Mänche. Nevertheless, Battalion Matthaei storms the train station and Battalion Ianssen the Northern Track Barracks.[36] [37]

The German account indicates that some success was experienced by the attackers during their assault on Station Redoubt and its outlying defences. Lieutenant Lamport's position had meanwhile been supplemented by men from the Royal Irish Fusiliers. However, the fog had caused such confusion as to give the Germans an overwhelming advantage and the position rapidly became untenable:

> The Infantrymen were eventually driven back onto my right gun position and when the enemy got to within bombing distance of that gun and its team, as the gun was no longer effective, I ordered the working parts to be buried and the gun itself was thrown down the shaft of a dugout. My left gun was still being used to keep back any of the enemy who appeared in front which was rarely now as they were lying down and firing on us with rifles. Eventually the enemy got to within bombing distance of my left gun and as the latter was now useless for keeping him back, I ordered the working parts of that gun to be buried also. We then retired a few yards to the left end of the trench and endeavoured to keep back the enemy with rifles but he seldom showed himself. After a few minutes, one of the Infantry Sergeants said to his men, 'They are calling us in, put your rifles down boys,' and he and his men did so. I, seeing that we could not hinder the advance of the enemy any further and also that he had only to throw a few bombs to finish the matter, considered that it would be needlessly throwing away my men's lives by refusing to go in and therefore went forward and surrendered on behalf of all shortly after 1.00 p.m.[38]

The excellent work performed by the combined efforts of the Machine Gun Corps, 1st and 9th Royal Irish Fusiliers ensured that Station Redoubt did not fall until an order to withdraw behind the St Quentin Canal was issued at 8:45 p.m. Prior to this,

---

35   *Feldhaubitze* translates as Howitzer.
36   The northern track barracks referred to are Station Redoubt, the 1st Royal Irish Fusiliers Battalion HQ.
37   Goes, (1933) *Der Tag X. Die Grosse Schlacht in Frankreich (21 Marz–5 April 1918)* p. 54.
38   TNA: WO 339/35055: Lieutenant Arthur James Lamport service record.

when the position looked to be under severe pressure, the reserve battalion of 109th Infantry Brigade, the 9th Battalion Royal Inniskilling Fusiliers, were ordered forward to reinforce 1st and 9th Fusiliers. They took up a position around 3:00 p.m. on the right of 9th Royal Irish Fusiliers, but as 41st Brigade of the adjacent Division still held the ground in front, they were not required and were withdrawn around 6:00 p.m. across the St Quentin Canal.

In the defence of Station Redoubt, 1st Royal Irish Fusiliers sustained 42 fatalities on 21 March. The oldest was 40 years old Serjeant Thomas Noblett 3274, from Dolphin's Barn, Dublin. In his will, he left all his property and effects to his wife, Bridget.

Later that evening following the order to withdraw, further confusion occurred within 9th Royal Irish Fusiliers due to the fog which had descended again in the early evening.

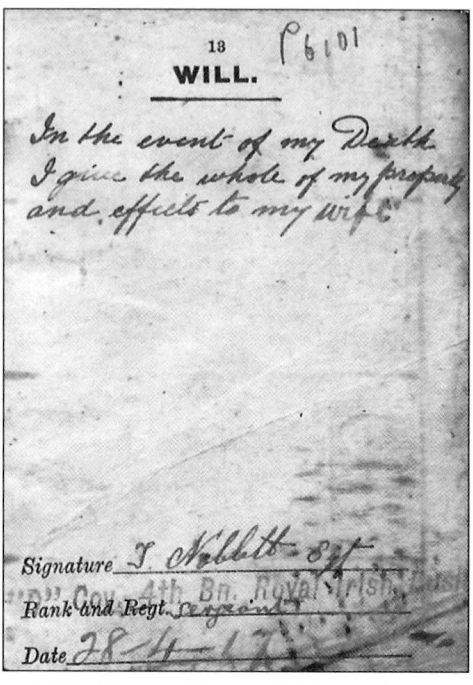

Will of Serjeant Thomas Noblett 3274 1st Battalion Royal Irish Fusiliers. (National Archives of Ireland)

A Company of the battalion could not be located despite a runner being sent out to find them. The Adjutant of the battalion, Captain Michael Henehan MC, a native of Tuam, Co. Galway, explained what happened next:

> At 11.00 p.m. night of 21-22nd orders were received from Brigade for the Battalion to withdraw to the Happincourt line as soon as possible. The enemy was at this time in the village of Grand Seraucourt and threatened our withdrawal. I sent out orders for Coy. Commanders to fall back without delay. The runner I sent to A Coy Commander returned after being about an hour absent and said he lost his way in the fog. My CO ordered me to go back with the runner and find the Coy. Commander. I did so and found him about 1:00 a.m. night 21-22. At about 1:30 a.m. I was returning with this Coy. when we were attacked suddenly by a large enemy patrol roughly about 200 strong. After a severe struggle, the Coy was practically wiped out. I with about 30 OR were taken prisoner.[39]

39   TNA: WO 339/54496: Captain Michael Henehan service record. Captain Henehan had enlisted in the Irish Guards in December 1914 and applied for a commission in December

Although Captain Henehan states that the Company was practically wiped out, the battalion sustained only seven fatalities that day, although more were wounded, and many others taken prisoner. Amongst those to fall was 27 years old 2nd Lieutenant Dalton Prenter, the second son of James and Clara Prenter of Fitzroy Avenue, Belfast. Second Lieutenant Prenter was a Clerk in the Linen business and had initially enlisted in the 14th (Service) Battalion Royal Irish Rifles (Young Citizen Volunteers) as a Rifleman with the service number 14/16946 and had embarked for France with the battalion in October 1915. He had been commissioned into the Royal Irish Fusiliers in June 1917. Second Lieutenant Prenter is commemorated on the Pozieres Memorial to the Missing.

Second Lieutenant Dalton Prenter 9th Battalion Royal Irish Fusiliers. (Great War Ulster Newspaper Archive)

107th Brigade

The 107th Brigade held the centre position in the 36th (Ulster) Division's frontage. The 15th (Service) Battalion Royal Irish Rifles (North Belfast Volunteers) held the Forward Zone, their battalion Headquarters being at Racecourse Redoubt. In some accounts uncovered during research, individuals refer to the Headquarters as Ascot Redoubt, the connotation being obvious. The railway line south from St Quentin ran through the centre of the Redoubt, the railway cuttings assisting in the defensive workings. This Redoubt was in line with and a mile to the left of Jeanne D'Arc Redoubt, held by the 12th Rifles. Around a mile to the left of Racecourse Redoubt was Boadicea Redoubt in 109th Brigade's area which was held by the 2nd Battalion Royal Inniskilling Fusiliers. The ground between the redoubts was undulating countryside and was picketed by a series of outposts and lightly held trenches. At the edge of Racecourse Redoubt on the left side, ran the road from the village of Grugies, skirting the hamlet of Contescourt and continuing to Grand Seraucourt, where the Headquarters of many of 36th Division units were based. Two miles directly behind the 15th Rifles, the 1st Battalion Royal Irish Rifles held the Battle Zone. Their Headquarters was at Quarry Redoubt, the edge of which rested on the Grugies-Grand Seraucourt Road and an outpost was in the Quarries on the opposite side of

1915 whilst a Serjeant. He was commissioned into the Royal Irish Fusiliers in July 1916 and was awarded the Military Cross in June 1917 for gallantry during a raid. He was repatriated in December 1918.

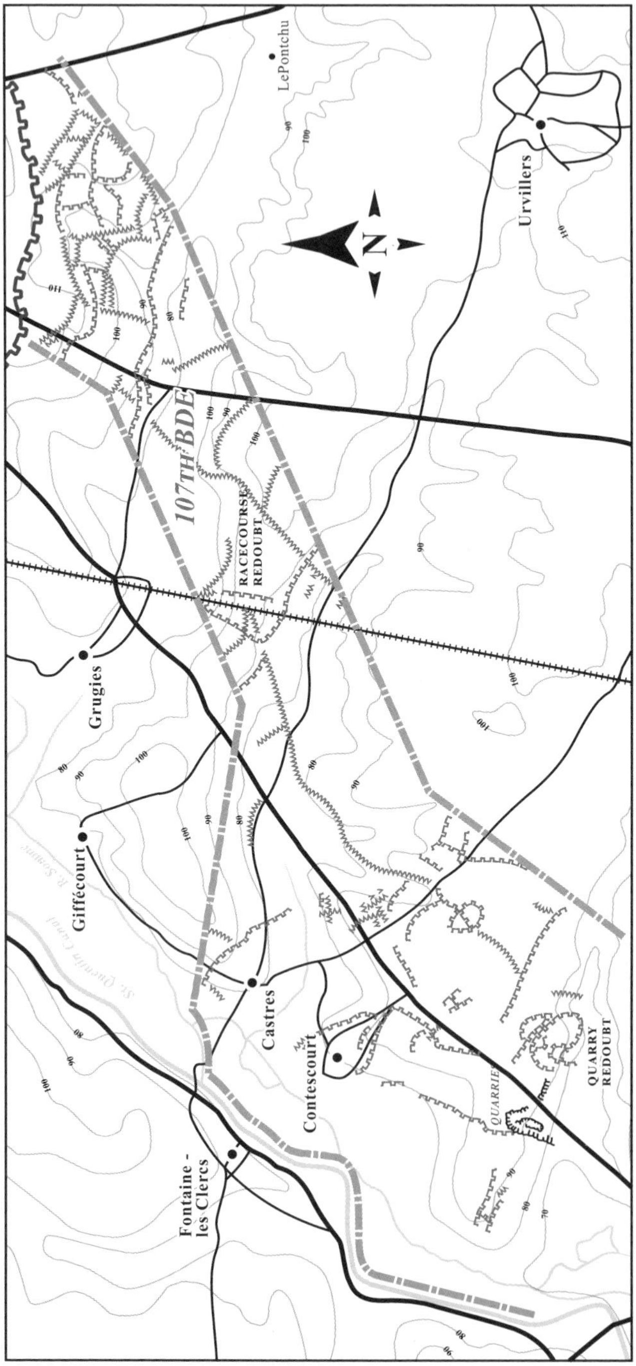

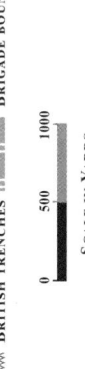

REFERENCE

BRITISH TRENCHES   BRIGADE BOUNDARY

SCALE IN YARDS

0   500   1000

Map 9 107th Brigade Defensive Zone.

the road. The 2nd Battalion Royal Irish Rifles were in the Reserve Zone at Grand Seraucourt with companies in the hamlet of Hamel, in dugouts on the banks of the St Quentin Canal and in Grand Seraucourt itself.

At this point it is worth considering the objectives of the Germans facing the Ulster Division opposite 107th Brigade. In his history of IR 463, Hoffmann (1930) recollected the operational plan:

> The 238th Infantry Division, in the position of the 18th army, is chosen as the battle division of the first encounter and has the task of travelling from south-west of St Quentin in a south-westerly direction, with their right flank along the Somme, and to break through to the 'Crozat' Canal. The width of the battlefield initially amounted to some 700 metres, later some two kilometres. The formation of the infantry: to the right 463rd Battalion, in the middle 465th, to the left 464th. The attack would commence at 4:40 a.m. with a heavy five-hour barrage of fire; a two-hour major gasification of the enemy battalion, then annihilating fire on the trenches, entanglements of wire and their support points etc. The artillery positions are in and around St Quentin and its outskirts.[40]

More specific instructions were given to the commanders of IR 463:

> The 463rd Infantry Regiment have orders to attack head-on, marching with their right flank along the road to Seraucourt in a 150m breadth (gradually to extend to a 500m breadth) and to penetrate the English position in this strip of the battlefield until the River Somme. The marshy easterly shore of the river reaches far into the regiment's field and affords the already strongly fortified British position natural protection. In this section there also lie eight villages which have been developed into substantial footholds. The extremely difficult task of the regiment is not to engage in battle across the full width of the battlefield. IR 465 and 464 have to conquer more favourable terrain without villages. The regiment gives the battalions the following orders for attack:
>
> 1st Battalion is to be the front line of attack, penetrating deep into the regiment's attack corridor, without regard to any support points to the left or right. Five groups of engineers, an accompanying artillery platoon and a *Flammenwerfer* are allocated to the battalion.
>
> 2nd Battalion initially follows close behind the 1st Battalion then moves to the right, namely towards position Gauchy, Grugies, then the allied positions in Giffecourt and Castres. From there they follow the 1st battalion as reserves. Nine groups of engineers, an artillery platoon and a *Flammenwerfer* are allocated.

---

40   Hoffmann, *Infanterie Regiment 463, 7000 Niedersachsen im Grosskampfe der Westfront*, p. 180.

3rd Battalion initially follows the 2nd. After the 2nd battalion's movement, the 3rd battalion is to follow the 1st, keeping a 400m distance and acting as a reserve.[41]

The attack frontage of IR 463 would bring them directly into contact with the Forward Zones held by 15th Royal Irish Rifles in the centre of the Ulster Division line and the 2nd Inniskillings on the left of the line. At this stage, we will deal with the attack on 15th Rifles.

The 15th Rifles had been commanded by Lieutenant Colonel Claude George Cole-Hamilton since September 1917. Born at Portaliffe, Killeshandra, County Cavan in January 1869, he had married Lucy Charlewood Thorold at Biarritz, France, in April 1893. The couple went on to have three daughters. His military career began as a Second Lieutenant in the Royal Irish Rifles in 1900. He served in the South Africa campaign between May 1901 and July 1902 as Captain in charge of the Mounted Infantry Company, 5th Battalion Royal Irish Rifles. He was Mentioned in Despatches in July 1902 and was awarded the Distinguished Service Order 'in recognition of services during operations in South Africa' in October of that year.[42] Following the South African War he reverted to the Army Reserve and whilst still a reservist, he became Chief Constable of Breconshire in 1912 and at the outbreak of war was called up, joining the 12th Battalion Royal Irish Rifles as second in command in February 1915. In August 1915, he was promoted Lieutenant Colonel and commanded the 8th (Service) Battalion Royal Irish Rifles (East Belfast Volunteers) until appointed to the regiment's 15th battalion.

Lieutenant Colonel Claud George Cole-Hamilton DSO 15th Battalion Royal Irish Rifles. (Great War Ulster Newspaper Archive)

There are two accounts of the progress of the battle from the 15th Rifles perspective written by Lieutenant Colonel Cole-Hamilton. The first was penned on 31 March 1918 from Karlsruhe Prisoner of War Camp, Germany, when events were

41   Hoffmann, *Infanterie Regiment 463, 7000 Niedersachsen im Grosskampfe der Westfront*, p. 181.
42   Lieutenant Colonel CG Cole-Hamilton DSO <https://www.angloboerwar.com/medals-and-awards/british/1884-distinguished-service-order> (Accessed 19 June 2017). Following his repatriation from Germany, he resumed as Chief Constable for Breconshire, a position he held until 1947. He died in 1957 aged 87.

obviously fresh in his memory. The second, which is a more sanitised version, was completed exactly a year to the day later, on 31 March 1919 for the Military Board of Enquiry into his surrender. For the latter, he was obviously more circumspect, but this account cannot be totally disregarded as whilst a Prisoner of War he would have met other officers from his battalion post the compilation of his first account, and would have been able to piece together events from what was obviously a chaotic situation. Portions of both reports will be used to highlight events. This initial passage is from the 31 March 1919 report and outlines the disposition of the Battalion within the defensive scheme:

> On the 21st March 1918, I was in command of 15th (S) Bn. RIR. The battalion was holding the 107th Bde sector of the front line and had been in the line 7 days. One Batt. From each brigade formed the Divisional Front Line, the 108th Bde being on the right, 107th in the centre and 109th Bde on the left, with their left on the River Somme. The Bn. was disposed as follows: two Coys in the front line in platoon posts and keeps, one counter-attack Coy in two keeps to rear of forward Coys with two platoons in each. Advanced HQ with details, signallers, runners, stretcher bearers, power buzzer station, stores etc in quarry in rear of counter-attack Coy. One Coy, Bn HQ, MG and Trench Mortar sections in Racecourse Redoubt at Grugies, further to the rear and to the left of the front line Coys. My orders were, speaking in the general sense, to hold on to our positions. There was to be no retiring. I was instructed not to expect assistance from the rear for at least 48 hours and that the Corps Commander hoped then to make his counter attack from the Battle Zone which was some 1500 yards to my rear. At about 4:30 a.m. the enemy began his bombardment and the redoubt was very heavily shelled with HE and Gas. There was an extremely thick fog which was intensified by smoke and gas shells. At the Redoubt, a man could not be seen at 10 paces up to 12 noon. Communications both to front and rear by wire and power buzzer were early interrupted and were maintained by runner only.[43]

The war diary of the 36th Ulster Division records that the final message was received from 15th RIR at 11:45 a.m. and read:

> At 10:30 a.m. enemy attack developed after heavy bombardment. They are still holding out. Enemy barraging Battle Zone. No Gas.[44]

The initial account of the commanding officer then refers to how the pattern of German attacks developed and how they were ultimately dealt with by the heroism

---

43   TNA: WO 339/8682: Lieutenant Colonel Claude George Cole-Hamilton service record.
44   TNA: WO 95/2492/2: 36th (Ulster) Division war diary.

of the Adjutant, Captain John Hazelton Stewart MC, a native of Waterford who had been residing at Eglantine Avenue, Belfast, prior to obtaining his commission:

> At 10:30 a.m. fighting became heavy all round us – shortly after this, the left of redoubt was overrun. This left us with only the portion of redoubt from Contescourt Communication Trench to Railway Cutting inclusive. The two platoons on left had all been killed or captured also. From that or about 10:40 a.m. we had very close fighting and were engaged by Flammenwerfer (4 attacks knocked out finally by the Adjutant with rifle grenades) machine guns heavy and light, and minenwerfers while the enemy infantry made several attacks over the open and along trenches with bombs. Every now and then they seemed to withdraw, then we were heavily shelled – then the infantry would attack again.[45]

This account is corroborated by that of Captain James Edmund Smith Condon, officer commanding D Company and a native of Dublin, who stated:

> It was now about 11:00 a.m. The sun was beginning to shine through the fog which had begun to lift. We were able to see about us. We saw the enemy passing on our right in close formation of about platoon strength and opened fire on them with good result. We also saw larger bodies of the enemy marching about one and a half miles behind us in the direction of the Battle Zone. The light enabled the enemy to discover a number of Communication Trenches leading into the trenches from Grugies. He attacked along these trenches using Flammenwerfer. Our Adjutant, Capt. Stewart destroyed the *Flammenwerfer* with grenades and the attack collapsed. Another effort was made along these trenches, but we beat it off and the enemy retired.[46]

Remarkably, these accounts are further corroborated by the Germans of IR 463:

> A different MG nest cannot be moved to surrender with hand grenades. Flame throwers set to work. The support point is peppered with concentrated loads. The brave Tommies throw hand grenades constantly and disable both flame throwers.[47]

For his gallantry in this action, Captain Stewart was awarded the Distinguished Service Order.[48]

---

45   PRONI: D961/8 Newton and Anderson family papers.
46   TNA: WO 339/53177: Captain James Edmund Smith Condon service record. Captain Condon was awarded the Distinguished Service Order for his gallantry on 21 March 1918.
47   Hoffmann, *Infanterie Regiment 463, 7000 Niedersachsen im Grosskampfe der Westfront* p. 188.
48   *The London Gazette,* 31 January 1920.

The relentless attack of IR 463 however cannot be stopped. Firstly, the outposts were overrun or forced backwards. As officer commanding D Company, Captain Condon had four platoons situated in outposts. The farthest from the redoubt was a position established in a trench at the village of Grugies which was held by a platoon under the command of Second Lieutenant Edmund De Wind. This outpost came under heavy attack and after a spirited defence the platoon was forced back to Racecourse Redoubt, Captain Condon reporting that 'the commander and a few men joined us about 11:00 a.m.'[49] As the German attacks intensified, De Wind and two non-commissioned officers performed repeated acts of heroism in driving back the enemy attacks which were recognised in both the accounts of Lieutenant Colonel Cole-Hamilton and Captain Condon. The commanding officer stated:

> 2nd Lt De Wind, Corporal Getgood and L/Cpl Walker did splendid work clearing Contescourt Communication Trench time after time. Twice they got out on top and walked along it clearing enemy out of it with rifle and rifle grenades. They all three won the VC several times. I fear De Wind was killed during one of the bombing stunts. L/Cpl Walker was wounded, I am not absolutely sure about De Wind.[50]

Research has identified one account that records how Edmund De Wind fell. Private Alfred Wright, 18/1714, D Company 15th Rifles provided the following account to the Red Cross from a prisoner of war camp:

> About 12 noon March 21st, the deceased officer was with his platoon in the battle position when a trench mortar landed and killed him instantaneously.[51]

Second Lieutenant De Wind was initially reported missing and his death was not confirmed by the War Office until September 1918, although the Red Cross had forwarded the above information to his mother a month earlier.

Second Lieutenant De Wind was recommended for the Victoria Cross by his Commanding Officer – as evidenced above in his report of 31 March 1918. Captain Condon was similarly praiseworthy:

> During the fighting, 2nd Lt De Wind (believed killed) Cpl Getgood and L/Cpl Walker (wounded) displayed the greatest gallantry, repeatedly clearing the enemy out of these trenches and to do so exposing themselves fearlessly.[52]

49   TNA: WO 339/53177: Captain James Edmund Smith Condon service record.
50   TNA: WO 339/8682: Lieutenant Colonel Claude George Cole-Hamilton service record.
51   TNA: WO 339/96433: Second Lieutenant Edmund De Wind service record.
52   TNA: WO 339/53177: Captain James Edmund Smith Condon service record

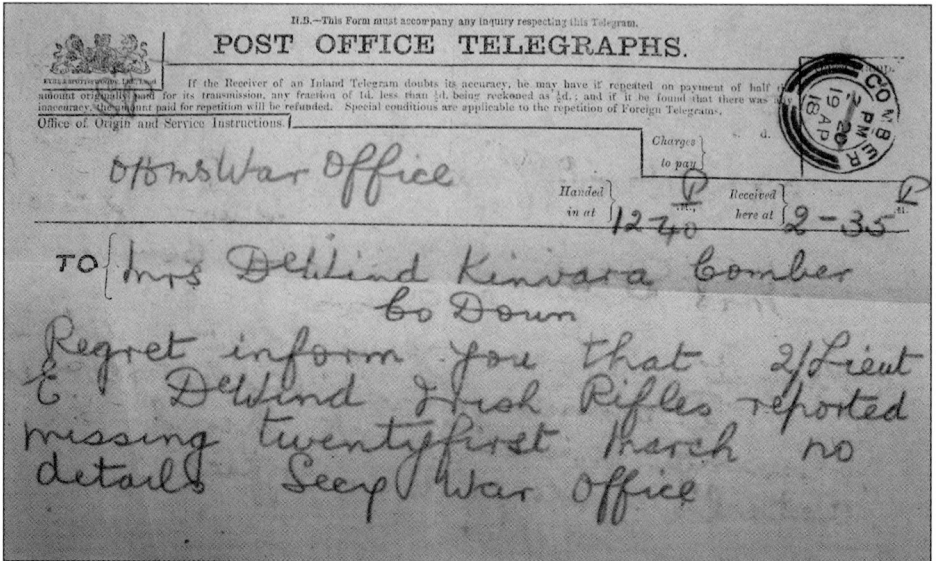

It is not known if all three were recommended for the Victoria Cross, but it was extremely unlikely that more than one was ever going to be awarded. As the man in command, Edmund De Wind received the honour albeit posthumously in May 1919, the medal being presented to his mother by King George V on 28 June 1919. The citation states:

> For most conspicuous bravery and self-sacrifice on the 21st March 1918, at the Race Course Redoubt near Grugies. For seven hours he held this most important post and though twice wounded and practically single-handed, he maintained this position until another section could be got to his help. On two occasions with two NCO's only, he got out on top under heavy machine gun and rifle fire, and cleared the enemy out of the trench, killing many. He continued to repel

Reported Missing Telegram, Second Lieutenant Edmund De Wind. (PRONI) Second Lieutenant Edmund De Wind VC 15th Battalion Royal Irish Rifles. (Great War Ulster Newspaper Archive)

attack after attack until he was mortally wounded and collapsed. His valour, self-sacrifice and example were of the highest order.[53]

Edmund De Wind was born at Comber, County Down on 11 December 1883. He was educated at Campbell College, Belfast and entered employment with the Bank of Ireland, being posted to County Cavan. On 1 November 1911, he emigrated to Canada, embarking at Bristol for Montreal. He gained employment with the Canadian Bank of Commerce at Edmonton, Alberta. He served for a time as a private soldier in a militia regiment, the 2nd Queen's Own Rifles of Canada and following the outbreak of war enlisted in the 31st Battalion Canadian Expeditionary Force (Alberta Regiment) at Edmonton, Alberta on 16 November 1914. On 11 December 1916 whilst on active service in France with the Machine Gun Section of 31st Battalion, Edmund de Wind applied for a commission, indicating that he wished to serve with the Royal Irish Rifles. He was appointed to the Royal Irish Rifles as a Second Lieutenant on 26 September 1917 and was posted to 15th Battalion.

An interesting point is that although born in Ireland and serving with an Irish regiment when he was killed, he is also claimed as a Canadian Victoria Cross winner.[54] In addition to memorials in Belfast and in his home town of Comber, Mount De Wind in Alberta, Canada was named after him in 1948.

Whilst Corporal Getgood and Lance Corporal Walker appear from the accounts to have been equally heroic, their exploits have been lost to history. Both were taken prisoner and following repatriation were each awarded the Distinguished Conduct Medal on 31 January 1920, there are however no citations to accompany the awards.

Samuel Getgood was born on 17 December 1894 at Gregg Street, Lisburn, County Antrim, the son of George and Mary Ellen Getgood. By 1911, the family were resident at 251 Crumlin Road, Belfast and Samuel was employed as a Linen Weaver. On Saturday 28 September 1912, along with many thousands of others, Samuel signed the Ulster Covenant, opposing Home Rule for Ireland, doing so at the City Hall, Belfast. He married a widow, Rachel Nelson at St Anne's Church of Ireland, Belfast on 8 June 1913 and the couple had a son named Samuel after his father, in April 1914. At that time the family were residing at Glentilt Street, Belfast.[55] Samuel enlisted in the 15th (Service) Battalion Royal Irish Rifles (North Belfast Volunteers) at its formation on 19 September 1914 being issued with the service number 15/1044. He embarked with the battalion for France in October 1915 and was promoted Lance Corporal in January 1916. On 18 February 1916, he was admitted to hospital with 'shock from shell', re-joining the battalion on St Patrick's Day of the same year. He saw action at

53 *The London Gazette* 15 May 1919.
54 Canadian Virtual War Memorial <http://www.veterans.gc.ca/eng/remembrance/memorials/canadian-virtual-war-memorial/Detail/7600006> (Accessed 22 June 2017).
55 Glentilt Street ran from the Old Lodge Road to Agnes Street, Belfast. It is no longer in existence.

the Somme in 1916; Messines and Langemarck in 1917 and was promoted Corporal in September 1917 before participating in the Battle of Cambrai in November that year.

Samuel was captured on 21 March 1918 and spent time at prisoner of war camps at Giessen in central Germany and at Meschede POW Camp in Westphalia, before being repatriated following the Armistice. As he had enlisted for the duration of the war, Samuel was demobilised in March 1919. In August 1926, Samuel emigrated to the United States with his family, setting up home in Philadelphia and gaining employment as an Ironworker. He became a United States Citizen in 1929 and remained in the United states until his death in New Jersey in 1987 aged 93. In addition to his Distinguished Conduct Medal, Samuel was also Mentioned in Despatches.

His comrade Lance Corporal Charles Hubert Walker was born at Garvagh, County Londonderry on 10 June 1896, the eldest son of John and Edith Walker. His father John Walker, a native of County Roscommon, was a Constable in the Royal Irish Constabulary. By 1911, the family was resident at Leopold Street, Belfast. Then aged 14, Charles had completed his education and was employed as a Clerk in a House Agent's office. Charles enlisted in the 15th Battalion Royal Irish Rifles

Corporal Samuel Getgood DCM 15th Battalion Royal Irish Rifles. (Great War Ulster Newspaper Archive) US Naturalisation Certificate – Samuel Getgood. (Open source)

and was issued with the service number 15/12170, embarking for France with the battalion in October 1915. He was also taken prisoner on 21 March 1918 and was taken to Limburg POW camp in central Germany. Following repatriation, he was demobilised in March 1919. In addition to his Distinguished Conduct Medal, Lance Corporal Walker had also been awarded the Military Medal for gallantry.

The speed of the German advance took the men of 15th Battalion very much by surprise. Serjeant William Finlay MM,[56] Regimental Medical Staff, was in an outpost at the quarries described by Lieutenant Colonel Cole-Hamilton. In a letter to his brother James he described how he was captured:

I was in the forward aid post on my own, the Doctor and my two orderlies being in the Aid post at HQ. About 4:00 a.m. in the morning a very fierce bombardment was opened on us by the Germans plentifully mixed with gas shells all along our front and support lines and right the way back to our reserve area five kilometres behind. It was a very misty morning and added to by the smoke and gas, it was impossible to see anything. The quarry where we were suffered severely, our signal station being knocked in by the constant concussion of the shells on its roof. Just before that happened, I wired through to the front line if there was any casualties or if the stretcher bearers required the assistance of the reserve stretcher bearers. The answer came back that there was nothing doing, it was very satisfactory considering the amount of stuff Jerry was delivering, and just as we were congratulating ourselves on that fact, in goes the roof of the signal station completely burying some of the poor chaps. I do not know how many, but I believe it was two. One got out with a slight bruise on his ankle, another we discovered with a beam across his chest and dead. Another one was buried all but his head, the frames forming a cave over him otherwise he would have been killed. It was while trying to extricate him that we heard rifle and machine gun firing in our rear and discovered it was the Germans who had flanked us in the mist and was coming up behind us. About 1 ½ kilometres behind us was an RAMC Advanced Post to whom we evacuated our wounded. These RAMC men and two Doctors the Germans had already taken prisoner and brought them along with them and passed them through under escort to St Quentin. As I passed from Signal Station to Aid Post to attend to one of our wounded, I did not expect to reach it with a sound skin as the Germans were 'Hocking' and shouting 'Tommy, Tommy, Arrest, Arrest' and firing away all the time. After a short time a German very cautiously lifted the gas curtain and presenting his rifle shouted, 'Arrest', but on seeing the Red Cross on the lamp and the Red Cross on my arm, he lowered his rifle and said 'Kamerade, carry on' which he made understand in broken English and by signs and so left me but soon returned again and taking a

---

56   Serjeant Finlay was awarded the Military Medal in December 1916 for carrying a wounded man two miles under enemy fire.

bottle out of his pocket he uncorked it and offered it to me to drink and was very angry seeming to be insulted, because I would not and so left and took up his post outside to guide the German wounded to the aid post.[57]

In a pragmatic move, the Germans realised that Serjeant Finlay was a man whose skills they could utilise and instead of being marched to the rear with the other prisoners, he was soon put to work under the supervision of a German Doctor:

> They were beginning to arrive plentifully too, and it looked like I was going to be kept more than busy when a German doctor and his orderly arrived and asked me how many wounded I had and to point out the worst cases and then told me I was relieved and could go outside. When I went outside I saw what was left of our chaps being formed up to march off. I expected to be put along with them but was told to stand where I was and they placed a sentry with me. A good many of British and German wounded were lying outside the aid post as it was full up inside and having my dressing bag stocked for emergencies, I commenced to dress them and when it ran done I went into the aid post for more. I went in three times for supplies and then the Doctor started 'Sacramentin' and said I was using too many dressings and they would not hold out until his supplies arrived. I quietly ignored him and went into an inner compartment where I had a supply of dressings for about 500 men. He would not follow me into the darkness but went and got his electric torch and then came in and was delighted when he saw the stock of dressings on the shelves, saying 'English wool, English wool, good, good'. By the way, German dressings and bandages are made of prepared paper.[58]

The magnificent defence of the 15th Royal Irish Rifles continued well into the afternoon, but with the Stormtroopers having passed well to their rear, it was only a matter of time before the redoubt was completely overwhelmed. However, the men had done their best and had delayed the German advance, forcing them to commit vital resources to overcome the defenders. Lieutenant Colonel Cole-Hamilton described how the end came:

> At 1:00 p.m. the fog cleared off and it was then seen that the enemy had passed well to the rear of us. The Redoubt on our right was evidently taken and the enemy were streaming through and past it to the rear. The Redoubt on our left held by the 2nd Royal Inniskilling Fusiliers (Lieutenant Colonel Lord Farnham DSO) was still holding out and I heard later held out until about 5:00 p.m. Around 1:30 p.m. I sent a message to the Bde by pigeon giving the position of affairs as I knew it. The enemy brought up several more trench mortars which

---

57   PRONI: D4101 Serjeant William Finlay papers.
58   Ibid.

did great damage to our defences. After considerable bombardment they again attacked, this procedure was repeated several times. The bombardment became so heavy and the trenches were so knocked about that the remains of the garrison were driven in bit by bit to a small area. At about 5:15 p.m. the enemy in our rear seemed to have overrun the Battle Zone. At about that time we sustained several casualties from heavy Trench Mortar bombs. I consulted my senior officers and we agreed that we could not hold the Redoubt should the enemy attack again. All papers, maps etc were destroyed and everything done we had time for to prevent the enemy profiting by anything of value. Shortly after this the Garrison was forced into the railway cutting where defence became impossible and rushed from all sides. This was at 5:45 p.m. Of the HQ and Coy of 15 RIR only about 30 officers and men could walk when captured and most of these wounded. Of the whole garrison, 55 were marched away.[59]

Following his capture, a German officer congratulated Lieutenant Colonel Cole-Hamilton on his defence and informed him that three battalions had been involved in attacking his redoubt and that one had been annihilated, another practically so and that the third had suffered heavy losses. The toll on the 15th Rifles was equally as heavy. The war diary of 15th Royal Irish Rifles is missing from 1 to 21 March 1918. It begins on 22 March by stating:

The battalion itself was gone, killed, wounded and missing.[60]

The vast majority of officers and men were taken prisoner. However, along with Second Lieutenant De Wind, a further 51 men fell. One of the few to have a known resting place is 28 years old Corporal James Charters who was attached to C Company. James, from Marine Street in the Docks area of Belfast is buried in Grand Seraucourt British Cemetery. His mother Margaret arranged for his headstone to be inscribed, 'A Gallant son of Ulster. Thy will be done.'

Lieutenant Colonel Cole-Hamilton was justifiably proud of the performance of his men and concluded his written account of 31 March 1918 with the following words:

Every man – Officer, NCO and man under my command did their damnedest and I am proud to have had the honour to have commanded such men.[61]

The 1st Battalion Royal Irish Rifles manned the Battle Zone position behind the 15th Royal Irish Rifles. Their strongpoint was known as Quarry Redoubt and was a mile outside the village of Grand Seraucourt and two miles behind the 15th Rifles

59   TNA: WO 339/8682: Lieutenant Colonel Claude George Cole-Hamilton service record.
60   TNA: WO 95/2503/5: 15th Battalion Royal Irish Rifles war diary.
61   PRONI: D961/8, Lieutenant AN Anderson papers.

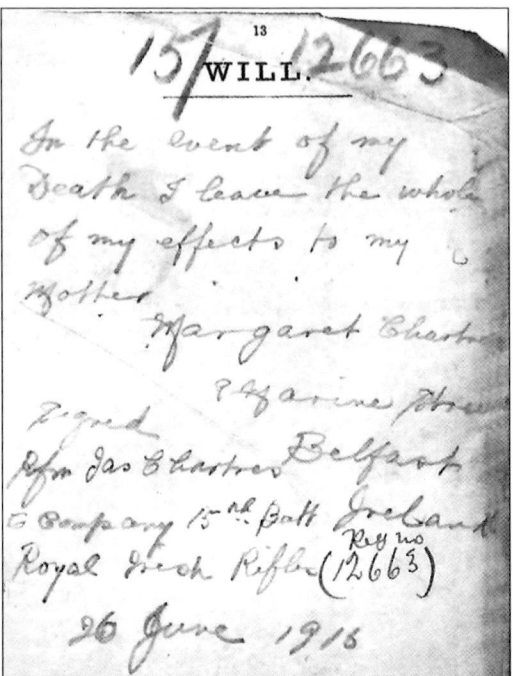

Corporal James (Jim) Charters 15th Battalion Royal Irish Rifles. (Great War Ulster Newspaper Archive), Headstone of Corporal James Charters Grand Seraucourt British Cemetery. (Author's Collection), Will of Corporal James Charters. (National Archives of Ireland)

strongpoint at Racecourse Redoubt. The battalion was commanded by Lieutenant Colonel Heffernan William Denis MacCarthy-O'Leary DSO MC. From an aristocratic Catholic family who resided at Coomlagane House, Millstreet, County Cork, Lieutenant Colonel MacCarthy-O'Leary's father had been killed leading his battalion of the South Lancashire Regiment at Pieter's Hill, during the South African War in February 1900. One of three sons, he attended Stoneyhurst College, Lancashire and then the Royal Military College Sandhurst before initially being commissioned into the Royal Irish Fusiliers. His younger brother, Lieutenant William Felix MacCarthy-O'Leary, Royal Munster Fusiliers had been killed in action in September 1916.

With the Battalion Headquarters at Quarry Redoubt, A Company held trenches to the front and right, whilst B Company held trenches to the front and left, close to the village of Contescourt. C Company was in counter attack trenches to the rear of the Redoubt and D Company was in position to the right of the Redoubt linking up with 1st Royal Irish Fusiliers at Station Redoubt.

When the initial German bombardment began, the Redoubt was heavily and accurately shelled, particularly with gas shells. A vivid description of the terror instilled by the bombardment was recorded by 19 years old Rifleman George Herbert Hill 18/271, from Surrey Street off the Lisburn Road in Belfast. A Signaller with 1st Royal Irish Rifles, he was rudely awakened from sleep in a dugout at Quarry Redoubt, as is graphically described in his wartime memoir, *'Retreat from Death. A Soldier on the Somme'* (2005):

> The Company Sergeant Major was nudging my backside with his boot. Looking up, cold and stupid from heavy, comfortless sleep on the floor, I tried sluggishly to get out of his reach. His lips moved, and I recognised familiar oaths forming themselves. But the words were lost. A tremendous roaring cataract of noise made the solid dugout shake… Bits of earth rained down from the roof, particles getting into my eyes. The air screamed as if in pain or on the point of reaching some wild transport of sound beyond human comprehension. Suddenly, out to the left, right at the limit of my vision, there was a lurid flash and a great column of black smoke sprang billowing into the mist. Falling to my knees, and still watching, I put my hands up to shield my face. The pillar hung motionless, wavered, and was slowly swallowed up. Rising to my feet I went on. I had seen my first actual shell-burst of the war. But my mask was awry as a result of the sudden movement and in my blindness, I tripped and fell headlong just as another great shell burst nearer the road. I hugged the ground, trying madly to claw into its hard surface as clods of earth rained down, striking my body dully. Something heavier struck my helmet and I lost consciousness.[62]

62   George Herbert Hill, *Retreat from Death: A Soldier on the Somme* (London: Tauris Parke Paperbacks, 2005), p. 86. George Hill survived the war and was discharged with the Silver War Badge in July 1919 suffering from Ulcerative Gingivitis – painful bleeding from the gums.

This bombardment slackened and then increased again in tempo around 9:00 a.m. just prior to the infantry assault. This bombardment accurately targeted the positions held by A and B Company. This was another example of the preparation and meticulous planning of the Germans who, being aware of the exact location of the Redoubt, targeted the positions on either side to isolate the strongpoint and to clear the way for the rapid advance of the stormtroopers.

When the infantry attack materialised, the Germans were able to advance rapidly, passing between the Forward Zone Redoubts held by 15th Royal Irish Rifles and 2nd Inniskilling Fusiliers to their left. It will be recalled that Lieutenant Colonel Cole-Hamilton of 15th Rifles was aware that the Germans were well to the rear of his position by 11:00 a.m. By 12:55 p.m. the 36th (Ulster) Division war diary recorded that the Germans had reached the village of Contescourt and that Divisional Artillery positions had been evacuated, the gunners blowing up their guns as they withdrew.[63]

This put B Company of the 1st Rifles directly in the path of the attackers of IR 463. To this time, the progress of the Germans had been rapid, passing the village of Castres en route to Contescourt, as their regimental history describes:

> At 1 o'clock in the afternoon the 5th and 7th company, under Lt. Hamann and Lt. Saßnick, advance well north of Castres in close combat with the Argonnen trenches, capturing Castres. Here the company sustains close range fire of medium calibre from the battalion located to the south of Contescourt. Proceeding through Contescourt the 7th company reaches 100m from the left flank of the Battalion. Shrill whistling. Tommy recognises the danger and occupies their defence trenches.[64]

The clash between IR 463 and B Company 1 RIR lasted most of the afternoon and was prolonged and vicious. On the German side 7th Company of IR 463 was in the vanguard of the attack:

> Fierce gun battle. The brave company then goes to battle against both flanks. In the close combat with guns and hand grenades, an English Officer and three men are killed, two wounded and the rest (all of six men) are captured. Two further English men are extracted from their refuge. Three intact guns and a large weapon store are captured.[65]

From research and available British military records, it is believed that the officer killed was the officer commanding B Company, 24 years old Captain John Brown, MC and Bar. Captain Brown was born at Oakland Avenue in the Bloomfield area of

63   TNA: WO 95/2492/2: 36th (Ulster) Division war diary.
64   Hoffmann, *Infanterie Regiment 463, 7000 Niedersachsen im Grosskampfe der Westfront* p. 192.
65   Ibid.

Belfast. He was a Section Commander in the Ulster Volunteer Force and enlisted as a Private in the 8th (Service) Battalion Royal Irish Rifles (East Belfast Volunteers) at their formation in September 1914. On enlistment, he also applied for a commission and was gazetted as a Second Lieutenant in 8th Royal Irish Rifles in November 1914. He was wounded on the first day of the Battle of the Somme with a gunshot wound to the right shoulder and was awarded the Military Cross. The citation was published in *The London Gazette* on 22 September 1916 and stated:

> For conspicuous gallantry in action. He led his platoon into the enemy's line with great dash and courage, subsequently driving off an enemy bomb attack from a post on his flank. He was wounded in doing this but carried on and completed his task.[66]

Whilst at home convalescing from this wound, he was awarded the Bronze Medal of the Royal Humane Society having saved a youth from drowning in the River Lagan, Belfast.

On 26 May 1917, he was awarded a Bar to his Military Cross, the citation stating:

> For conspicuous gallantry and devotion to duty. He went forward with a machine-gun team and some men from his platoon and engaged two enemy machine-guns, one of which was captured. He set a fine example of courage and initiative.[67]

Captain Brown was posted to 1st Battalion Royal Irish Rifles on 11 December 1916. He was initially posted as 'Missing' on 21 March and following the battle, enquiries were made as to his fate. Statements were taken from three men from his Company. Their disparate accounts indicate the confusion engendered by the course of the battle:

> Rifleman J McFall 18/161 – Capt. J Brown MC was my Company Commander. I was beside him on the morning of 21 March. When the Germans attacked Capt. Brown ordered us to fix bayonets and charge. A few minutes afterwards when getting out of the trench, I saw Capt. Brown lying dead, shot through the head.
>
> Rifleman R McBurney 12354 – On the morning of 21st March 1918, B Company 1st Battalion Royal Irish Rifles to which I belonged and which Captain J Brown MC commanded, was standing to in the trenches at Contescourt. Capt. Brown came to me and ordered me to go to the other side of the road I was on. A few moments afterwards we were surrounded by the enemy and I saw Capt. Brown firing his rifle. I was cut off by the enemy and did not see him again.

66 *The London Gazette*, 22 September 1916.
67 *The London Gazette*, 26 May 1917.

Serjeant McGuigan 9257 – I remember the 21st March 1918, I was in charge of No 6 Platoon at Contescourt. At about 1:00 p.m. Capt. J Brown came to where I was and remained in the trenches for about two hours. The Germans at this time got behind us and owing to the clouds of smoke from the shells we could not see them. They got into the trench where we were and I saw a German Officer throw a bomb at Capt. J Brown which fell at his feet and killed him instantaneously. I was about 10 yards from him at the time and was afterwards taken prisoner with the remainder of my platoon.[68]

Captain Brown has no known grave and is commemorated on the Pozieres Memorial to the Missing. His sacrifice is also commemorated on the Roll of Honour at Ballymacarrett Presbyterian Church, Belfast. Along with Captain Brown, another four officers and 40 men from the battalion were killed that day. Only 10 have a known grave, with the remainder being commemorated with Captain Brown on the Pozieres Memorial.

The remnants of the Battalion fought the Germans to a standstill and although A and B Companies had been decimated, they withdrew in the evening to Quarry Redoubt and fought on. It was not until 11:00 p.m. that the Redoubt was ordered to be abandoned as part of a planned withdrawal and the remainder of the battalion made its way to a pre – arranged position at Hamel on the outskirts of Grand Seraucourt.

At the opening of the German bombardment, the 2nd Battalion Royal Irish Rifles were in the Reserve Zone of 107th Brigade at Grand Seraucourt. The Battalion had been commanded since January of 1918 by Major Richard de la Ros Rose MC, of Ardue House, Limerick. Major Rose had been awarded his Military Cross for gallantry with the battalion in June of 1917 and had been Mentioned in Despatches in December of that year.

Father Gill who was in a dugout at the 2nd Rifles battalion headquarters, had retired to bed the previous evening with a feeling of uncertainty. In the early hours of the morning, he got a rude awakening:

The first indication that the attack had begun was the scream of a shell which burst in the middle of the billets. Presently the bugles rang out the alarm, it had begun. I got hold of my batman and along with another who was on his way up we set out to join the rest. There was a most unusual and very thick fog. It was nearly impossible to make our way with shells falling all along the road, the journey was not pleasant. Soon we had to put on our gas masks. This made things still worse. I lost my pipe![69]

68   TNA: WO 339/17471: Captain John Brown service record.
69   IJA/CHP1/27 p. 160.

Captain John Brown MC and Bar 1st Battalion Royal Irish Rifles. (Great War Ulster Newspaper Archive), Obituary of Captain John Brown MC and Bar. (*The Belfast News Letter*)

FATE OF CAPTAIN JOHN BROWN, M.C.

Captain John Brown, M.C., 1st Battalion Royal Irish Rifles, who was reported wounded and missing on 21st March, 1918 (the day on which the great German offensive opened), is now officially reported to have been killed on the battlefield at Contescourt on that date. This gallant officer was the second son of Mr. Samuel S. Brown, Ailsa Terrace, Strandtown, the Assistant Postmaster of Belfast. On the opening of the war in August, 1914, he was in the employment of Messrs. Richardson, Sons, & Owden, Ltd. He obtained a commission in the East Belfast Battalion on the formation of the Ulster Division, and was wounded in the shoulder at the opening of the Battle of the Somme on 1st July, 1916, being awarded the Military Cross for conspicuous gallantry in action upon that occasion. While home on leave in September following he gained the bronze medal of the Royal Humane Society for his bravery in saving a boy from drowning in the River Lagan. On recovering from the effects of his wound he returned to the front, and received a bar to his Military Cross early in 1917. A young man of splendid physique—he was well over six feet in height—Captain Brown invariably set a fine example of courage and initiative, and he enjoyed the warm regard of the officers not only of the East Belfast Volunteers, but also of the distinguished line battalion in which he was serving when he fell in action. As unassuming as he was daring, he inspired the men under his command by his skill and resource in leadership, and his personal popularity with the rank and file was unquestioned. One of his cousins, Second-Lieutenant Robert M'Dowell, North Staffordshire Regiment, won the Military Cross in Mesopotamia, and subsequently was killed in action in that theatre of war. Widespread sympathy will be extended to Mr. S. S. Brown and the other members of the family in their bereavement.

The journey Father Gill was undertaking was to join the remainder of Battalion Headquarters at a pre – designated position on the outskirts of Grand Seraucourt. It soon became evident to Father Gill that the Germans had carried out meticulous preparation prior to the attack:

> We found the men and officers in dugouts made in the side of the chalk quarry. As an indication of the way in which the Germans had mapped out the ground it is interesting to note that at the very beginning of the attack this quarry was heavily shelled, although it had been left alone before that. The shells fell with an accuracy which proved that the range had been fully noted beforehand.[70]

The German bombardment of the Reserve Zone consisted of both High Explosive and Gas Shells in a deliberate attempt to incapacitate those who would have been in a position to provide support to the battalions further forward. Amongst those who

---

70 Ibid. p. 161.

suffered from the effects of the gas shells was 19 years old Lieutenant Cecil Robert Walter McCammond. Lieutenant McCammond from Innisfayle, Donegall Park Avenue, Belfast had had an interesting military career up to that date. He was the son of Lieutenant Colonel Walter McCammond, who was the officer commanding 3rd Battalion Royal Irish Rifles during the Easter Rising in Dublin in April 1916. Cecil McCammond enlisted as a Private in the Royal Irish Rifles in June 1915 when he was 16 years of age. He applied for a commission in October of that year claiming he was 18. He was appointed as a Second Lieutenant in the 19th (Reserve) Battalion in January 1916 still aged 16. In April of that year at the outbreak of the Easter Rising he was visiting his father in Dublin and as Falls (1925) records:

> Lieutenant McCammond had been in Dublin and about noon, when returning on horseback to barracks was set upon by rebels at Portobello Bridge. These had established themselves in Davy's Public House, which overlooked the bridge and commanded the Rathmines Road and Richmond Street. A number came out of the house to attack him, while others fired at him from the windows. Fortunately, they were incredibly bad marksmen. Lieutenant McCammond got clear, only slightly wounded and rode on to barracks to give the alarm.[71]

Cecil McCammond was promoted Lieutenant in July 1917 and joined the 2nd battalion that month. The *Belfast News Letter* of 25 March 1918 recorded that he was admitted to hospital at Rouen on 23 March suffering from a gunshot wound to the right ear and severe gas poisoning.[72] Lieutenant McCammond went on to survive the war, despite being further wounded and was discharged in April 1919, still aged only 20.

As all communication had been lost due to the German shelling, confusion reigned at battalion headquarters and it was imperative that a clear picture of the situation could be obtained. Father Gill recorded that:

> A young 'Intelligence Officer' was sent up the road to find out what was happening, he never came back. He was an excellent young fellow, most popular with everyone.[73]

This officer was 20 years old Second Lieutenant Maurice Anderdon McFerran MC. He had set off in the direction of Grugies but was never heard from again. It is most likely that he ran into a party of advancing Stormtroopers and was killed. Second Lieutenant McFerran was from Stafford, the county town of Staffordshire and his

---

71   Cyril Falls, *The History of the First Seven Battalions the Royal Irish Rifles in the Great War* (Uckfield: Naval & Military Press reprint of 1925 edition), p. 88.
72   *The Belfast News Letter*, 25 March 1918. Ulster and the War column.
73   IJA/CHP1/27 p. 161.

father was a serving Major in a reserve battalion of the Royal Engineers. McFerran also has no known grave and is commemorated on the Pozieres Memorial to the Missing.

At around 2:00 p.m. the 2nd Rifles were ordered to take up a position on the Grand Seraucourt – Essigny Road. This position would have provided much needed support to the Battle Zone positions of 1st Royal Irish Rifles. By 4:00 p.m. however, the battalion resumed its former position at the Quarry east of Grand Seraucourt. At 7:00 p.m. D Company advanced in support of 1st Battalion to try to recapture the village of Contescourt which had been in German hands for a number of hours. The commanding officer of 1st Battalion cancelled the order for the attack just as it began, but the order never reached D Company, who were decimated.[74] The abortive attack was witnessed by *Vizefeldwebel* Wilhelm Prosch of IR 463:

> By early evening, we had taken the main positions, but we paused a while at the foot of a slope about 10 metres high near Contescourt. Our lookouts on top of the slope raised the alarm – a counter-attack! We fought this off and caused many casualties. The survivors crawled back to the nearest trench. The enemy fire stopped when our medical orderlies went forward to attend to the wounded. Their opposite numbers came out too, which impressed us a lot.[75]

The remainder of the battalion remained in position until around 11:00 p.m. when they retired as part of a general withdrawal to the Le Hamel-Happencourt Road, where positions were held for the remainder of the night, which passed quietly. In the action that day the battalion had 11 men killed although many others, particularly of D Company, were wounded and taken prisoner. The greatest test for the 2nd Battalion Royal Irish Rifles was to come however, in the following days as the withdrawal continued.

109th Brigade

The position of the 109th Brigade was different geographically from those of the other two brigades in the Division, in that the battalions were disposed on both sides of the River Somme and St Quentin or Crozat Canal, which was hardly ideal defensively. To complicate matters, the ground between the two watercourses was marshy which hindered any attackers heading in that direction, but also made the movement of troops either forward, or to the rear more difficult. On the left of the Brigade on

---

74   One of the officers of D Company who was killed was 20 years old Lieutenant William Leonard Price Dobbin MC. He had been in Dublin during the Easter Rising and was Guard Commander in an infamous incident when Captain Bowen-Colthurst of the Royal Irish Rifles shot the pacifist journalist Francis Skeehy Sheffington at Portobello Barracks.
75   Middlebrook, *The Kaiser's Battle*, p. 292.

the far side of the canal were the 21st Brigade of 30th Division. In the Forward Zone of 109th Brigade's sector were the 2nd Battalion Royal Inniskilling Fusiliers, who had taken over the position of the evening of 19 March. Their strongpoint in the Forward Zone was known as Boadicea Redoubt, which was around three quarters of a mile to the left of the 15th Royal Irish Rifles at Racecourse Redoubt. The Battle Zone was held by 1st Battalion Royal Inniskilling Fusiliers, their strongpoint being named Ricardo Redoubt, after the former Brigade Commander, Brigadier General Ambrose St Quintin Ricardo who had returned to the United Kingdom following the Battle of Cambrai in November 1917 due to ill health. The 2nd Inniskillings position was particularly isolated as the Battle Zone positions of 1st Inniskillings were around two and a half miles to the rear and across the River Somme and the St Quentin Canal. The ground to the 2nd Inniskillings left in the river valley was marshy and the battalion in the Reserve Zone, the 9th Inniskillings were based at Artemps, 5 miles to the rear.

The 2nd Battalion Royal Inniskilling Fusiliers were commanded by Lieutenant Colonel Arthur Kenlis Maxwell DSO, the 11th Lord Farnham, of Farnham estate, County Cavan. Aged 38 at the time of the battle, Lord Farnham had been educated at Harrow School and the Royal Military College Sandhurst, being commissioned into the 10th (Prince of Wales Own Royal) Hussars in 1899. He resigned his commission

due to ill-health in 1905 and was appointed as Captain in the North of Ireland Imperial Yeomanry, the forerunner of the North Irish Horse, in May of that year. Prior to the war, Lord Farnham commanded B Squadron of the North Irish Horse and was also the commander of the County Cavan Ulster Volunteer Force.[76]

Lord Farnham embarked for France on appointment to the Divisional Staff of the 36th (Ulster) Division and following a period again with the North Irish Horse, he was appointed as Lieutenant Colonel commanding the 10th Inniskillings in September 1917. On disbandment of 10th Inniskillings in February 1918, Lieutenant Colonel Lord Farnham was appointed to command 2nd Inniskillings. As a major figure in civil society in County Cavan, he was a social acquaintance and near neighbour of the 36th Division Commander, Major General Nugent.

Lieutenant Colonel Lord Farnham 2nd Battalion Royal Inniskilling Fusiliers. (Cavan County Museum)

76   The North Irish Horse in the Great War <http://www.northirishhorse.com.au/NIH/Images/People/Full%20pictures/Lord%20Farnham.htm> (Accessed 29 June 2017).

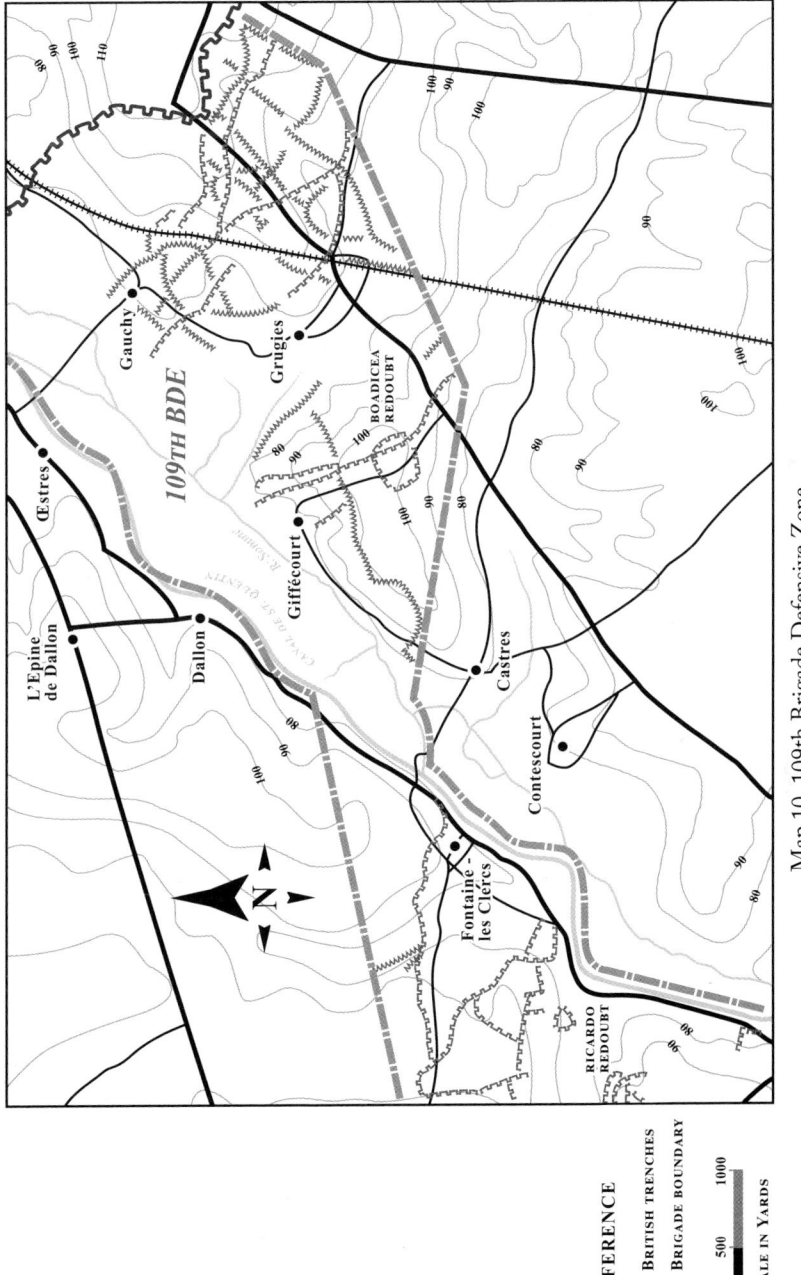

Map 10 109th Brigade Defensive Zone.

REFERENCE

BRITISH TRENCHES

BRIGADE BOUNDARY

SCALE IN YARDS

0   500   1000

The war diary of the 2nd Inniskillings is unsurprisingly, sparse in detail:

> On the morning of the 21st inst., a terrific bombardment was opened by the enemy at about 4:30 a.m. – this continued throughout the day.[77]

Thereafter, the war diary only refers to Transport and QM Stores personnel as the rest of the battalion was cut off and killed, wounded or taken prisoner. However, a reasonable account can be established from accounts of individuals and the German regimental history. When the bombardment commenced, Captain Charles Miller was in a fortified position a short distance to the right from Battalion Headquarters. He was initially puzzled by the pattern of the German artillery bombardment:

> I had with me a subaltern and a full platoon. My strongpoint consisted of about 150 yards of trench with one deep and very spacious dugout quite capable of holding us all and protecting us from the effects of shellfire, but a death trap if the enemy infantry got in before we could get out of it… There was one fairly strong belt of wire running in a half circle right round the front of the strongpoint and ending about twenty yards wide of the two stops at the end of the trench. Had that wire been thicker and stronger it would have been a much more formidable little place for a frontal attack, and of course by rights the wire should have been all round it. I knew that the enemy would be pretty close behind his bombardment, but it seemed to me that his barrage was at the moment stationary and concentrated on our front – line wire. The intensity of the bombardment was terrific, and I also gathered that his long-distance guns were passing our artillery positions. He seemed to be pouring *minenwerfers* on our front line and I had great fear for the so-called strongpoint that I had visited. As a matter of fact, practically all that luckless platoon were buried in the ruins of their strongpoint. We ourselves were escaping comparatively lightly though probably not for long. I burnt my maps and papers and then put myself on the top stair of the dugout with the men behind me ready to dash out the moment the barrage seemed to lift at all. It was now getting on towards dawn and there was a heavy mist, the noise was terrific, but I came to the conclusion that either there was some flaw in their battery work and our position was not getting its full share, or else the barrage was beginning to move forward. It was impossible to tell which.[78]

It was not long however, before evidence of the German infantry attack presented itself and fierce hand to hand fighting subsequently ensued:

---

77   TNA: WO 95/2510/2: 2nd Battalion Royal Inniskilling Fusiliers war diary.
78   IWM Doc.4118: Captain Charles C. Miller papers.

The night was alive with noise and explosions everywhere, but I thought it advisable to get out into the trench. The first thing I did was to send one party to the stop at one end of the trench and myself take a party to the stop at the other end. I had hardly got there when I saw my first German. He was just at the point where the wire ended outside the stop and was groping his way forward through the mist. But for the shape of his helmet, it would have been impossible to know if he was German or British on account of the mist, but the helmet was unmistakeable. He had disappeared into the mist again before I had time to fire, but he was followed by another and another and the stop at the post proceeded to shoot them as fast as they appeared. What had happened was obvious. The attacking Germans had come on the semi-circular belt of wire that surrounded our post. They could not see that it was comparatively weak and therefore were feeling their way round it, this inevitably brought the nearest ones for a moment or two within sight of our men at the end of the trench, giving us the chance to shoot them before they disappeared into the mist again. The attackers groping their way through the murk hardly knew from where they were being shot. For the moment, the advantage was with the defence so far as we were concerned. On the other hand, I had no illusions, it was obvious that they were through and advancing in vast numbers and as soon as the mist rose we should get what was coming to us. I dashed off to the stop at the other end of the trench and found exactly the same thing happening there – my men picking off the dim figures of Germans as they passed by in the mist. As a matter of fact, the first attackers were into the trench long before the mist lifted. I was so occupied with the flanks that I barely saw them before they appeared out of the mist and leaped down into the trench and in a moment, we were all mixed up in hand to hand fighting. I remember vaguely that I had two men coming at me with their bayonets one of whom I think I shot with my revolver, whilst a Sergeant of mine standing just behind me shot the other at point blank range with his rifle barrel over my shoulder, but almost at the same time a German stick bomb came whistling into the trench from the parapet right into the bunch of us, and killed or wounded practically the whole lot of us, English and German alike. Whether it was actually this bomb or a bayonet stab that gave me the wound in my neck, I don't know, it might have been either. For the moment we were clear, but there was a nasty little shambles round us. Sergeant Adcock who had just saved my life having his head blown off.[79]

The NCO killed was 28 years old Lance Serjeant Frank Adcock 42280. He was from Rugby Place in Brighton. Serjeant Adcock had previously served with the Army Ordnance Corps before transferring to the Inniskillings and is commemorated on the Pozieres Memorial to the Missing.

79   IWM Doc.4118: Captain Charles C. Miller papers.

It was only a matter of time before Captain Miller's position was overrun by superior numbers:

> There was a tremendous hubbub further down the trench and on my way there, I got involved in a sort of a private duel with a man carrying a flamethrower. I got the best of that and then came into another shambles further down the trench. There again we had settled them for the moment, but a lot of our men were out too. I felt awfully weak and discovered that a river of blood was flowing from my neck. I tried to bandage it but the bandage wouldn't hold and in my giddiness, I remember realising that the sun was getting up which meant the end of us. Before they attacked again they brought up some trench mortars and knocked seven bells out of us and then swarmed into the trench. By that time there were only a handful of us left on our feet and all I suppose wounded. I got another wound from a stick bomb which put a bit of metal into my thigh, but I think it was loss of blood that put me out. Before I collapsed I tried to give the surrender signal and hope I succeeded in saving a few lives.[80]

From his account, it would appear that Captain Miller's outpost surrendered around lunchtime and the remaining Inniskillings retired to the main Redoubt. By this time however, the leading Germans had streamed far past Boadicea Redoubt and were already in Contescourt, over a mile to the rear of the Inniskillings position, a fact acknowledged by the Divisional Commander who penned a letter to his wife at 12:30 p.m. on 21 March, lamenting the fate of his neighbour, Lieutenant Colonel Lord Farnham:

> The latest is the Germans have got all our forward lines along the whole front of attack as far as I can make out. From our second position we can see the Germans on the ridge in front, where our front line was. There is no doubt it is all captured and Kitty dearest, Arthur was in front. He must be either dead or a prisoner. Poor Arthur and poor Aileen. It is terrible. I am afraid there is no hope that he got away. He would not have left his men and all his line is gone. We know that.[81]

At the time however, Lord Farnham was very much alive and continuing the fight, supported by accurate suppressing fire from four teams from the Machine Gun Battalion under the command of 33 years old Lieutenant Thomas Graham Weall from Watford:

80   IWM Doc.4118: Captain Charles C Miller papers.
81   PRONI: D3835/E/2/17/11 Farren Connell papers.

I was in command of four machine guns on the left front of a Battalion keep near Boadicea Corner. On 21 March, it was too misty to see far, all communication was completely cut by the barrage and at 9:30 a.m. I learnt that we were completely surrounded, the keeps on each flank having given way and very soon after the enemy were in position on the high ground in rear of us. After conferring with Colonel Lord Farnham, I moved up to better protect the keep as the guns on the right flank had been put out of action... I arrived in position in the keep about noon, and worked in conjunction with the Lewis guns to defend the approaches, more especially the sunken road where we had to put a German MG out of action at a range of about 40 yards. From then onwards we fired on scattered parties of Germans who we could easily see now that the weather had cleared, and also during the afternoon engaged Field Artillery in action on the Racecourse and various lots of transport passing up the road; fair results could easily be observed. During the afternoon, we were also able to assist in driving off enemy aeroplanes flying very low over us.[82]

The excellent defensive action by Lieutenant Weall and his men is corroborated by the account of IR 463:

All efforts from Lieutenant Colonel Prinz, to direct artillery fire onto the enemy are in vain. Even the Second Minenwerfer Artillery is absent. The Battalion's combined telephone groups and the three assigned artillery liaison officers are unable to establish a connection. All attempts are thwarted by the English disruption fire, which had meanwhile accrued in strength greatly. Leutnant Beckedorf receives the command to skirt around Giffecourt hill with his Sixth company and attack the enemy from behind. The Second company is located north of the allies position, under the courageous leadership of Leutnant Thümecke amid intense fighting with a strong enemy M.G nest. The company is crouched in a communication trench, which cuts perpendicular to the English position, and is directly opposite an enemy M.G. The company attempts to approach the trajectory range of the hand grenades however, they suffer bloody losses. When the brave messenger, Lance Corporal Knabe pulls himself together, he crawls forward, pulls the pin of his hand grenade, straightens up and throws – he sustains a shot to the heart and collapses without a sound. The hand grenade of the brave fallen comrade explodes three meters in front of the English nest. The Fourth company is unable in its unfavourable position, to disengage from the enemy, to mount an attack on their flank. In fact, they remain engaged in gruelling battle until the evening and dwindle further.[83]

---

82   TNA: WO 339/106124: Lieutenant Thomas Graham Weall service record. Lieutenant Weall was a Land Agent in Hong Kong at the outbreak of war and a Lieutenant in the Hong Kong Volunteer Corps.

83   Hoffmann, *Infanterie Regiment 463, 7000 Niedersachsen im Grosskampfe der Westfront*, p. 192.

The Inniskillings stout resistance was causing the Germans serious problems. Although the advance was by now far behind the Redoubt, it simply had to be dealt with to enable the Germans to bring up reserves and supplies. Having battered at the Redoubt all day, the Germans decided to try another tack, as recalled by Lieutenant Weall:

> At about 5:30 p.m. a German Officer with white flag was admitted and after conferring with Colonel Lord Farnham we were given 10 minutes to decide whether to surrender or not. Colonel Lord Farnham called all officers together and it was unanimously decided to surrender as it was hopeless to hold out longer in the position and equally hopeless to fight our way back, even by night seeing that the Germans were then beyond Grand Seraucourt and were in great strength.[84]

This account is corroborated by that of the Battalion Signal Officer who was based in Boadicea Redoubt, 24 years old Lieutenant Frederick William Davidson from Laurel Villas, Castlederg, County Tyrone, although he puts the time at 6:00 p.m.[85] The account of IR 463 emphasises the delight of the Germans in capturing the Redoubt without having to incur further loss of life:

> At around 5:15 pm Leutnant Floß, Eighth company, with VFW Volkenstorff, Corporal Arnold and two English speaking soldiers with Lieutenant Colonel Prinz come forward. They shall urge the enemy to surrender through negotiation, they receive the command to advise the enemy that the German front line already lies to the southwest, kilometres from the allied position, that any further defence is useless and heavy artillery, primed to attack, would fire on their position if surrender did not immediately take effect. Under the protection of the white flag the brave soldiers advance. A short time of breathless tension passes. And lo and behold, in a long procession the Tommies come out from their small stronghold: a Lieutenant Colonel, three Captains, seven Lieutenants and 241 men! They relinquish their position, with 41 machine guns and a mortar. The Colonel lovingly carries a small white dog in his arms. He requests of Lieutenant Colonel Prinz confirmation that he and his troops defended themselves bravely before he gave himself up. He receives it. German chivalry honours the brave enemy with their due recognition.[86]

84   TNA: WO 339/106124: Lieutenant Thomas Graham Weall service record.
85   TNA: WO 339/1256: Lieutenant Frederick William Davidson service record.
86   Hoffmann, *Infanterie Regiment 463, 7000 Niedersachsen im Grosskampfe der Westfront*, p. 192.

Notification of the fall of Boadicea Redoubt came to 36th Divisional Headquarters when two messenger pigeons were released by the Germans and returned to the Divisional HQ at Ollezy. One of the pigeons carried the message, 'Have captured the Redoubt and have got the battalion commander a prisoner.'[87] As there were three redoubts, General Nugent was keen to clarify further as he explained in a letter to his wife:

> I sent to our pigeon loft to ask the pigeoneer if he remembered which battalion the pigeon was sent to and he was able to say it was Arthur's battalion. There is therefore no reason to doubt that Arthur is safe though a prisoner and if he had been wounded, I expect the German would have mentioned it.[88]

The defence of and subsequent surrender of Boadicea Redoubt, along with that of Racecourse Redoubt was commented on with a degree of pride by Falls in, *The History of the 36th (Ulster) Division* (1922):

> The resistance of Racecourse and Boadicea Redoubts affords a rare example of that 'cold courage', unsupported by the ardour and excitement of an advance or the hope of ultimate victory, which has been so often displayed by soldiers of British race in all periods of the history of the British arms.[89]

The defence of Boadicea Redoubt particularly, has drawn criticism, sometimes implied and sometimes overt from other respected commentators. In his outstanding 1978 book, *The Kaiser's Battle*, Martin Middlebrook outlines the account of the German plan to engineer a surrender:

> It is not known how many casualties the redoubt garrison had suffered; the total fatal casualties of the whole battalion – of which at least two and a half companies were not in Boadicea Redoubt were 47 men.[90] No officers were amongst the killed.[91]

The implication here is that had an effective defence been carried out, officers would have appeared as fatalities, the examples of Second Lieutenant Edmund De Wind and Lieutenant Colonel Elstob of 16th Battalion Manchester Regiment, both of whom

---

87   PRONI: D3835/E/2/17/12A Farren Connell papers.
88   Ibid.
89   Falls, *The History of the 36th (Ulster) Division.* p. 201.
90   Commonwealth War Graves Commission records indicate that 49 men from the 2nd Battalion died that day. One of these however, Private T Morris 7687, is buried in Ste Marie Cemetery, Le Havre and it is most likely that he succumbed to wounds previously sustained, in one of the five hospitals in the town.
91   Middlebrook, *The Kaiser's Battle*, p. 268.

were posthumously awarded the Victoria Cross for their actions are cited. It is true that of those killed, the highest rank is that of Serjeant. However, the evidence is clear that it was only through good fortune that officers were not killed. To take the example of Captain Miller, as highlighted in his account he was wounded in the thigh and neck in hand to hand fighting and weak from loss of blood, was still not out of danger:

> Meantime I was in a state of oblivion in which I knew I was moving but knew very little else, until I received a shattering blow to my hand. Actually, I was being carted across 'no man's land' between one of our wounded men and a German stretcher bearer towards the enemy's rear. In my holster was an empty revolver and one of the advancing enemy concluding that I was armed proceeded to take a pot shot at me. The bullet hit me just above the back of my thumb and came out the front of my hand below the base of my thumb. Actually, I had been using my revolver at the start of the scrap, but, having emptied it had shoved it into the holster not having time to reload and had picked up a rifle. The chap who had shot me now approached covering me and relieved me of the revolver, after which I was carted to an advanced German Dressing Station where a German Doctor succeeded in dressing my neck.[92]

Further in his narrative however, Middlebrook recognises the value of not throwing away lives unnecessarily:

> The vital weapon leading to the fall of the redoubts had been the mobile German mortars and the light howitzers which had been brought up to safe positions within easy range and had then proceeded to send bombs or shells into the redoubts. There was no answer to this and the commanders who surrendered saved many lives.[93]

In his comprehensive, *Retreat and Rearguard Somme 1918, The Fifth Army Retreat*, Jerry Murland (2014) is more overtly critical. He highlights that Lieutenant Colonel Lord Farnham had only been in command of 2nd Inniskillings for a matter of weeks and continues:

> There is some controversy over the surrender of Boadicea Redoubt…Quite how long Farnham and his men held out for is unclear, Cyril Falls in the divisional history says it was 5:50 p.m. when three captains, seven subalterns and 241 men filed out of the redoubt after the Germans threatened to bombard the position. Apparently, Farnham asked for – and was given – a document of evidence that

92   IWM Doc.4118: Captain Charles C Miller papers.
93   Middlebrook, *The Kaiser's Battle*, p. 292.

he and the garrison had put up a good fight before they were marched off into captivity! When compared to the action at Le Pontchu and Racecourse Redoubt it does leave one wondering how events at Boadicea Redoubt could possibly be described in the divisional history as a 'rare example of cold courage.'[94]

Murland is correct in his assertion that Lieutenant Colonel Lord Farnham had only been in command of 2nd Inniskillings for a matter of weeks however, he neglects to mention that he had been in command of 10th Inniskillings for five months, including through the Battle of Cambrai in November 1917. His assertion of 'quite how long Farnham and his men held out for is unclear,' shows in this instance a lack of in-depth research. In the *Official History 1918*, Vol. I (1935) Edmonds states:

> The most easterly of the redoubts, situated on the Essigny-St Quentin road and garrisoned by the 12/R Irish Rifles, was overwhelmed before noon, and others soon followed; but two – one on the railway south of Grugies (15/R Irish Rifles) and the other near the western end of the line (2/R Inniskilling Fusiliers) – held out against repeated heavy attacks until after 6 pm.[95]

As we have already seen, the account of IR 463 indicates that their plan to negotiate a surrender was put in to effect around 5:15 p.m. With time to approach the redoubt, deliver the offer and give time to consider, 6:00 p.m. may be an accurate time of surrender. Similarly, Lieutenant Weall of the Machine Gun Corps indicates that the German party was admitted to the redoubt at 5:30 p.m. and following negotiation, the defenders were given 10 minutes to decide their course of action. In his account, Lieutenant Davidson the battalion Signals Officer, also puts the time of surrender at 6:00 p.m. From this evidence from a number of sources, I would contend that Boadicea Redoubt held out until around 6.00 pm.

The most serious implication from Murland's account is that the actions of Lieutenant Colonel Lord Farnham were somehow less than honourable as he surrendered with 250 men, instead of fighting to the end. However, the evidence once again contradicts this view. The initial German Infantry attack streamed past the Redoubt on the left and right, dealing with Captain Miller's party as they passed. By 1:00 p.m. Lieutenant Colonel Cole-Hamilton of 15th Royal Irish Rifles to the right of Boadicea Redoubt was aware that the Germans were far to the rear of his position. By 12:55 p.m. the 36th Division recorded that the Germans were in Contescourt, a mile to the rear of Boadicea Redoubt. On the left of the Inniskillings and across the River Somme and St Quentin Canal, the 2nd Battalion Wiltshire Regiment were holding the Forward Zone as part of 21st Brigade, 30th Division, in a redoubt at L'Epine de Dallon. Their commanding officer, Lieutenant Colonel Archibald Martin

94   Murland, *Retreat and Rearguard: Somme 1918*, p. 57.
95   Edmonds, *Military Operations France and Belgium 1918*, p. 176.

recorded that his right-hand company (which would have been immediately to the Inniskillings' left) were attacked mid – morning from the rear, confirming that the Germans had infiltrated deep between the Wiltshires and the Inniskillings.[96]

The accounts of Lieutenant Weall of the MGC and Lieutenant Davidson indicate that the 2nd Inniskillings continued to give a good account of themselves against anything German that moved, up until they were called upon to surrender.

It would have been quite obvious to Lieutenant Colonel Lord Farnham, even before he was informed of the facts by the Germans, that the redoubt position was hopeless. The Inniskillings' party was completely surrounded and there was no hope of escape. To continue fighting against overwhelming odds would have had only one outcome. In the circumstances, Lieutenant Colonel Lord Farnham took the only option open to him, and in doing so saved countless British and German lives. Whilst he surrendered with 250 men, other battalions surrendered with more. As we have seen, the 12th Rifles lost 588 men, the vast majority being taken prisoner and of the entire comple- ment of 15th Rifles, none escaped death or captivity.

No adverse comment in the performance of Lieutenant Colonel Lord Farnham and the 2nd Inniskillings was passed at official level where it appears to have been recognised that the German attack was so swift and overwhelming, that little could have been done about it. The final words on this situation will be left to the Commander Fifth Army, General Gough. On the afternoon of 21 March, he visited the Headquarters of XVIII Corps and its Commander, Lieutenant General Sir Ivor Maxse. Of the Divisions in this Corps, which included the 36th, General Gough stated:

> His XVIII Corps had done magnificently, and after desperate fighting still held its Battle Zone intact. The nine battalions, however, holding its Forward Zone had sacrificed themselves, bravely and stoutly and had been almost annihilated in doing so.[97]

As highlighted earlier, research indicates that 48 men from the 2nd Inniskillings were killed on 21 March. Few of them have a known grave, with the majority being commemorated on the Pozieres Memorial to the Missing. One who has an identi- fied resting place is 22 years old Lance Corporal Thomas George McIlroy MM from Upperlands, Co. Londonderry. A Farmer's son, McIlroy originally enlisted in the 10th (Service) Battalion Royal Inniskilling Fusiliers (Derry Volunteers) and embarked for France in October 1915. Attached to D Company, he was awarded the Military Medal on Christmas Eve 1917 for gallantry during the Battle of Cambrai, before transferring to 2nd Inniskillings in February 1918 on disbandment of 10th Inniskillings. He was

---

96   TNA: WO 374/46357: Lieutenant Colonel Archibald Victor Powell Martin service
       record.
97   Gough, *The March Retreat*, p. 85.

initially buried in Urvillers German Cemetery and after the Armistice in a consolidation process carried out by the Imperial War Graves Commission (forerunner of the Commonwealth War Graves Commission), his remains were exhumed and reburied at St Souplet British Cemetery.[98]

The 1st Battalion Royal Inniskilling Fusiliers held the Battle Zone position of 109th Brigade. As already mentioned, their position was somewhat unique in that they were the only Ulster Division unit to have their strongpoint on the western side of the River Somme and St Quentin Canal. Their colleagues in the Forward Zone, 2nd Inniskillings being to their north-east. The battalion strongpoint, Ricardo Redoubt, was situated at a bend in the canal, a mile south of the village of Fontaine-les-Clercs. Two miles to the north of this following the canal was the strongpoint of the 2nd Battalion Wiltshire Regiment, 21st Brigade, 30th Division.

Headstone of Lance Corporal Thomas McIlroy MM, St Souplet Cemetery.
(Author's collection)

The 1st Inniskillings were commanded by an officer with vast military experience – Lieutenant Colonel James Norman Crawford DSO. Born at Dublin in 1874, his father Henry was a Major in the Regiment. James Crawford attended the Royal Military College, Sandhurst and was gazetted as a 2nd Lieutenant in the Royal Inniskilling Fusiliers in October 1893. At the outbreak of war, he was a Captain in the regiment's 2nd battalion and embarked for France on 10 August 1914. Promoted to Major, he commanded the battalion (in the absence of the commanding officer) at the Battle of Festubert in May 1915, when the 2nd Inniskillings casualties numbered two-thirds of the battalion, including 264 killed.[99] He was awarded the Distinguished Service

98   Lance Corporal McIlroy is commemorated on the Roll of Honour at Maghera Presbyterian Church. His name does not appear on the war memorial in the Diamond, Kilrea which commemorates local men who fell. However, relatives have left an addendum. See <http://www.ulsterwarmemorials.net/html/kilrea__county_londonderry.html> (Accessed 30 June 2017).

99   For a detailed account of the Inniskillings' involvement at Festubert, see *It was an awful Sunday: The 2nd Battalion Royal Inniskilling Fusiliers at the Battle of Festubert 15-17 May*

Order in January 1916 and on promotion, Lieutenant Colonel Crawford commanded the 2nd Battalion from February 1916 until May 1917 when he was invalided. Following convalescence, he was posted to command 1st Inniskillings in January 1918.

As the 1st Inniskillings position was somewhat isolated from the remainder of the Division, the action that affected the other battalions in the Forward and Battle Zone largely passed them by. This sense of isolation was compounded from about 12 noon on 21 March by the destruction of the road and foot bridges at Fontaines-les-Clercs by 121st Field Company Royal Engineers. The Inniskillings were certainly heavily shelled in the initial bombardment by High Explosive and Gas shell and sustained some casualties from this. However, no infantry attack materialised on their positions, primarily as the Germans advancing against 2nd Inniskillings were being delayed by the defence there, and also by the fact that the Germans were unable to negotiate the marshy ground of the River

Lieutenant Colonel James Norman Crawford DSO, 1st Battalion Royal Inniskilling Fusiliers. (Inniskillings Museum)

Somme and St Quentin canal basin. The resolute defence of the 2nd Wiltshires at L'Epine de Dallon certainly stymied the German advance and as Lieutenant Colonel Powell of the Wiltshire's remarked, his position was not overcome until 2:50 p.m. Shortly after this, the Germans were seen massing at Fontaine-les-Clercs but were heavily engaged by British artillery and made no attempt to mount an attack on the Inniskillings position for the remainder of 21 March. The 1st Battalion consolidated their position as best they could and awaited what the morning would bring.

The Battalion in the Reserve Zone of 109th Brigade were the 9th Inniskillings. They were commanded by an experienced officer who had been with the battalion since its formation. Lieutenant Colonel Warren John Richard Peacocke DSO and Bar aged 28, was from Skevanish, Innishannon, County Cork. Pre-war, he had had nearly three years' service with the Grenadier Guards. Appointed as a Captain to C Company 9th Inniskillings, he was awarded the Distinguished Service Order for leading a daring trench raid at Thiepval in May 1916. On the 1st July 1916 at the Somme he commanded his Company with great gallantry defending the position known as 'the

1915 (Eastbourne: Reveille Press, 2015) by the same author.

Crucifix' under sustained German attack.[100] On 1 December 1916 he was promoted Lieutenant Colonel and appointed to command the battalion, which he continued to do throughout the Battles of Messines, Langemarck and Cambrai in 1917, being awarded the French Croix de Guerre in July of that year. He was Mentioned in Despatches in December 1917 and was awarded a Bar to his DSO in January 1918.

On the morning of 21 March, the battalion was in reserve positions at Artemps on the St Quentin Canal to the south of Grand Seraucourt. As the bombardment commenced, the battalion stood to and marched to positions known as 'Somme Dugout' just south of Grand Seraucourt. With the enemy reported to be in Contescourt, the battalion was ordered to cross the canal to the village of Happencourt. Just as they arrived, further orders were issued detailing them to cross back over the canal and make their way through Grand Seraucourt to support the 9th Royal Irish Fusiliers of 108th Brigade near Essigny, as it appeared that the right flank of the Division was in danger, due to the Germans forcing a wedge between it and 14th Division. This position was reached around 3:00 p.m. and was held for around five hours under sporadic German attack. During this period, two companies were detached to support 107th Brigade at the Grand Seraucourt-Essigny Road.

On 21 March, records indicate that the 9th Inniskillings sustained 11 fatalities.[101] Closer examination of this figure however, shows the confusion that existed in the face of the sustained German attack. Two of those listed, 23 years old Private John Douthart from Ballycastle, County Antrim and 32 years old Private James Gore from Carnalea Street, Belfast, are both interred at Noyon New British Cemetery with their headstones both indicating the date of death as 21 March 1918.

Noyon New British Cemetery is however, 25 miles from where the 9th Inniskillings were in action on 21 March. Research of other existing military records indicates that the exact date of death of both men is given as 21-29 March 1918, giving rise to the probability that both men were killed later in the withdrawal. These however, are not the only cases where research has identified that the date of death recorded by the Commonwealth War Graves Commission is most likely not correct. Others identified in a similar manner will be commented on as they occur in the narrative.

Whilst the battalions of 36th (Ulster) Division were fighting for their very existence, those in command were monitoring the scale and scope of the German advance closely. The Commander Fifth Army, General Gough, rapidly recognised the danger posed by the infiltration of the German attack between 36th and 14th Divisions. Having only two Divisions in reserve, he placed one of these, the 20th (Light) Division, at the disposal of Lieutenant General Maxse, Commander XVIII Corps at 1:00 p.m. 21 March. The promised assistance from the French agreed by Field

100 The 9th Inniskillings sustained 222 fatalities on 1 July 1916. Commonwealth War Graves Commission <http://www.cwgc.org.> (Accessed 19 October 2016).
101 Commonwealth War Graves Commission <http://www.cwgc.org.> (Accessed 19 October 2016).

Headstone of Private John Douthart, Noyon
New British Cemetery. (Author's collection)

Headstone of Private James Gore, Noyon
New British Cemetery. (Author's collection)

Marshal Haig and General Petain in the event of a major attack was not forthcoming. The French officer in charge of liaison with the British, General Humbert, apologised profusely to General Gough, stating that he had no resources to give. It was not until midday on 22 March that three French Divisions were ready to move into position. Having to make do with what resources were available, Lieutenant General Maxse placed one Brigade of 20th Division at the disposal of Major General Nugent. This was the 61st Brigade, commanded by Brigadier General James Kilvington Cochrane, formerly of the Leinster Regiment. The Brigade comprised the 7th Battalion Somerset Light Infantry, 7th Battalion Duke of Cornwall's Light Infantry and 12th Battalion King's (Liverpool Regiment).

On the morning of 21 March, the 61st Brigade was at Freniches, nine miles south of the 36th Division's HQ at Ollezy. The Brigade war diary records the initial events of the day:

> The order – '18th Corps manning Battle Stations' was received at 5:14 a.m. On receipt of this order all units were to be prepared to move at one hour's notice, transport to be loaded in preparation of a move to the 'Rear Zone' of defences in the event of an enemy attack on the Fifth Army Front.[102]

102 TNA: WO 95/2125/3: 61st Infantry Brigade war diary.

To ensure that his front did not collapse completely, General Gough put into effect a plan that he had agreed with Field Marshal Haig, to withdraw some of his forces behind the St Quentin or Crozat canal. This affected 36th Division due to the gap forced by the Germans between them and 14th Division. As 14th Division (part of III Corps) were moving behind the canal, it was necessary for 36th Division to move also to maintain the integrity of the front line.

The St Quentin Canal in the area held by the 36th Division formed the rough shape of an 'L', from St Quentin in the north, south past the position held by 1st Inniskillings near Fontaines-les-Clercs, past the villages of Grand Seraucourt, Artemps and Tugny, shortly after which there was a fork and the relevant branch of the canal took a sharp turn eastwards, past St Simon to the village of Jussy, which was in the area held by 14th Division. At the same location, a separate branch of the canal turned westwards. Named the Somme Canal, this watercourse ran initially to the west past the town of Ham before turning to the north-west in the direction of the town of Peronne.

The 61st Brigade were put under the command of 36th Division at around 1:30 p.m. and were immediately ordered to secure the bridgeheads at Tugny and St Simon. The Brigadier and Brigade Major proceeded in advance to St Simon calling at 36th Division HQ at Ollezy on the way for news. The 61st Brigade war diary recorded the directions of 36th Division command:

> Information was received that the Redoubt Line in the rear of the Battle Zone was the line being held at that time which was around 4:30 p.m. The positions occupied were as follows, Bde HQ at St Simon, 7th DCLI were on right holding the main line of resistance, 12th Kings were on left of Bde. front guarding the Tugny bridge. 7th Somerset LI were in Bde Reserve. 61st MGC were in position in depth guarding the Brigade front. The remainder of the day was spent digging in and consolidating.[103]

On the evening of 21 March, the withdrawal as ordered by General Gough was put into operation. The position of the 36th Division at this point was as follows; the battalions in the Forward Zone had carried out their duty beyond expectations and the three battalions manning the Forward Zone – 12th and 15th Royal Irish Rifles and 2nd Royal Inniskilling Fusiliers ceased to exist as fighting forces, their complement either killed, wounded or as was the case for the vast majority, taken prisoner. This effectively reduced the fighting strength of 36th Division by a brigade. The sacrifice of these battalions however, had ensured that their comrades manning the Battle Zone were able to withstand the German assault, the weakest position in this line being around Contescourt which saw attacks by the Germans against 2nd Royal Irish Rifles up until 9:00 p.m. To affect the withdrawal, it was decided to pivot the Division on 1st Inniskillings, who were still 'holding the fort' so to speak, at Ricardo redoubt. Edmonds (1935) records the timing of the withdrawal:

---

103 TNA: WO 95/2125/3: 61st Infantry Brigade war diary.

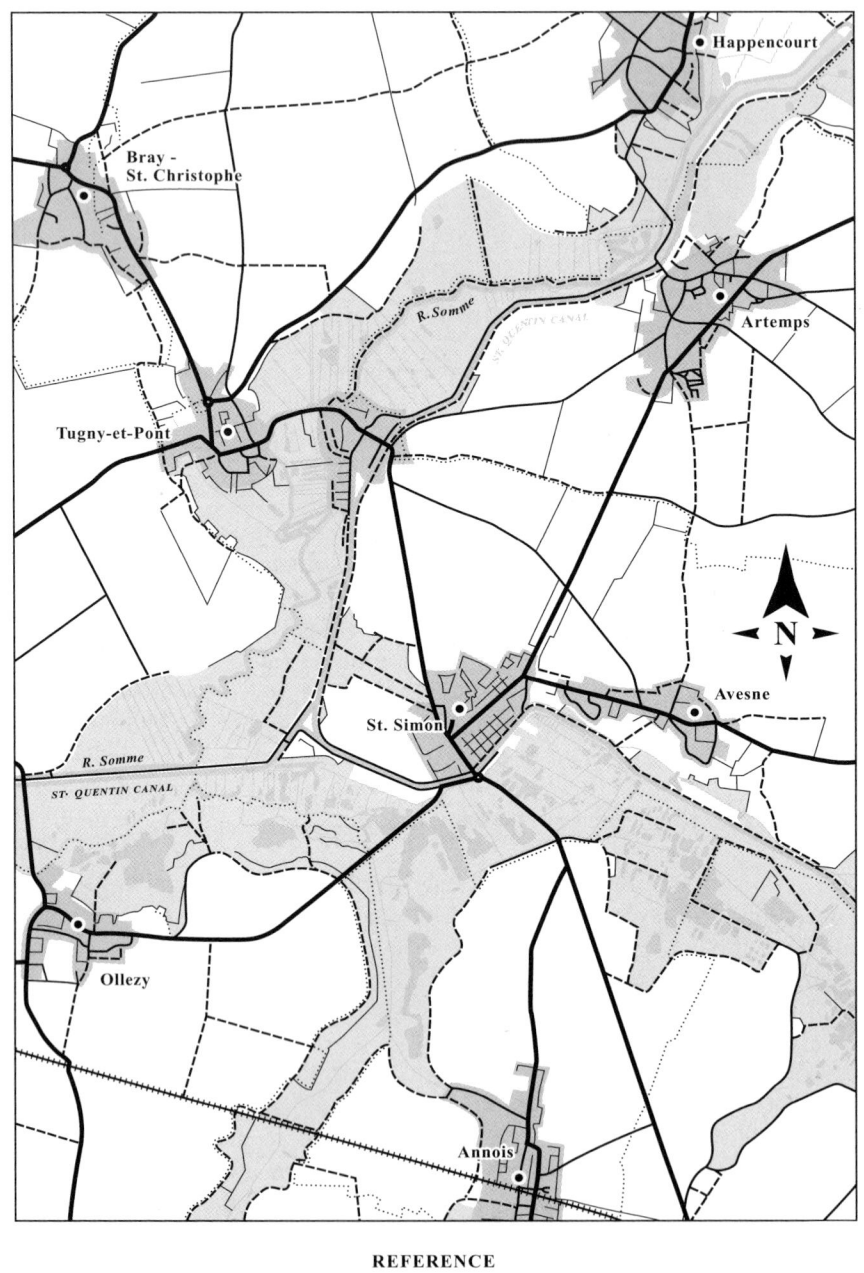

REFERENCE

0   0.5   1

SCALE IN MILES

Map 11 Somme and St Quentin canals and vicinity.

Although orders did not reach brigades until 8:00 p.m. the withdrawal of the
36th Division was carried out without interference from the enemy between
10:30 p.m. and 4:15 a.m. on 22nd.[104]

The term 'without interference' would certainly not be agreed with by Captain
Henehan of 9th Royal Irish Fusiliers who, as it was seen earlier in the chapter, ran
into a strong party of advancing Germans as he sought to locate one of his companies
in the fog which had again descended. In addition to three platoons from 9th Royal
Irish Fusiliers, a platoon from 1st Royal Irish Fusiliers failed to make the crossing,
having been surrounded and captured. Nevertheless, the vast majority of the Division
was able to retire to the western side of the canal. Which left the disposition of the
Division from north to south along the St Quentin Canal as follows: 1st Inniskillings
at Ricardo Redoubt, then 9th Inniskillings, then 107th Bde, then 108th Bde. The
attached 61st Brigade filled the gap between 108th Brigade and the left of 14th
Division which had retired across the canal near Jussy.

The question of how the weather conditions and particularly the thick fog influ-
enced the first day of the battle has been the subject of much argument and conjecture
by learned historians attempting to answer the question; 'Which side benefitted most
from the fog?' There appears to be no clear answer on this, but it is important in telling
the story from the 36th (Ulster) Division perspective that the issue is addressed.

Firstly, it can be stated that research for this book has failed to find a single instance
where anyone from the Ulster Division thought that the fog was of assistance in deter-
mining the outcome of the day. There were instances of short duration such as that
described by Captain Miller, 2nd Inniskillings who related how his men were able
to pick off individual Germans feeling their way round the barbed wire defences in
the murk, but these had no defining impact on the progression of the battle. Major
General Nugent writing to his wife on 21 March stated:

> It is the first real fog there has been for months and it is disastrous that it should
> have come today. We are the people who suffer from it. This time it is the
> Germans who are attacking. They know where they want to go, and we don't so
> it is all against us.[105]

The Germans certainly knew where they wanted to go but trying to get there in the fog
was not particularly easy. There is the example of ingenuity as described by Captain
Adamson of 12th Royal Irish Rifles, of German units ringing bells to identify each
other in the fog, however, this initiative does not appear to have been widespread. The
initial German Artillery bombardment was certainly effective in that it was designed
to incapacitate and disorientate rather than completely destroy the British defences.

---

104 Edmonds, *Military Operations France and Belgium 1918*, p. 212.
105 PRONI: D3835/E/2/17/11 Farren Connell papers.

The infantry attack by the stormtroopers had progressed, but it could only progress as fast as the men could move in the fog and the creeping barrage meant to proceed and protect it was not completely effective, for fear of hitting their own men. There are a number of accounts of Germans being taken prisoner as they literally stumbled into British defensive positions. It is open to consideration that if there had been no fog, the stormtroopers could have penetrated more deeply, more quickly.

The counter argument to that is, that if there had been no fog, the British machine-gunners would have wreaked havoc on the attackers. Middlebrook (1978) in addressing the issue, highlights that the majority of British casualties on 1 July 1916 were caused by just 200 German machine guns. On 21 March, the entirety of the British front line had 2,000 machine guns in the Forward Zone and 4,000 in the Battle Zone.[106] There may be some value in this argument when one considers the damage caused by Captain Johnston's men of the 12th Rifles at Le Pontchu when the fog lifted, or of the description of the damage wrought by the gun teams of Lieutenant Weall, MGC at Boadicea Redoubt when visibility improved.

It is of no doubt that had there been no fog, German casualties would have been much higher. General Gough addressing the issue in Shaw Sparrow (1921) states:

> My opinion is that at first, say for a couple of hours, fog was a great disadvantage to the defence. Had it not been present, many of our machine-guns very skil-fully hidden, would have taken a terrible toll… But as soon as the foe had broken through the first lines of resistance and was pushing on, he must have found that command, co-operation and communication became increasingly difficult.[107]

The fog had an undoubted impact on the casualty figures. Analysis by Middlebrook (1978) indicates that the total casualties for both sides on 21 March were remarkably close, around 40,000. The starkest difference between categories of casualty though, were in those taken prisoner. Only 300 Germans were taken prisoner against 21,000 British.[108]

Accounts from each of the battalions in the Forward Zone of the Ulster Division indicate that the fog assisted the Germans, in that they were each surrounded before they knew the Germans were attacking and this single fact had the greatest impact on the outcome of the day from an Ulster Division point of view. That the fighting capacity of the Division was reduced by a third by their inability to see their attackers is evidence that the view of General Gough in his first sentence above is correct. By the time the fog had lifted sufficiently, too much damage had been done for the situation to be retrieved. To compound matters, the fog descended again in the early evening of 21 March.

---

106 Middlebrook, *The Kaiser's Battle*, p. 331.
107 Walter Shaw Sparrow, *The Fifth Army in March 1918* (London: Bodley Head, 1921), p. 59.
108 Middlebrook, *The Kaiser's Battle*, p. 332.

6

The Retreat Continues

---

*We had now been holding the Germans at bay and moving steadily back for six days.
We were withdrawn at last and marched five or six miles to the rear. The Battalion was
sleeping on its feet. I walked into the man in front and cut my face on his steel helmet.*[1]
Corporal Jim Donaghy 23292, 9th Royal Inniskilling Fusiliers
(late 10th Royal Inniskilling Fusiliers) describing the state of
utter exhaustion felt after fighting and retreating for six days

In this chapter, I aim to cover the retreat of the Ulster Division until they were finally
relieved and withdrawn from action on 29 March. The objective is to cover the main
events which took place on each day which will give the reader an appreciation of how
the withdrawal progressed, how initiative was displayed, fighting discipline maintained, and of some instances of the heroism of the officers and men involved.

22 March 1918

As the units of the 36th Division withdrew across the St Quentin Canal, the Divisional
Engineers began at 3:00 a.m. to destroy all the bridges north of Grand Seraucourt.
The noise of the demolition and the constant movement of men ensured that for the
defenders of Ricardo Redoubt, there was little rest to be had. A and B Companies 1st
Inniskillings held the ground in front of the Redoubt, A on the right closest to the
canal and B on the left, with C Company slightly behind them. D Company remained
in the redoubt along with battalion HQ. At around 4:00 a.m. the German Artillery
began to bombard the defensive positions. This bombardment continued throughout
the morning until about 11:00 a.m. when German Infantry were seen approaching
from Fontaines-Les-Clercs. A Company bore the brunt of the initial frontal infantry
attack as the enemy tried to work their way between the Company and the canal bank
in an attempt to get behind the redoubt. The attack was made by the German 1st Foot

---

1   Mitchell, *Three Cheers for the Derry's*, p. 160.

Guard Regiment, part of the 1st Guard Infantry Brigade of the 1st Guard Infantry Division. This was a Prussian unit and one of the elite of the German Infantry. The Inniskillings however, repulsed repeated attacks from the Prussians with both A and B Companies involved in a ferocious defence.

In the early afternoon, the high casualty rate combined with the repeated attacks forced A and B Companies back to the C Company position and then eventually, the survivors had to fight their way into the Redoubt where D Company and Battalion HQ were still holding out. Around 3:00 p.m. realising that their position was untenable and that the Redoubt – already surrounded on three sides was in danger of becoming completely encircled, Lieutenant Colonel Crawford gave an order for those who could do so, to attempt to make their way to the rear. One of those was Serjeant Andrew Rice 10032, of B Company:

> About 30 of us together started to get through a gap in our wire on our left rear and about 20 got through. I went back until I came upon two machine guns of 20th Division and was sent by them to 9th Inniskillings and then to Brigade HQ.[2]

As he negotiated the gap out of the redoubt, Serjeant Rice noted around 30 German dead in the vicinity, testament to the ferocious defence being undertaken.

The Germans then began to storm the redoubt using scaling ladders to cross the barbed wire defences. They were repulsed where possible by the dwindling band of defenders, who retreated to another part of the redoubt when a position became untenable. Both Falls (1922) and Fox (1928) record an instance whereby Privates Bailey and Conway[3] charged and drove out a party of enemy bombers who had gained a foothold in the redoubt.[4]

The Inniskillings had done all that was humanly possible to delay the German advance and to give their comrades a chance to reorganise. Having fought the 1st Foot Guard Regiment to a standstill, it was the 3rd Foot Guard Regiment, part of the same Guard Brigade, who made the final assault, finally quelling the gallant resistance at 4:40 p.m.

In a letter to his wife, Major General Nugent was unstinting in his praise of the battalion:

2   PRONI D3835/E/10/8/35: Serjeant Rice survived the war and was demobilised in March 1919.
3   Despite research carried out by the author and by volunteers at the Inniskillings Museum, neither Privates Bailey nor Conway have been positively identified. Neither was killed on 22 March and neither appear to have been awarded any form of gallantry medal for their heroic action.
4   Falls, *The History of the 36th (Ulster) Division*, p. 205 and Fox, *The Royal Inniskilling Fusiliers in the World War*, p. 138.

The 1st Battn Inniskilling Fusiliers are the heroes of this Division. They are one of the regular battalions. Their duty was to hold a redoubt in the main line and they held it to the end. No man came back from it. They beat back 12 different attacks made we believe by the 1st Guard Division of the Prussians and at the last those who were watching from other places said that the Germans just poured over in a wave, but none of the Inniskillings came back. They were ordered to hold the line and they held it to the end. All the officers and men died where they stood. It is a great and gallant story.[5]

The battalion war diary records that the battalion sustained 551 casualties, dead, wounded and missing on 22 March.[6] The majority, including their commanding officer became prisoners of war, however, 82 made the supreme sacrifice. This included three officers and 79 other ranks. Of this total, only 10 have a known grave, with the remainder being commemorated on the Poziéres Memorial to the Missing. Surprisingly, there is no record of Lieutenant Colonel Crawford receiving any official recognition of his exemplary leadership of the battalion in the valiant defence.

Of those to fall, nine were from the city of Londonderry. One of the officers to fall was 21 years old Lieutenant Arthur James Seaber Dick attached to B Company. Born at Foyle College, Londonderry where his father was Headmaster, he was educated there and at Hastings, Sussex, before obtaining a commission in the Cambridgeshire Regiment in 1915, transferring to the Inniskillings in 1916. His final moments are recorded in Condon (2010):

A brother officer wrote, 'The Coy Commander had just been wounded and he (Lieut. Dick) had to take command. The enemy at this moment were attacking in force on his left: he rushed forward to see what could be done; he ordered his men to hold on and, in a few moments, had broken up the advancing waves of Germans. A few seconds later he was taking observation through his glasses when he received the fatal wound. His last words were, 'stick it out lads, we are beating him.'[7]

Of those in the ranks from the city, Corporal William McClay MM, was 28 years old when he was killed. A Flour Miller prior to enlisting, William was the eldest son of Thomas and Elizabeth McClay from East Avenue. He had married a local girl, Martha Campbell in May 1912 and the couple were resident at Fountain Hill in the Waterside area. William had enlisted in the 10th Inniskillings and transferred to 1st Battalion during the 1918 reorganisation. He is commemorated on the Roll

5   PRONI D3835/E/2/17/12A: Farren Connell papers.
6   TNA: WO 95/2510/1 1st Battalion Royal Inniskilling Fusiliers war diary.
7   Jim Condon, *Officers of the Royal Inniskilling Fusiliers in World War 1* (Enniskillen: Royal Inniskilling Fusiliers Museum, 2003), p. 78.

Corporal William McClay MM,
Royal Inniskilling Fusiliers. (Great
War Ulster Newspaper Archive)
Londonderry Memorial Records
– Corporal William McClay MM.
(PRONI)

of Honour at Ebrington Presbyterian Church and on the city War Memorial at the Diamond.

Another who had originally enlisted in 10th Inniskillings was 23 years old Serjeant Thomas Parkhill. The second son of Thomas and Elizabeth Parkhill of Ferguson Street, Londonderry, Thomas was a Box Maker prior to enlisting. One of the few who has a known resting place, Thomas is buried in Savy British Cemetery. His elder brother Robert aged 28, who had enlisted with Thomas on the same day was killed in action six months after Thomas, whilst serving with 2nd Inniskillings. Both brothers are commemorated on the Roll of Honour of Londonderry City Methodist Mission and on the Diamond War Memorial.

Whilst the 1st Inniskillings were making their courageous stand, the Royal Engineers continued in their systematic programme of destroying all the bridges across the St Quentin Canal. There was now a degree of urgency in this task as the Germans were advancing at speed and in force towards the Canal. The bridges around Grand Seraucourt were destroyed beginning at 3:00 a.m. by 121st Field Company, Royal Engineers. South of this towards the fork in the canal, two officers of 150th Field Company, Royal Engineers, Lieutenant Cecil Leonard Knox and Second Lieutenant John Bryan Stapylton-Smith were tasked with destroying a system of bridges at

 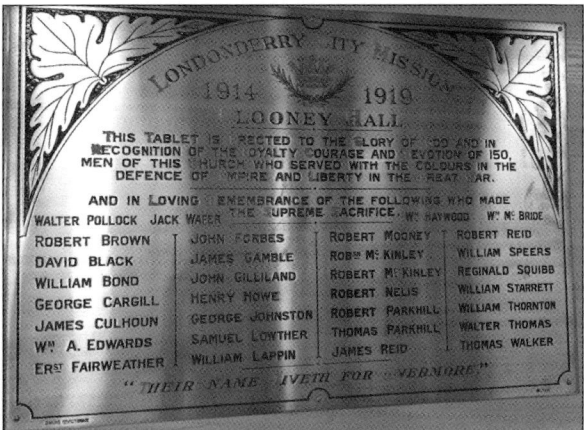

Headstone of Serjeant Thomas Parkhill Royal Inniskilling Fusiliers, Savy British Cemetery.
(Author's Collection) Londonderry Methodist City Mission Roll of Honour.
(Author's Collection)

Artemps, Tugny-et-Pont and Saint Simon, being given the task of destroying 12 each. The Company war diary records that following the alarm being raised on the morning of 21 March, sections were dispatched to prepare all the road and foot bridges for demolition.[8] This having been accomplished, on the morning of 22 March it was a relatively straightforward task for the Engineers to set the fuses and detonate the charges. The complicating factor was that the Germans were hot on the heels of remnants of units who were rushing to cross the canal before being cut off. Murland (2014) describes how the remnants of an artillery unit under the command of Major Kenneth Cousland arrived at the main bridge at Tugny-et-Pont with the Germans in sight as Lieutenant Knox was about to demolish it around 9:00 a.m.

> I had to use my authority to force him to let us cross over before he pressed the button. A few minutes later and we would all have been stranded.[9]

With the artillery detachment safely across and the Germans approaching the bridge, Lieutenant Knox pressed the detonator. To his horror however, nothing happened. Without hesitation, he ran forward under fire and ripped the existing fuse away, replacing it with an instantaneous fuse which he immediately detonated. The bridge was destroyed and by any circumstances, Lieutenant Knox should have been killed in

---

8   TNA: WO 95/2497/3: 150th Field Company Royal Engineers war diary. The bridges would already have had explosive charges placed and were ready for a means of detonation to be attached.

9   Murland, *Retreat and Rearguard: Somme 1918*, p. 139.

the explosion however, by some miracle he survived without serious injury. For this act of the utmost heroism, Lieutenant Knox was awarded the Division's second Victoria Cross in two days. The citation published in *The London Gazette* of 4 June 1918 stated:

> When entrusted with the demolition of twelve bridges along the Somme Canal he successfully carried out the task with the exception of a steel girder bridge where the time fuse failed to ignite. As the Germans began to cross, he ran to the bridge under heavy fire and lit an instantaneous fuse, knowing the grave risk to himself, but the bridge was blown, and he escaped relatively unscathed.[10]

Cecil Knox was born at Nuneaton, Warwickshire in May 1889, the son of James and Florence Knox. His father, an Engineer by profession, was the Managing Director of a Brick and Tile Company. Cecil was one of nine sons who served, two of whom were killed in the war.[11] A Civil Engineer prior to enlisting, Cecil Knox had spent three years working on the railways in British Columbia, Canada. He joined the Royal Engineers as a Sapper in May 1916 and applied for a commission in November that year, being appointed to 150th Field Company Royal Engineers as a Second Lieutenant in June 1917 and was promoted Lieutenant in February 1918. He was presented with his Victoria Cross by King George V in the field in August 1918. Lieutenant Knox survived the war and relinquished his commission in June 1919. He died on 4 February 1943 when his motorcycle skidded on an icy road close to his home and he sustained fatal head injuries.

Lieutenant Cecil Leonard Knox VC. (Open source)

Further down the canal at St Simon, Second Lieutenant John Bryan Stapylton-Smith was charged with destroying the bridges at the village. As the last of 61st Brigade personnel crossed the bridge, the Germans were again in hot pursuit. Lieutenant Stapylton-Smith waited until the Germans

---

10   *The London Gazette*, 4 June 1918.
11   Second Lieutenant Andrew Ronald Knox, 185th Tunnelling Company Royal Engineers was killed in action at La Boisselle in December 1915 and Lieutenant Colonel James Meldrum Knox DSO and Bar was killed in action commanding the 1/7th Battalion Royal Warwickshire Regiment on the Asiago Plateau, Italy in September 1918.

Main Bridge at Tugny-et-Pont 2017. (Author's Collection)

were on the bridge before demolishing it, causing the enemy many casualties. For his gallantry, he was awarded the Military Cross, the citation of which was published in *The London Gazette* of 29 July 1918:

> For conspicuous bravery and devotion to duty when entrusted with the demolition of twelve bridges. He waited under heavy shell and rifle fire until the enemy were about to cross and then successfully demolished all the bridges.[12]

John Bryan Stapylton-Smith was born in the Cape Colony, South Africa in 1892. He moved to the United Kingdom and was resident in England in 1911 when he was employed as a Gas Engineer. Following the Armistice, he resumed this career working in Toronto until the late 1940s.

Meanwhile, the 9th Inniskillings who were immediately behind the 1st Inniskillings, also came under concentrated attack from the Germans during the morning of 22 March. They were attacked both by the enemy who were swarming past Ricardo Redoubt on the west bank of the canal, but also by German infantry who had reached the east bank following the withdrawal overnight. Several attacks were beaten off by No's 2 and 4 Companies who lost several officers and other ranks during the assault, but it was soon realised that the position was rapidly becoming unsustainable. Several of the battalion's outlying posts were overrun, one being held by a party under Second Lieutenant John Francis Regis Darbyshire, who later recorded:

12 *The London Gazette*, 29 July 1918.

Bridge at St Simon 2017. (Author's Collection)

About 2:00 a.m. on the 22 March 1918 No 3 Coy were detailed to take up a position in front of Le Hamel to prevent the enemy crossing the canal and in the event of getting in touch with the enemy to hold him for three hours and then withdraw to a position in rear of Happencourt. We dug ourselves in during the night along the canal bank, there was a very thick fog all night and till about 11:00 a.m. on the morning of 22nd. About 11:00 a.m. the fog lifted and we saw the enemy advancing along the canal bank in close formation. We immediately opened fire and continued to hold our position till about 2:30 p.m. 22 March 1918. In the meantime, the enemy had worked round to our flanks and rear and opened fire with machine-guns on our position. The enemy artillery shelled us heavily and about 3:00 p.m. 22 March 1918 I was knocked senseless by the concussion of a shell bursting on the parapet of the trench we held. When I recovered, I found myself a prisoner.[13]

13   TNA: WO 339/30237: Second Lieutenant John Francis Regis Darbyshire service record. Born in Manchester in 1890, 2nd Lieutenant Darbyshire had a varied and interesting military career. He enlisted in the Sherwood Foresters at the outbreak of war and following a successful application was commissioned into the 10th North Staffords. He was required to resign over 'untrustworthiness in money matters' in February 1916, was court martialled and acquitted. He enlisted again in the Royal Marine Light Infantry and again applied for a commission, being appointed to the Royal Inniskilling Fusiliers in July 1917. He survived his period of captivity and relinquished his commission in December 1919.

The Germans who had worked their way past the 1st Inniskillings at Ricardo Redoubt were those who, as Second Lieutenant Darbyshire stated, were attacking the flanks in overwhelming numbers. In danger of being surrounded themselves, the 9th Inniskillings withdrew initially to Happencourt. These positions were held until the evening with the battalion under artillery fire and subject to at least one sustained attack by German infantry which was repulsed. The 9th Inniskillings sustained nine fatalities during the day's action, three of whom were officers;

- Second Lieutenant William Edgar Barton aged 31, was from Carrickmacross, County Monaghan. A Clerk in the London and Brazilian Bank, he had enlisted in the Leinster Regiment in September 1915 as a Private. Wounded in March 1916, he applied for a commission in February 1917, joining the 9th Inniskillings in November of that year.
- Lieutenant Arthur James Starr aged 25, was from Newtownhamilton, County Armagh. He had joined from the 11th Inniskillings and been with the battalion just over a month before he was killed.
- Second Lieutenant Henry Norman Thompson aged 22 was from Melrose Terrace, Londonderry. The eldest son of Thomas Henry and Susan Thompson, his two younger brothers also fell during the war.[14]

Lieutenant Arthur James Starr 9th Royal Inniskilling Fusiliers. (Great War Ulster Newspaper Archive), Headstone commemorating Thompson brothers, Londonderry City Cemetery. (War Graves Ulster Project)

14 Corporal Victor Logan Thompson S/40434 8th Battalion. Black Watch was killed in action on 19 October 1916 aged

As this defensive action was continuing, those in command had difficult decisions to make, as the relentless German offensive was rapidly wearing out the defenders. General Gough outlined the next steps that Lieutenant General Maxse was forced to take on 22 March to protect his forces:

> Many German attacks were repulsed and, on several occasions, when they succeeded in gaining a foothold in our lines, gallant counter attacks by the few troops in reserve often succeeded in temporarily recapturing the lost ground. But the battalions were suffering heavy casualties and Maxse felt that they could not hold on against the persistent attacks of Von Hutier's Army without being eventually overwhelmed. He had also received the Army order to fight a rear-guard action and therefore at 1:00 p.m. he issued an order to his Corps to retire behind the Somme. The brigades broke off the fight therefore and commenced to retire a distance of eight or nine miles covered by the 20th Division, but this was only done at the cost of much severe fighting.[15]

The 36th Ulster Division received the order to move at 3:30 p.m. but it was a difficult matter to immediately disengage and retire and some had to remain in the firing line and cover the withdrawal. The 2nd battalion Royal Irish Rifles maintained their position south-east of Happencourt to enable the withdrawal to proceed, coming under heavy shellfire during the afternoon and early evening. During this attack the commanding officer, Major Richard de la Ros Rose MC was severely wounded by shellfire, sustaining a fractured skull, fractured jaw and penetrating chest wounds.[16] He was medically evacuated, but his war was over. He was awarded a Bar to his Military Cross for the action in which he was wounded, the citation being published in *The London Gazette* of 13 September 1918:

> For conspicuous gallantry and devotion to duty in command of the battalion. He made personal reconnaissances of the position after several officers were wounded and was eventually severely wounded when attempting to regain touch with the unit on his left.[17]

18 during the Battle of the Somme. Private Thomas Boyd Thompson 20747 1st Battalion Royal Dublin Fusiliers, died on 10 October 1918 aged 19 when the SS *Leinster* on which he was returning from leave, was torpedoed in the Irish Sea with the loss of 500 lives. Private Thompson is buried in Londonderry City Cemetery and all three brothers are commemorated on the War Memorial at the Diamond, Londonderry and on the Roll of Honour at Ebrington Presbyterian Church in the city.
15   Gough, *The March Retreat*, p. 97.
16   TNA: WO 339/12582: Major Richard de Ros Rose service record. Major Rose was medically retired to his home in Limerick where he died in 1939.
17   *The London Gazette*, 13 September 1918.

Major Rose was replaced as commanding officer by Captain Thomas John Chichester Conyngham Thompson DSO, a native of Markethill, County Armagh, who had initially joined the battalion in October 1915.[18]

Eventually, the whole of the Division was withdrawn behind the Somme by 11:00 p.m. Father Gill, still co-located with the 2nd battalion Royal Irish Rifles was somewhat circumspect:

> It was evident that a retirement was in progress, but there was no sign of any panic, neither was there any sign of reinforcement.[19]

It would be prudent at this stage to outline the location and strength of the Division following two days constant engagement with the enemy and the consequent withdrawal.

On the evening of 22 March, the 36th Division held a line along the St Quentin canal from around a mile north-west of Jussy, east past the fork where the St Quentin canal became the Somme Canal to a position a mile beyond the village of Sommette-Eaucourt.

From east to west, the Division was positioned as follows:

From the position near Jussy – 61st Brigade with 7th battalion Somerset Light Infantry on right, 7th battalion Duke of Cornwall's Light Infantry on left and 12th King's (Liverpool) Regiment in reserve. This position put the Somerset Light Infantry at the far right of the Divisional line where they should have met with 41st Brigade of the 14th (Light) Division.

Next to 61st Brigade was 108th Brigade who held the line from Ollezy to Sommette-Eaucourt with 9th battalion Royal Irish Fusiliers on the right and 1st battalion Royal Irish Fusiliers on left. A composite battalion held the line to the left of 1st Royal Irish Fusiliers. This battalion was formed from the remnants of 12th Royal Irish Rifles and other units complemented by clerks, cooks, those returned from courses, from leave and from hospital. This battalion was commanded by Lieutenant Colonel Patrick Godfrey Ashley Cox DSO, a Boer war veteran who had commanded 2nd Royal Irish Rifles early in 1918 before becoming temporary commander of 108th Brigade.

To the left of this battalion, 36th Division was meant to join with 30th Division. By a quirk of fate, this position was allocated to one of the battalions temporarily attached to 30th Division, the 21st Entrenching battalion, which had left 36th Division following the reorganisation a matter of weeks before. The battalion was at full strength, comprising over 1200 officers and men of 8/9th and 10th Royal Irish Rifles

---

18   TNA: WO 339/40568: Captain Thomas John Chichester Conyngham Thompson service record. Captain Thompson had been wounded twice and received his DSO for an action at the Battle of Messines in June 1917.
19   IJA/CHP1/27 p. 163.

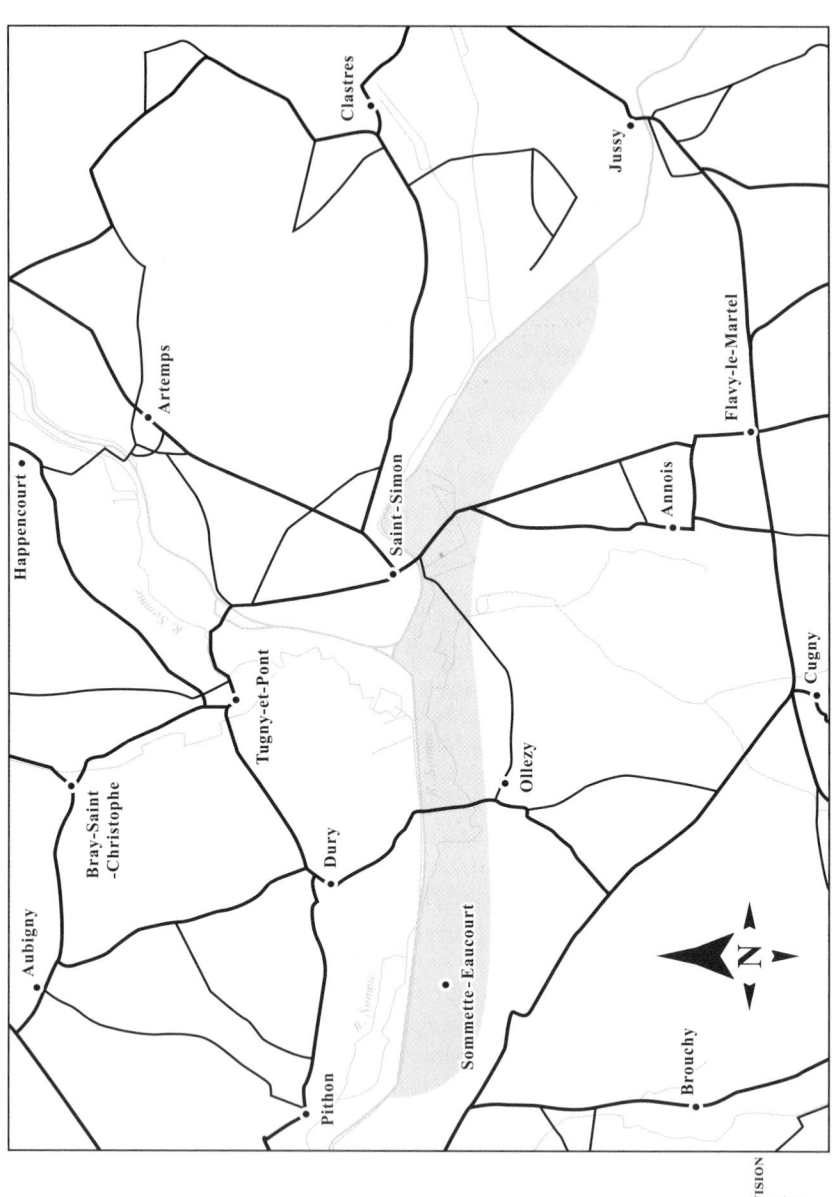

Map 12 Area of Operations – Evening 22 March 1918.

REFERENCE

POSITION HELD BY
36TH (ULSTER) DIVISION

SCALE IN MILES

0   1

and 10th Royal Inniskilling Fusiliers. From this time until the end of the withdrawal, the 21st Entrenching Battalion remained attached to 107th Brigade as it could not physically get in touch with its parent Division, the 30th. The battalion was commanded by Major John Dunwoodie Martin McCallum DSO, who had been in command of the 8/9th Royal Irish Rifles prior to their disbandment. Prior to receiving his commission, Major McCallum from Windsor Avenue, Belfast, had been a solicitor in the city.

Both battalions of the Royal Irish Rifles – what remained of 107th Brigade, crossed the Somme Canal using the railway bridge at Pithon at around 11:00 p.m. The 1st battalion went into billets at Sommette-Eaucourt, whilst the 2nd battalion marched three and a half miles south-east to billets in the village of Cugny.

Major John Dunwoodie Martin McCallum, 21st Entrenching Battalion. (Great War Ulster Newspaper Archive)

The 9th Inniskillings were all that remained of 109th Brigade. On crossing the Somme Canal, the battalion marched to the village of Brouchy, two and a half miles south of Sommette-Eaucourt, where they were able to get a few hours well-earned rest.

Research of available records indicates that by midnight of 22 March, the Division had retired nine miles from its positions on the morning of 21 March. This was a massive distance when one considers that successful advances in the era of trench warfare were usually calculated in terms of yards gained. The strength of the respective Brigades was as follows:

107th Brigade
15th Royal Irish Rifles – Transport and Quartermaster personnel only remained, supplemented by some returning from leave and courses and a draft of 100 other ranks who fortunately had arrived from the Divisional Base Depot at Harfleur. This composite unit was commanded by Captain Percy Maurice Miller MC, a native of Surrey.
1st Royal Irish Rifles – Five officers and 180 other ranks.
2nd Royal Irish Rifles – Six officers and 340 other ranks.

108th Brigade
12th Royal Irish Rifles – Transport detail of the battalion only existed.
1st Royal Irish Fusiliers – about 250 men remaining.
9th Royal Irish Fusiliers – about 250 men remaining.

109th Brigade

2nd Royal Inniskilling Fusiliers – remnants only, part of composite battalion under Lieutenant Colonel Cox DSO.

1st Royal Inniskilling Fusiliers – remnants only, in process of consolidating.

9th Royal Inniskilling Fusiliers – Still close to full strength,[20] although 20 men had been killed and many more wounded.

Divisional Troops

16th Royal Irish Rifles – around 500 officers and men.

36th Machine Gun Battalion – the battalion had ceased to exist as a fighting unit, although individual teams were attached to battalions, coming under the command of battalion commanding officers.

121st, 122nd and 150th Field Company's Royal Engineers – still up to strength.

Artillery – Most of the artillery units had been detached from the Division following the initial day's withdrawal and were attached to 20th Division. A small element consisting of seven batteries from 91, 153 and 173 Brigades Royal Field Artillery remained, supplemented by two howitzers.

23 March 1918

The weather on the morning of 23 March was the same as it had been for the previous two mornings – thick fog. This again assisted the Germans as they resumed their attack along the line held by 36th Division. At the eastern end of the line, they continued to exploit the weakly held point where 36th and 14th Divisions met, by forcing a crossing of the St Quentin Canal at Jussy at around 9:15 a.m.[21] The 7th Battalion Somerset Light Infantry under the command of Lieutenant Colonel Cecil John Troyte-Bullock DSO, were now in an invidious position. They were being attacked frontally by the Germans who had forced the crossing at Jussy, but also on the flank from the enemy who had reached the far canal bank and who were attempting to affect a crossing. Eventually, the Germans succeeded in crossing the canal and forced a breach in the line between the Somersets and the Duke of Cornwall's Light Infantry (DCLI) on their left. In danger of being surrounded, the remnants of the Somersets tried to force their way back to join with the DCLI at Annois. The situation is graphically described in Murland (2014) by Captain George McMurtrie of A Company, 7th Somerset Light Infantry:

---

20   TNA: WO 95/2510/3: The battalion war diary for 1 March denotes battalion strength as 1200 officers and men.

21   The crossing was forced by 1st Bavarian Regiment. From this time onwards, the 36th and 14th Divisions no longer formed a continuous line.

The Huns attacked us and for about an hour we kept shooting at them and kept them at bay. The CO [Lt Col Troyte-Bullock] was shot through the neck by a rifle bullet and Berry, [Captain Samuel Berry, battalion Adjutant] who was next to me firing away, got up to look over the bank over which we were shooting. He got a bullet right through the head and was killed instantly, falling on top of me with a groan. I was very upset to see him killed. I now had to take command of battalion headquarters. Ammunition was given out and the Germans were gradually working round us and threatening to surround us at any minute. I considered it would be a waste of life to hold on any longer, having done all we could to delay the enemy for as long as possible…I decided it was time to withdraw.

Captain McMurtrie and most of his Company managed to escape, the only ones from the battalion to do so. In addition to the Adjutant, 15 other men from the battalion were killed on 23 March with only two having a known grave.

This was probably the most crucial time in the entire battle to date for the Division. By shortly after 10:00 a.m. the Germans had forced a crossing of the canal in many places held by 36th Division and were advancing rapidly. The entire Divisional line was in danger of collapsing as units became separated from each other. It was only through calm, confident leadership that a disaster was averted. To the east, the Germans were exploiting the gap at the end of the divisional line to advance in the direction of Cugny, via Flavy-le-Martel. To combat this, the 1st battalion Royal Irish Rifles joined and extended the line of the regiment's 2nd battalion on the outskirts of Cugny. The 1st Rifles commanding officer, Lieutenant Colonel MacCarthy-O'Leary described the chaotic events of the afternoon:

The 2nd RIR proceeded to occupy a defensive position E and NE of the village astride the Cugny-Flavy-le-Martel road. Another battalion, I believe belonging to the 14th Div. [possibly 11th South Lancashire Regiment (Pioneers)] were on their right prolonging the position southwards. 1 RIR under my command were held in readiness on the high ground south of Cugny. During the afternoon, large bodies of Germans were observed collecting. The 1st Bn. had by this time occupied a position I had selected. To the best of my recollection, it was about 3:45 p.m. that the enemy's advance commenced. This was preceded by an intense machine-gun bombardment which continued until the light began to fail. About 4:30 p.m. large numbers of men belonging to the battalion in front, to which I referred, commenced a somewhat disorderly withdrawal through the left of my battalion. I went forward to find out what was happening and met the Colonel of this battalion being carried back on a stretcher in a dying condition. His men were now retiring hastily. It was now dusk and getting dark quickly. The noise of musketry and German shouting and cheering was great. They had broken through on my left front (there being no troops left there to stop them) and were firing at us in enfilade at short range. Shortly afterwards they charged us from the front and the left. They were in superior numbers and we were overrun. In the turmoil, I was hit and knocked down. I shouted to all I saw to retire south along the road. A few hundred yards back I was able to collect the majority of the battalion. I then decided to withdraw to the next high ground which was in the vicinity of Beaulieu… The men had had no rest since 20th and were very tired, however they fell to and before long had made a passable attempt at a defensive position by digging isolated holes.[22]

The 2nd battalion Royal Irish Rifles had received a welcome boost on the morning of 23 March with an unexpected draft of 67 other ranks, which enhanced their depleted numbers to just over 400. They too came under heavy attack late in the afternoon and survived as the war diary records, with a spirited defence accompanied by a bit of ingenuity:

12 noon. Reports that enemy cavalry had entered Flavy-le-Martel and brigade orders directed that Cugny was to be held at all costs. With the exception of minor attacks, the afternoon passed quietly. Hostile aeroplanes were however much in attendance. 6:00 p.m. the enemy attacked in force, but after a stiff fight was repulsed on our front, but later succeeded in driving back the troops on our right and he occupied positions between the battalion and the village. 8:30 p.m. a party of C Coy under Lieutenant RB Marriott-Watson returning to the village came in contact with a strong party of the enemy. Lieutenant Marriott-Watson spoke to the enemy in German and succeeded in allaying their suspicion, thus enabling the party to get to close quarters to rush and disperse the enemy. 10:00 p.m. the battalion withdrew to a line 300 yards west of the village.[23]

Just over four miles to the west, the 9th Inniskillings were billeted at Brouchy having arrived there at 1:00 a.m. By 8:00 a.m. they had marched just over a mile north to the outskirts of the village of Aubigny and had the 21st Entrenching battalion on their left, the 1st battalion Royal Irish Fusiliers being on their right. Rifle and machine-gun fire heralded the arrival of the Germans and after a short exchange, the 9th Inniskillings were driven out of the village. The Headquarters of 109th Brigade were on the northern outskirts of Brouchy and the Brigade Commander, Brigadier General Hessey had a clear view of the action. On observing a company of the Inniskillings retiring from Aubigny, he immediately sent a runner forward, ordering them to re-take the village. It is not known if this message had reached them when the Brigade

22   TNA: WO 95/2502/3: 1st Battalion Royal Irish Rifles war diary.
23   TNA: WO 95/2502/4: 2nd Battalion Royal Irish Rifles war diary. 2nd Lieutenant Richard Brereton Marriott-Watson MC, from Guildford, Surrey, was commissioned into 13th Battalion Royal Irish Rifles and was wounded at the Somme. He transferred on return from convalescence to 2nd Battalion in November 1916. TNA: WO 339/2172: 2nd Lt RB Marriott-Watson service record.

British Munitions Dump at Aubigny, captured by the Germans in March 1918.
(Bundesarchiv.Bild 183 – S11744)

Major, Major George James Bruce MC and Bar[24] galloped forwards on his horse from Brouchy and rallying the men, led them in a successful attack to retake the village. A short time later however, the Germans retook the village. A second counter-attack was organised and the Germans were again driven out with heavy casualties being incurred on both sides. Due to the pressure being exerted by the Germans to the left and right of 9th Inniskillings, they had to eventually give up this hard-won ground and withdraw with the 21st Entrenching battalion to south of Brouchy, the village they had left some 12 hours earlier.

The Commonwealth War Graves Commission records that the battalion sustained five fatalities that day, all of whom held rank:

24   Born at Cork, Major Bruce was resident in Belfast when he obtained a commission in 13th Royal Irish Rifles. He embarked for France with the Division and during 1916 and 1917 was attached to the 16th (Irish) Division during which time he was awarded a Military Cross and Bar. For his action on 23 March and the following day he was awarded the Distinguished Service Order. Details of the award were published in *The London Gazette* of 13 September 1918, the citation stating: 'For conspicuous gallantry and devotion to duty during an enemy attack. He rallied a company and rode in front as it once more advanced and took a village. Next day he galloped to two companies under heavy fire and directed them. When the Brigade withdrew he was the last to leave and covered the withdrawal with Lewis Gun sections under his personal supervision. Throughout he displayed high qualities as a Staff Captain with total regard for personal safety.'

- Captain John Forsyth Harvey aged 24 from Downshire Road, Cregagh, Belfast.
- Second Lieutenant Thomas Lipton Clements aged 21 from Omagh, Co. Tyrone
- Second Lieutenant Joseph John Fawcett aged 20 from Clones, Co Monaghan
- Company Serjeant Major Robert Hamilton DCM MM aged 22 from Londonderry
- L/Cpl Alexander Deane aged 22 from Bruckless, County Donegal.

That only five relatively senior personnel were identified as being killed is unusual, but may indicate that the command element of a company was wiped out. Both Second Lieutenant Clements and Lance Corporal Deane had joined 9th Inniskillings from the 11th battalion on its disbandment. It is the inclusion of CSM Hamilton, who had joined from 10th Inniskillings however, which is of greatest interest. Most records indicate that CSM Hamilton was killed on 23 March, however, there are some which indicate that he was killed in the days following. The war diary for the battalion referring to the day's action at Aubigny states:

> One light and two heavy machine guns were captured, and many casualties inflicted on the enemy.[25]

It is believed that CSM Hamilton was awarded his Distinguished Conduct Medal for action on this date, the citation stating:

Captain John Forsyth Harvey 9th Royal Inniskilling Fusiliers. (Inniskillings Museum), Headstone of Second Lieutenant Joseph John Fawcett, Ham British Cemetery, Meuille-Villette. (Authors Collection)

25   TNA: WO 95/2510/3: 9th Battalion Royal Inniskilling Fusiliers war diary.

For conspicuous gallantry and devotion to duty. During an attack, he captured an enemy machine gun and three of its crew single-handed. **While holding the line in the following days** he rendered valuable assistance in reorganising the company and getting forward supplies of bombs and ammunition, on several occasions under fire. His example and cheerfulness throughout were magnificent.[26]

This award was published in *The London Gazette* 28 March 1918 and confirmation of it was published in *The Belfast News Letter* of 30 March 1918. In her reply to the letter seeking approval for the inclusion of her son's name on the Londonderry War Memorial, his mother Ellen has corrected the date of death on the form by hand, amending it from 23 to 26 March. Canning (2006) in his history of the 9th Inniskillings in the Great War also states that CSM Hamilton was killed on 26 March (Interestingly, he also claims that Second Lieutenant Clements was also killed on that date and not 23 March.)[27]

Whatever the date of his death, what is not in dispute is that Robert Hamilton was an exceptional soldier. Robert was born on 20 August 1895 at Dernaflaw, Dungiven, County Londonderry, the second son of James and Ellen Hamilton. By 1911 the family was residing at Bishop Street, Londonderry and Robert was an Apprentice in a Monumental Works. He enlisted in the 10th Inniskillings at their formation and embarked with them to France in October 1915, when already a Corporal. He was awarded the 'Ulster Divisional Certificate for Bravery' on 1 July 1916, the citation stating:

> For great gallantry in the attack of July 1, 1916 in the Thiepval sector. At about 7:00 p.m. the Germans counter attacked, and his platoon officer being killed, he rallied the men round him and broke up the counter attack. He led another counter attack later in the evening.[28]

He was promoted Serjeant and was awarded the Military Medal for gallantry in December 1916. In November 1917, he was promoted Company Serjeant Major and joined the 9th Inniskillings on the disbandment of 10th Inniskillings in February 1918. On hearing of his death, a friend and colleague, Corporal Jim Donaghy paid this fitting tribute:

> Bobby was the bravest man I have ever met. The bravest man who ever stood in a pair of boots ... Bobby was a great friend of mine and was highly respected by all

---

26   *The London Gazette* 28 March 1918
27   Canning, W.J., *A Wheen of Medals: The History of the 9th (Service) Battalion The Royal Inniskilling Fusiliers (The Tyrones) in World War One* (Antrim: W.J. Canning, 2006), p. 187.
28   Mitchell, *Three Cheers for the Derry's*. p. 198.

15572 C.S.M. R. HAMILTON, M.M., Royal Inniskilling Fusiliers, 77 Fountain Street, Londonderry.

For conspicuous gallantry and devotion to duty. During an attack he captured an enemy machine-gun and three of its crew, single handed. While holding the line during the following days he rendered valuable assistance in reorganising the company and getting forward supplies of bombs and ammunition, on several occasions under fire. His example and cheerfulness throughout were magnificent.

MEMORIAL REGISTER.

No. 288

The whole of this Form should be filled up to the RIGHT OF CENTRAL LINE and returned as early as possible to the address printed on the back.

PLEASE WRITE CLEARLY.

Surname	Hamilton
Rank	Co, Sergeant Major
Christian or Forenames (in full)	Robert
Regimental Number	15572
Military Honours	D.C.M., M.M., Ulster Division Certificate
Particulars of Company, Battery, etc., and, in case of Naval Units, the name of the Ship should be given	B Company B.
Regiment	10th Batt, Royal Innis, Fus.
Nature of death (if desired and if particulars are available)	Killed in Action
Date of death	26th March, 1918.
Native place of deceased (if not a native of Londonderry state connection with City)	City.
Any other particulars in reference to Soldier (if desired)	Killed in B Coz. get Bn. Royal Innish Fus.

PLEASE WRITE CLEARLY.

Signed) Ellen Hamilton   Relationship Mother

Address 77 Fountain St,

Londonderry.

Company Serjeant Major Robert Hamilton DCM MM (Great War Ulster Newspaper Archive), Londonderry Memorial Records – Company Serjeant Major Robert Hamilton. (PRONI)

the men. Several times in the freezing cold conditions in the trenches he brought a big dixie of warm cocoa up on his back for his men on duty. What other man of his rank would have done this for his men?[29]

CSM Hamilton was not the only NCO of the Division to be awarded the Distinguished Conduct Medal that day. On the right of 9th Inniskillings were the 1st battalion Royal Irish Fusiliers and then the regiment's 9th battalion who were the closest unit of the Division to the Somme Canal at Ollezy. Both came under severe attack during the afternoon of 23 March, the 9th Royal Irish Fusiliers being supported by what

29   Mitchell, *Three Cheers for the Derry's*. p. 158. Robert's elder brother James emigrated to Canada and enlisted in the 2nd Battalion Canadian Infantry in February 1915. In January 1917, he was severely wounded in France with gunshot wounds to the left arm, thigh and shoulder which necessitated the amputation of his left arm. After convalescing he returned to live in Londonderry. The author's father-in-law remembers him driving a horse and cart and he was known to the locals as 'one wing' on account of the loss of his arm. Canadian service record Private James Alexander Hamilton. See <http://www.bac-lac.gc.ca> (Accessed 20 May 2017).

remained of the Division's Pioneer battalion, the 16th Rifles. On this date Company Quartermaster Serjeant James Hughes MM, a native of Portadown, was awarded the Distinguished Conduct Medal for gallantry in defence of the battalion's position. The citation reads:

> For conspicuous gallantry and devotion to duty. He went forward with a Lewis Gun and knocked out an enemy machine gun which was firing on our left flank. When his team were disabled, although wounded himself, he kept the gun in action until reinforcements came up.[30]

In common with CSM Hamilton, 9th Inniskillings, CQMS Hughes was also killed in the retreat and there is also debate over his date of death with some records indicating that his death took place between 21-29 March, whilst his headstone at Roye New British Cemetery indicates that he died on 21 March.

Throughout the afternoon a fierce defence was put up by all units of the Division, including those composite units comprised of cooks, clerks and storemen. Mutual assistance was also not confined to units within the Division in the hour of need. As what remained of 109th Brigade fell back on Brouchy, they were assisted by two batteries of 91st Brigade Royal Field Artillery, who were attached to 20th Division.

By the end of the day the Divisional line ran from the Ferme de Bonneuil on the outskirts of Golancourt to Brouchy, then to the outskirts of Cugny, whereupon the line went north sharply to Sommette-Eaucourt and then to Ollezy. The Divisional line formed what resembled the letter 'S' which in military terms was far from satisfactory. Worse still, both ends of the line were 'in the air' as contact could not be established with either 30th Division on the left, or 14th Division on the right.

24 March 1918

The morning of 24 March dawned much as the previous mornings had, with a heavy mist which was slow to clear. Brigadier General Hessey commanding 109th Brigade and Brigadier General Cochrane, commanding 61st Brigade, had developed a plan which was intended to straighten the line and involved assaults to retake the villages of Brouchy and Aubigny by 109th Brigade, and Eaucourt[31] by 61st Brigade. To supplement his sparse resources, General Hessey had been given a composite battalion containing the remnants of 1st Inniskillings and stragglers from other units, under the command of Major Robert Sinclair Knox DSO, 9th Inniskillings.[32] Another

---

30 *The London Gazette*, 3 September 1918.
31 The hamlet of Eaucourt is not to be confused with Sommette-Eaucourt. Eaucourt is two miles south of this village and one and a half miles east of Brouchy
32 Thirty-eight years old Robert Sinclair Knox was from Ballymoney, County Antrim. He was to finish the war in the rank of Lieutenant Colonel and one of the most decorated

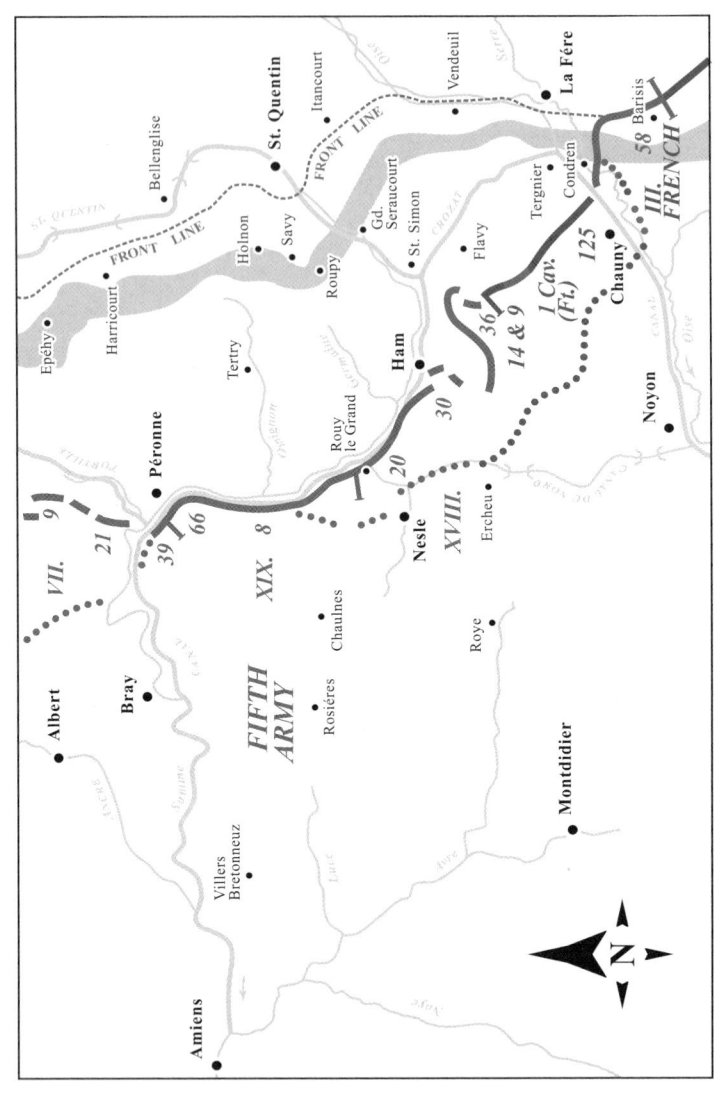

Map 13 36th (Ulster) Division position 24 March 1918.

REFERENCE

BRITISH LINE
24TH MARCH 1918

BRITISH LINE
25TH MARCH 1918

FRENCH LINE
24TH MARCH 1918

FRENCH LINE
25TH MARCH 1918

FRONT LINE

BATTLE ZONE

SCALE IN MILES

composite unit numbering around 300 and formed from officer's servants, grooms and the Divisional Signal School under the command of Major General Nugent's Aide de Camp and Staff Officer attached to Divisional Headquarters, was sent to join 109th Brigade – indicative of the last ditch defensive effort that was being made. On his part, Brigadier General Cochrane had 100 men from the 284th Army Troops Company Royal Engineers attached, under the command of two of his own officers.

Any attempt to straighten the line was however, doomed to failure as there was a yawning gap on both the left and right of the Division through which the Germans were free to manoeuvre. Once they had secured the crossings of the Somme Canal, the Germans were faced with open, rolling countryside, tailor-made for a rapid advance and also desperately difficult to defend as there was little cover available. For the next few days, the concept of trench warfare which had characterised the Western Front for the previous three and a half years was abandoned. For the men of all units in General Gough's Fifth Army, open warfare was an alien concept. The great majority of officers and men who were familiar with such tactics from the South African war and the early days of the war in summer 1914 were now mostly dead. Those in command on the ground now had to rely on their own initiative.

Major Knox intended to manoeuvre his troops into position via the village of Golancourt during the hours of darkness and launch a surprise attack to retake the village of Aubigny around 8:00 a.m. The Germans however, had taken Golancourt during the night and met Major Knox' detachment with heavy machine gun fire, ensuring that they could advance no further.[33]

The failure of this attempt to advance, meant that the attack proposed by Brigadier General Cochrane could not proceed due to a lack of mutual support. His troops soon came under severe attack and around 11:00 a.m. he ordered them to withdraw. This was not before time, as they were nearly surrounded and had to fight a desperate rear-guard action to escape. The description in the war diary of 7th Battalion Duke of Cornwall's Light Infantry epitomises the pressure the units of the Division came under on 24 March:

> 10:00 a.m. Received order to withdraw from Railway Embankment south of Ollezy at 11:00 a.m. and take up position between Cugny and Eaucourt – as withdrawal was about to commence, the unit on our right retired in a disorganised manner and we had to fight a hard rear-guard action – the enemy suffered very heavily. The position was taken up as ordered, but was only held for a short time, unfortunately for us, both our flanks retired very quickly, and we were again called upon to fight a rear-guard action to a sunken road NE of Villeselve.

soldiers in the army with the DSO and three bars. These are the same decorations that were awarded to Lieutenant Colonel 'Paddy' Blair Mayne in World War Two.

33 The detachment under Major Knox' command joined what remained of 9th Inniskillings.

Village of Cugny 2017. (Author's Collection)

> This position was attacked in force and a stiff fight ensued in which both sides lost heavily.[34]

To the right of 7th DCLI, 2nd battalion Royal Irish Rifles were still holding their position 300 yards to the west of the village of Cugny.

The bizarre situation from a military point of view which now existed, was that 2nd Royal Irish Rifles with 1st battalion to their left were facing the village of Cugny, where the Germans could be seen advancing. The 7th DCLI and 9th Inniskillings to their left were facing Golancourt, from where the Germans who had halted the advance of Major Knox' detachment were pouring fire on the exhausted Ulster Division men. The units were therefore at a right angle to each other, forming two sides of a square, a situation which was clearly untenable. The 12th King's (Liverpool) Regiment of 61st Brigade were meant to be on the right of 2nd RIR, but in the confusion touch was never established with them.

In an attempt to straighten the defensive line, at around 9:05 a.m. the units of 61st Brigade were ordered to begin a gradual withdrawal to the village of Villeselve, the withdrawal to begin at 11:00 a.m. At the same time, the beleaguered 14th Division was in the process of being relieved, the long awaited arrival of French reinforcements

---

34   TNA: 95/2126/1: 7th Battalion Duke of Cornwall's Light Infantry war diary. 7th DCLI lost 12 men killed on 24 March and their commanding officer was taken prisoner.

having begun to take place during the night. The arrival of the French 9th and 10th Divisions and a dismounted Cavalry Division was woefully inadequate however, as they were in a state of total unpreparedness, with no artillery or reserve stocks of ammunition.

This was perhaps the most dangerous time in the entire withdrawal, as the Germans, lightly armed and moving at speed, took advantage of the reliefs and withdrawals to attack, causing chaos and confusion. The events of the next five hours were to prove crucial in the course of the entire German offensive.

Lieutenant Colonel MacCarthy-O'Leary, in charge of 1st Royal Irish Rifles at Montalimont Farm between Cugny and Brouchy, described the confusion which existed:

> Little happened on my immediate left until early afternoon but our troops from Eaucourt and Ollezy could be seen retiring. About 1:30 p.m. messengers from my right Coy. brought news that the enemy had got in behind us through the woods on that flank and that French MG'rs in support had retired. I immediately sent word to the OC 2 RIR to withdraw and we would cover their retirement, but I doubt if the messages were ever received. MG fire from the high ground south of Cugny had become heavy. The Germans were known to be behind us on our right while on our left at a distance of about 300 yards they were in strong force and had commenced to fire at us in enfilade. At this point I gave the order to withdraw... Fell back to Villeselve. The village was now being heavily shelled. A Lieutenant Colonel on the staff suddenly appeared on the scene. We debated whether we should retire and decided to issue orders for the move back to the high ground near Guiscard. **The troops however did not wait for orders and fell back in confusion through the village. Two officers went ahead in an ambulance and formed up the remnants of the Division as far as possible by units.**[35]

That some in the Ulster Division came close to breaking at this time was confirmed by the war diary of 107th Infantry Brigade:

> 4:35 p.m. from Bde Major. All troops are retiring in disorder except 1 & 2 RIR. 2 RIR appear to be cut off and it is doubtful if 1 RIR can get away as troops on both flanks have retired.[36]

The concern for 2nd Royal Irish Rifles was well founded. The first enemy attack came at around 10:00 a.m. but was repulsed. The official history of the regiment by Falls (1925), gives a graphic account of what followed:

35   TNA: WO 95/2502/3: 1st Battalion Royal Irish Rifles war diary.
36   TNA: WO 95/2502/1: 107th Infantry Brigade war diary.

By this time however, there was a shortage of ammunition and orders were given to fire at good targets – that is, at considerable groups of Germans only. In view of the isolated position, orders were given for the outlying companies to consolidate in the centre. In executing this movement, D Company had heavy losses, Lieutenant Marriott-Watson being among the killed. Soon after, Captain Thompson [Acting Commanding Officer] met a like fate…Captain JC Bryans[37] now assumed command and took advantage of a short lull to reorganise the line. This had hardly been completed when a new attack began. Colonel MacCarthy-O'Leary sent forward messengers with orders for the 2nd Battalion to withdraw through the 1st. No answer was received, runners all being killed or wounded. In any case, Captain Bryans had orders to fight to the last[38] and had moreover, come to the conclusion that an attempt to retire over open ground with machine guns on either flank would mean annihilation… The attack, accompanied by a flight of low-flying aeroplanes, swept in in overwhelming strength from the left and a desperate hand to hand fight ensued. When the Germans finally closed, many men had not a round left to fire. They sprang from their entrenchments and met the enemy with their bayonets. In a few minutes, it was all over. The defenders were simply engulfed by superior numbers.[39]

An officer in C Company 2 RIR, 38 years old Second Lieutenant Eric Charles Strohm[40] gave a first-hand account of the action and particularly of the tactics employed by the Stormtroopers, following his capture:

No 9 Platoon was in support of C Company 50 yards in rear of the front line. Enemy MG's were established on both our immediate flanks, he advancing his men in short rushes all the morning, our fire was very damaging. Early in the afternoon he brought his TM's [Trench Mortars] into action registering on our line, he also registered 'whiz bangs'[41] About 2:00 p.m. the enemy was observed about 2000 yards to our right and well to our rear. About 3:00 p.m. he was well

37   Taylor, *The 2nd Royal Irish Rifles in the Great War* p. 207. Captain Joseph Charles Bryans was a native of Liverpool. Aged 27, he had originally enlisted with the Liverpool Regiment and on obtaining a commission was appointed to the Royal Irish Rifles. He had joined 2nd Battalion in November 1917.

38   Gough, *The March Retreat,* p. 109. An order had been issued from GHQ on 23 March at 5:30 p.m. which stated, 'Fifth Army must hold the Somme at all costs. There must be no withdrawal from this line.'

39   Falls, *The History of the First Seven Battalions The Royal Irish Rifles in the Great War*, p. 142.

40   2nd Lieutenant Strohm was married and resided at Thornbank Road, Catford, London. A Broker, he had resided in Vancouver pre-war. Prior to obtaining his commission he had enlisted in 1916 in the 28th Battalion London Regiment (Artists Rifles) Repatriated in December 1918, he relinquished his commission in March 1919.

41   Whiz Bangs was the slang term given to small calibre artillery shells, so named after the sound they made.

View from Cugny to Villeselve 2017. As Captain Bryans 2 RIR noted, there was no cover to assist a withdrawal. (Author's Collection)

to the rear on our left. About this time his TM and MG fire was very persistent, my men were running short of ammunition. About 4:00 p.m. he put down an intense barrage comprising the former with the addition of artillery which lasted about half an hour, he then came over. I observed an officer and about 20 men falling back on our left, this apparently gave him an opening which he followed up and was through on our left – seemingly within a few minutes he was through our line and we were all mixed up, he seemed to pass right through and we were just mopped up by the second wave. I was taken about 5:00 pm. I had no ammunition and what remained of my men had none.[42]

In the relevant volume of *The Official History of the War, Military Operations France and Belgium 1918* (1935), Edmonds indicates that the remnants of 2nd Royal Irish Rifles were attacked by two Regiments of the German Guard Division from 10:00 a.m. on 24 March.[43]

Father Gill watched the action from near the village of Villeselve:

From my observations, I was convinced the battalion was gone. I found the ration party about to set out when I returned. I told them I did not believe they would find the battalion. I proved to be right. They had got the order to hold Cugny at all costs and had done so. Of the whole 750 or so only a very few came back. They were all either killed or taken prisoner.[44]

42 TNA: WO 339/69183: 2nd Lieutenant Edward Charles Strohm service record.
43 Edmonds, *Military Operations France and Belgium 1918*, p. 405, footnote 1.
44 IJA/CHP1/27 p. 166.

Father Gill's estimate of the strength of the battalion on 24 March is wildly optimistic. Accounts of the strength of the battalion vary but at this stage a figure of between 200-250 is probably accurate. The battalion war diary indicates that of this total, 10 wounded and 10 unwounded came back.[45] Of the remainder, the Commonwealth War Graves Commission records that 96 were killed, the inference being that the rest were taken prisoner.

Due to the confusion engendered by the retreat, the full story of the heroism of the officers and men of 2nd battalion Royal Irish Rifles on 24 March did not become known until well after the Armistice, by which time many were keen to put the war to rest. The term 'fought to the last man' is often used to describe a heroic action. The actions of 2nd Royal Irish Rifles on 24 March are truly worthy of that expression.

Captain Bryans when taken prisoner, was congratulated by a German officer on the stand of the 2nd Rifles and was assured by him that Captain Thompson and Lieutenant Marriott-Watson would receive a proper burial in Cugny churchyard. If this turned out to be the case, their graves were subsequently lost. Of those who fell, only 13 have a named grave, with the remainder being commemorated on the Pozieres Memorial to the Missing. Of those who fell, five were known to have been 19 years of age:

- Rifleman Victor Barnes 10516, whose sister resided at Dandy Street, Whitehouse, Co. Antrim
- Rifleman John Best 1379, from Woodford Street, Belfast[46]
- Rifleman Henry Clifford 10350, from Joseph Street, Londonderry
- Rifleman Timothy Coleman 9859, from Cork, Co. Cork
- Rifleman William Matthews 6174, from Chapel Hill, Lisburn, Co. Antrim

Rifleman Victor Barnes 2nd Battalion Royal Irish Rifles and Rifleman John Best 2nd Battalion Royal Irish Rifles. (Great War Ulster Newspaper Archive)

45   TNA: WO 95/2504/1: 2nd Battalion Royal Irish Rifles War Diary.
46   Rifleman John Best enlisted in the Royal Irish Rifles in 1916 and was appointed as a Signaller, being posted to the 10th (Service) Battalion Royal Irish Rifles (South Belfast Volunteers). He joined 2nd Irish Rifles in February 1918 on the disbandment of 10th Battalion and was killed a month to the day before his 20th birthday.

The disorganised retreat which was taking place had the potential to turn into a full-scale rout. For the most part, the men were exhausted, having had no sleep for four days and no food apart from what they could scrounge during that period. Control was in serious danger of breaking down completely. Most units and remnants of units were falling back on the village of Villeselve and Brigadier General Cochrane, 61st Brigade realising that action needed to be taken to avoid a potential disaster, sent an urgent message to 36th Division HQ at 3:35 p.m.

> Situation 3:00 p.m. very obscure. Germans have been seen on the edge of the wood (W Cugny). Germans appear to be pressing from the north. Great mixture of troops very disorganised and difficult to control and considerably demoralised. To readjust situation fresh troops to act as rallying points are essential. Our men withdrawing out of control is on some instances affecting the morale of the French.[47]

The problem was, as had been seen with the problems of French reinforcements there were no fresh reserves left, especially on the British side.

Help however, was about to arrive from a truly unexpected source and the action which followed undoubtedly bought the 36th Division a few vital hours to reorganise.

For close on four years, the Cavalry had been onlookers on the Western Front. With the advent of trench warfare their role had become virtually redundant and particularly with the advent of the machine gun, their role looked like being consigned to history. To many in the Infantry, they had become a source of irritation, as Major General Nugent commented following the Battle of Cambrai in November 1917:

> The papers are full of what the Cavalry has done. It is a fact that the Cavalry have done absolutely nothing except block the roads and follow the Infantry. It makes us all so furious to read the frantic efforts made to boost the Cavalry, which is as much out of date in this war as a naked man with a stone axe.[48]

Earlier in that year, the Army Council had come to much the same conclusion and ordered that six cavalry units should be dismounted to become infantry, one of those being the 2nd North Irish Horse which joined the 9th Battalion Royal Irish Fusiliers becoming the 9th (North Irish Horse) Battalion Princess Victoria's (Royal Irish Fusiliers) in the Division's 108th Brigade.

By March 1918, much of the 3rd Cavalry Division was operating as dismounted troops, however, they maintained a mounted element which acted as a support to operations. The mounted element was known as Harman's Detachment after the Division's commanding officer, Brigadier General Antony Ernest Wentworth

---

47   TNA: WO 95/2492/2: 36th (Ulster) Division war diary, Appendix 10.
48   PRONI D3835/E/2/15/20: Farren Connell papers.

Harman, and included the 6th Cavalry Brigade which comprised elements of 1st Royal Dragoons, 10th Hussars and 3rd Royal Dragoons. In his comprehensive *History of the 6th Cavalry Brigade* (1922), Lieutenant John Bickersteth describes the actions of the brigade on 24 March:

> About 2:00 p.m. on 24th the 6th Cavalry Brigade mounted detachment which was then at Berlancourt was ordered by Lieutenant Colonel R W Paterson DSO (Fort Garry Horse who commanded the 3rd Cavalry Division detachment) to make a mounted attack on some hostile infantry and machine-guns. The Infantry were very shaky, and it was hoped that a successful mounted attack would regain some of the ground which had been lost, and also restore confidence. The detachment (roughly equal in numbers to a squadron) moved along the main road to Villeselve, taking the sunken track running north into Collezy. On approaching Collezy the Squadron came under heavy machine-gun fire from the direction of a large farm at the south-east exit of the village. The squadron which was under the command of Major EH Watkin Williams (10th Hussars) with Captain CW Turner (Royals) 2nd in Command was formed into three troops by regiments, the 3rd Dragoon Guards under Lieutenant ABPL Vincent MC, the 10th Hussars under Lieutenant the Viscount Ednam and the Royal Dragoons under Lieutenant the Hon. WH Cubitt. The plan of attack had been explained to troop leaders on the way. Lieutenant Vincent was ordered to move towards Copse B. He was to charge any Germans he encountered and secure the right flank. The 10th Hussars and Royals were to make the main attack towards Copse A. The 3rd Dragoons moved off immediately and almost at once came under machine gun fire. They advanced at a steady pace and soon encountered parties of German infantry, some of whom ran into the copse where they were followed on foot. Many were shot at point blank range as they ran away. Twelve prisoners were handed over to the infantry and the right flank secured. As soon as the 3rd Dragoons were on their way the 10th Hussars and Royals started. The formation was troops in line, first the 10th Hussars and then the Royals about 150 yards behind. When the charge started the men were knee to knee but owing to machine gun fire and the fast pace, they tended to open out and by the time the enemy was reached, were more or less extended. On clearing the farm, the column wheeled slightly to the left and passed through a few scattered parties of our infantry. The Germans were then clearly seen in front of Copse A. The distance to be covered was about 600 yards, the last 200 yards being over plough. There was considerable machine-gun fire from the left flank. The 10th Hussars advanced steadily and when the enemy saw mounted troops headed towards them and heard the men cheering they began to surrender freely. The 10th Hussars rode straight through the enemy, the Royals following and mopping up small parties who had run together. After the melee, 'Rally' was sounded, prisoners collected, and the Squadron returned to the main Berlancourt-Villeselve Road, wounded being picked up. Ninety-five prisoners were brought in by the

10th Hussars and Royals making a total of 107 in all. The number however was really greater, as small bodies of the enemy kept giving themselves up to the infantry who followed up the charge…Besides the prisoners, between 70 and 100 Germans were sabred. The casualties of the Squadron were about 73 out of 150, but comparatively few were killed… The manoeuvre gave the infantry renewed confidence and they were able to push forward their line well beyond the limits of the charge thus enabling the remnants of two battalions who had been fighting near Cugny to retire on Villeselve and reform.[49]

The Germans in question were from the 5th Guard Division and following on from their annihilation of 2nd Royal Irish Rifles outside Cugny were moving rapidly across country, by-passing the village of Villeselve which retained large numbers of British troops from various units frantically trying to reorganise. Having exited the two copses which comprised the Bois de Bossemont, the Stormtroopers were in open countryside. Flushed with success at the speed of their advance, German tactics had unwittingly proved to be their own undoing. As the British withdrawal continued, tactics had changed from holding defensive strongpoints to open warfare, which was ideal Cavalry territory. Caught in the open, what the Stormtroopers saw emerging from behind the farm buildings in front of them must have looked like a vision from Hell.

Farrier Serjeant Bertram Turp, 1st Royal Dragoons from Grays, Essex, was one of the participants in the charge:[50]

Shortly after noon our patrols reported that German infantry were advancing from some woods about 500 or 600 yards away on our flank – a perfect cavalry situation, with infantry in the open. A Major of the 10th Hussars gave us the order to draw swords and to hold them down along our horse's shoulders so that the enemy would not catch the glint of steel and we were told to lean down over our horse's necks. A moment later we wheeled into line and then with a loud yell, it was hell for leather for the enemy! We had of course been taught that a cavalry charge should be carried out in line, six inches from knee to knee, but it didn't work out like that in practice and we were soon a pretty ragged line of horsemen at full gallop. We took the Germans quite by surprise and they faced us as best they could, for there can't be anything more frightening to an infantryman than the sight of a line of cavalry charging at full gallop with drawn swords. I cannot remember if I was scared, but I know that all of us were really excited, and so were the horses. The Germans had taken up what positions they could in

49   Bickersteth, *History of the 6th Cavalry Brigade, 1914-1919*, pp. 84-86.
50   Bertram Turp enlisted in the Cavalry in 1902, serving in India and South Africa before the outbreak of war. He survived the war, being awarded the Meritorious Service Medal in 1919.

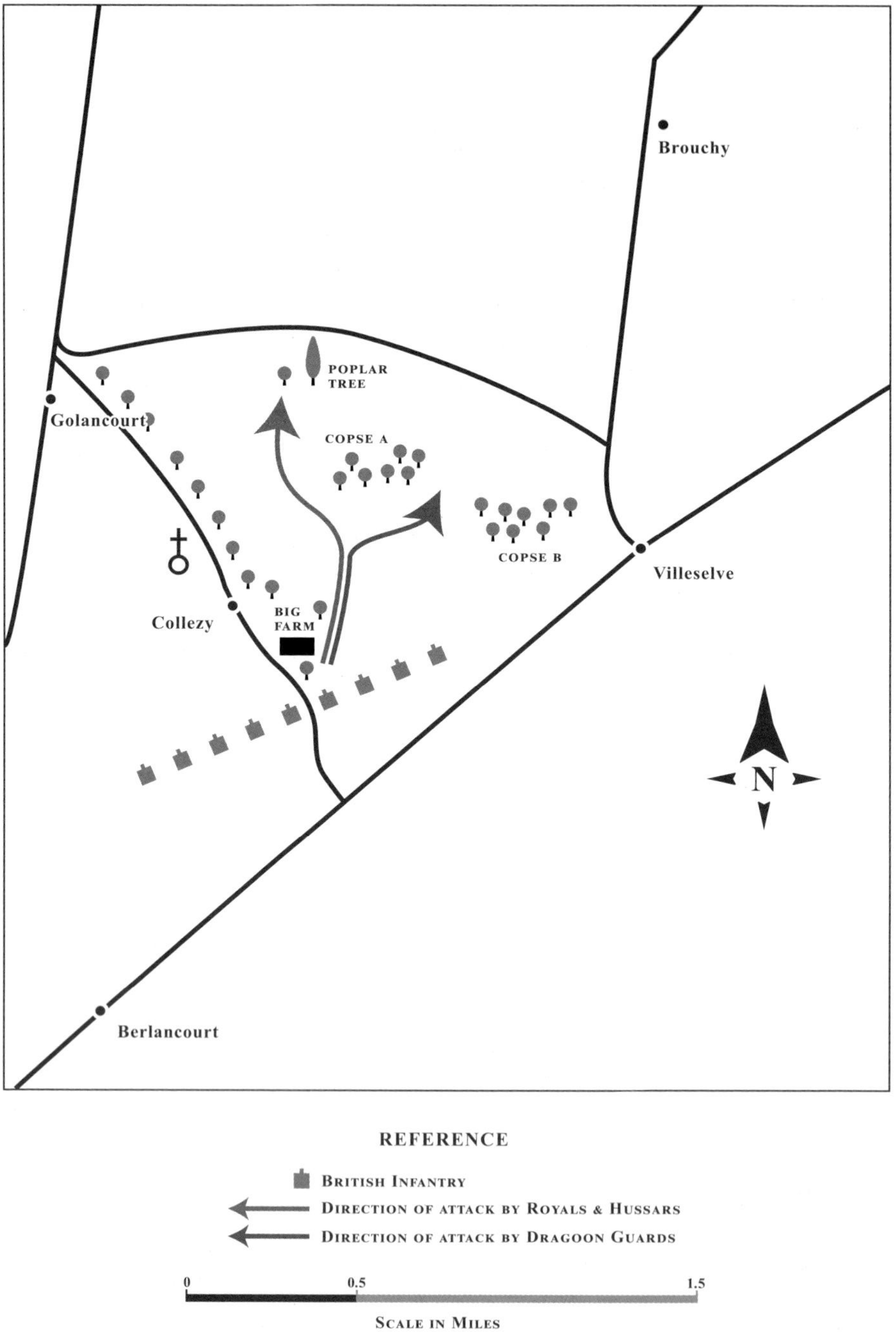

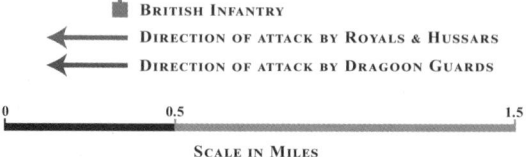

Map 14 Vicinity of cavalry charge, 24 March 1918.

View of Cavalry towards Copse A. (Author's Collection 2017) Farm buildings where Cavalry began advance, still in use 2017. (Author's Collection)

the open and I remember seeing three or four machine-guns and each of them seemed to be pointing at <u>me</u> as they opened up! Men and horses started going down but we kept galloping and the next moment we were amongst them. Oddly enough, at this moment of the real thing, I remembered my old training and the old sword exercise. As our line overrode the Germans I made a regulation point at a man on my offside and my sword went through his neck and out the other side. The pace of my horse carried my sword clear and I then took a German on my nearside and I remember the jar as my point took him in the collarbone and knocked him over. As we galloped on the enemy broke and ran and I gave a German a jab in the backside which couldn't have hurt him much but sent him sprawling. We kept galloping and, circling the woods on the far side, we halted while some of the 3rd Dragoon Guards who had got round to the flank cleaned up what was left of the enemy.[51]

Quickly realising the significance of the moment, troops from the 1st and 9th Royal Irish Fusiliers and 9th Royal Inniskilling Fusiliers, who had moments before been in a state of demoralisation, seized the initiative and quickly followed up the Cavalry charge, taking a number of prisoners and providing temporary respite in the withdrawal. The cavalry themselves rightly regarded the charge as a complete success. In the regimental history of 10th Royal Hussars, Whitmore (1920) describes the aftermath:

> The rally was sounded, and the squadron returned to the Berlancourt – Villeselve Road and the wounded were collected. 94 prisoners were brought by the 10th Royal Hussars and 1st Dragoons. To this should be added 12 brought in by 3rd Dragoon Guards. Three machine-guns were also captured. About 100 Germans were killed at the point of the sword. The mounted detachment suffered heavy casualties including Lieutenant the Hon. H Cubitt (died of wounds) who was in command of the Royals detachment, the losses being 73 out of 150, but the attack gave a wonderful moral effect on the infantry, who had suffered so severely during the retreat and the price the detachment paid was well rewarded.[52]

The casualties amongst the Cavalry referred to by Whitmore seem horrendous at close to 50 percent. However, only three men were killed. One of those who died was, as mentioned above, the commander of the Royal Dragoons detachment, 21 years old Lieutenant the Honourable William Hugh Cubitt, known as Hugh. The third son of Baron and Lady Ashcombe, of Dorking, Surrey, Hugh was educated at Eton

---

51   John Cusack MM & Ivor Herbert. *Scarlet Fever. A Lifetime with Horses* (London: Cassell & Company, 1972) pp. 74-5.
52   F.H.D.C. Whitmore. *The 10th PWO Royal Hussars & The Essex Yeomanry during the European War 1914-1918* (Colchester: Benham, 1920), p. 145.

and entered the Royal Military College, Sandhurst in 1914. William's two elder brothers pre-deceased him in the war, Captain the Honourable Henry Archibald Cubitt, 3rd Battalion Coldstream Guards was killed in action on 15 September 1916 and Lieutenant the Honourable Alick George Cubitt 15th (The King's) Hussars was killed in action on 24 November 1917. Severely wounded in the charge, Hugh died in No 46 Casualty Clearing Station at Noyon and was buried in Noyon New British Cemetery.

This respite, although welcome was however, only temporary. The overwhelming numbers of the enemy soon made up the ground lost and the 36th Division units consolidated in and around Villeselves were forced to withdraw again. The initial withdrawal was westwards to Berlancourt and then Guiscard, but both these villages were subjected to heavy enemy shelling in the early evening. At 11:00 p.m. orders were received that the troops of the Division were to be relieved by the French 62nd Infantry Division. To facilitate this process, the 9th Royal Irish Fusiliers made a stand at the village of Guiscard to cover the withdrawal. Here they were subjected to heavy shelling from all calibres of artillery but held the village until the rest of the Division was clear. Only then could they withdraw through the French lines. In this action, when several of the officers were wounded, Company Serjeant Major Robert Lucas MM took control and rallied the men, ensuring that the defence of the village could continue. For his actions he was awarded the Distinguished Conduct Medal, the citation stating:

Lieutenant the Honourable William Hugh Cubitt, 1st Royal Dragoons. (Public Domain) Headstone of Lieutenant the Hon. WH Cubitt – Noyon New British Cemetery. (Author's Collection)

For conspicuous gallantry and devotion to duty. Displayed great coolness and courage in rallying the line round a village and by his fine example was instrumental in saving a critical situation.[53]

CSM Lucas was a 35 years old married man from Loughgall, County Armagh. A Postman prior to enlisting, he had also been a member of the Ulster Volunteer Force. He had been awarded his Military Medal for gallantry on 1 July 1916. He survived the war and was discharged due to sickness in December 1918.[54]

The beleaguered troops of 36th (Ulster) Division when withdrawn, moved southwest to the area of the village of Sermaize, three miles north of the town of Noyon having on 24 March retreated under constant enemy harassment, a distance of 12 miles.

The Artillery of 36th Division were similarly depleted after four days of hard fighting and were returned from 20th Division on 24 March. Operating due to losses under the names of their commanding officers,[55] they provided vital cover to both French and British troops during the retreat, particularly near the town of Berlancourt where they covered the retreat until the Germans were actually in the town. On the evening of 24 March, the artillery was put at the disposal of the French 9th and 62nd Infantry Divisions.

25 March 1918

The decision to withdraw the Ulster Division was a consequence of deliberations at General Headquarters which had been gathering pace since 23 March. The gradual withdrawal of Fifth Army troops under the onslaught of the German attack created a situation whereby a redrawing of Army areas of responsibility could take place. Using the Somme as a natural boundary, it was proposed to transfer responsibility for all operations north of the river from Fifth Army to Third Army, under the command of General the Hon. Sir Julian Byng. South of the Somme, responsibility for operations passed from General Gough to the French General, Marie Emile Fayolle. The order for the change in responsibility was issued at 3:00 a.m. 25 March.[56]

Whilst General Gough was still in command of Fifth Army, operational control was ceded to the French. As in all major military operations which do not go well, the hunt was on for a scapegoat and General Gough was in the firing line. On 23 March, the Commander in Chief, Field Marshal Sir Douglas Haig had visited General Gough at his HQ. Later that day he wrote in his diary:

53   *The London Gazette* 3 September 1918
54   CSM Lucas' medals are on display in the Royal Irish Fusiliers Museum, Armagh.
55   The artillery units were named, Erskine, Eley and Potter.
56   Edmonds, *Military Operations France and Belgium 1918,* p. 419.

I was surprised to learn that his troops are now behind the Somme and the River Tortille. Men very tired after two days fighting and long march back. On first day they had to wear gas masks all day which is very fatiguing, but I cannot make out why Fifth Army has gone so far back without making some kind of stand…[57]

No cognisance was being given to the fact that Gough's Army held a longer portion of the line with less troops and faced a greater concentration of attacking German forces. For his part, General Gough thought the decision nonsensical, but must have realised that he was under close scrutiny. In his 1934 book, *The March Retreat*, he described his thoughts:

25 March. Very early in the morning before 2.00 a.m. orders arrived from GHQ placing all the troops north of the Somme, with VII HQ under the Third Army and at the same time informing me that it had now been arranged that the French should take over up to that river, under General Fayolle, who was commanding the group of armies in that area. The Fifth Army was thus cut off from GHQ as regards military operations and GHQ gave up all responsibilities for the British troops under my command south of the Somme… Placing the Fifth Army under Fayolle's group of armies made no material difference. He issued no orders to me and I saw him only once for a few minutes.[58]

The Ulster Division war diary records that it was at 10:00 a.m. on 25 March that orders were received placing the Division under the command of the French 62nd Infantry Division. The immediate task was to reorganise behind the French lines and be ready for use as a reserve if necessary.[59] As part of this reorganisation, 61st Brigade was ordered to return to 20th Division, which was under the operational control of the French 22nd Infantry Division. In a move which demonstrated that not all organisational functions had broken down, motor lorries were provided to take the remnants of 61st Brigade to re-join 20th Division.

The Brigade left with the warm wishes and heartfelt thanks of 36th Division. The officers and men of the Somersets, DCLI and King's (Liverpool) Regiment had proved themselves skilled fighters and admirable comrades. Along with the units of 36th Division, they too had suffered heavily in the withdrawal. The 61st Brigade war diary recorded the toll that had been exerted on the brigade:

The brigade was then organised into a composite battalion of four Companies, each company comprising of men from a battalion in the brigade with a HQ

57   Sheffield & Bourne, *Douglas Haig. War Diaries and Letters*, p. 391.
58   Gough, *The March Retreat*, pp. 127-128.
59   TNA: WO 95/2492/2: 36th (Ulster) Division war diary.

company in addition. The strength of the battalion mustered nine junior officers and 440 other ranks.[60]

In the three and half days which the 61st Brigade had been attached to the Ulster Division, they had had 103 men killed,[61] many more wounded and a greater portion taken prisoner.

There was little time for the men of the Ulster Division to reorganise and for most, the details of the reorganisation came as the Division was again on the move on the morning of 25 March. On that day, the remnants marched west for 15 miles arriving in the evening at the village of Guerbigny. Some however had a lucky break. Due to the severe casualties suffered by 61st Brigade, a number of lorries were left over from their move back to 20th Division. These were used to convey some of the weary Ulstermen to Guerbigny, which the majority reached around midnight. One of the lucky ones was Corporal Jim Donaghy, 9th Inniskillings, from Drumahoe outside Londonderry:

> We had been holding the Germans at bay and moving steadily back for six days. We were withdrawn at last and marched five or six miles to the rear. The battalion was sleeping on its feet. I walked into the man in front and cut my face on his steel helmet. We were met on the road by a fleet of lorries which transported half the battalion to a village. We were billeted in the school and had a rest at last.[62]

Following this necessary reorganisation, 36th Division's establishment was as follows:

107th Brigade
1st Royal Irish Rifles, numbering around 150.
2nd Royal Irish Rifles numbering eight officers and 40 men.
15th Royal Irish Rifles comprising a small party of Transport and Quartermaster personnel commanded by Captain Miller.
16th Royal Irish Rifles numbering around 500 officers and men.
21st Entrenching Battalion numbering around 250 officers and men.
121st Field Company Royal Engineers numbering around 150 officers and men.

108th Brigade
12th Royal Irish Rifles. Transport and Quartermaster detail only.
1st Royal Irish Fusiliers, numbering around 150 officers and men.
9th Royal Irish Fusiliers, numbering around 200 officers and men.
122nd Field Company Royal Engineers numbering around 150 officers and men.

60   TNA: WO 95/2125/3: 61st Infantry Brigade war diary.
61   Commonwealth War Graves Commission <http://www.cwgc.org> (Accessed 15 May 2017).
62   Mitchell, *Three Cheers for the Derry's*, p. 160.

109th Brigade
1st Royal Inniskilling Fusiliers (including Brigade HQ element and remnants of 109th Trench Mortar Battery) eight officers and 147 other ranks.
2nd Royal Inniskilling Fusiliers. Transport and Quartermasters detail only.
9th Royal Inniskilling Fusiliers, numbering around 670 officers and men.[63]

The action and subsequent retreat of 24 March combined with the change in operational control had a sobering effect on the Divisional Commander. The letter that he wrote to his wife on 25 March exhibits a level of despondency not seen in previous letters:

> It is all a ghastly nightmare. I cannot credit that it is only five days ago that we were holding the trenches just in front of St Quentin. Yesterday was a bad day for the French and British Armies. We lost much ground, a great deal of guns and ammunition have been captured … What is left of my Division had terribly heavy fighting yesterday and we had to fall back again in common with French and British… A very heavy fight is going on just in front of us. I pray the French will be able to hold the Germans. My men have had no food, some of them for two and three days. They have had no sleep for five nights. They are absolutely beat. We are in support of the French but if they call on us before I am reorganised and before the men have had at any rate one good night's sleep, we shall be of no help to them. This is truly Armageddon. Unless we stop the German attack soon, I fear it will be the end. It is a funny situation, as I am now part of the French Army. I hope we shall not fail them…I feel more than anything the attitude of the French towards us. They hardly pretend to be civil and I can hardly wonder. We have let them down disastrously.[64]

Whilst the majority of the Division had arrived in the vicinity of Sermaize at around 2:00 a.m. the 9th Royal Irish Fusiliers, following their stand at Guiscard had spent the night marching and did not arrive until 8:00 a.m.

The problem that emerged on the morning of 25 March concerned the relief by the French infantry. In *The History of the 36th (Ulster) Division*, Falls (1922) who witnessed events first hand, was critical of the lack of understanding between the two armies:

> The fighting of March 25th exhibited in lamentable fashion the difficulties that occur in a retreat when two armies, using different methods, speaking different languages, based upon different lines of communication, with different apprehensions preoccupying the minds of their commanders, are being forced back before a victorious and powerful enemy. The French were retiring south-west,

63   Figures of battalion and company strengths gleaned from war diaries and official histories.
64   PRONI D3835/E/2/17/13A: Farren Connell papers.

the British west. Sooner or later a gap was inevitable, it occurred on the evening of 25th at Roye.[65]

The lack of coordination saw the dog-tired men of the 36th Division march in the morning to positions near Cantigny as previously agreed with the commander of the French 62nd Division, only to be redirected on arrival to Avricourt, some 15 miles away. There was to be no rest there either as the Division was required to fill the gap between the British and French armies to the north-west of Roye. This necessitated further marching until the totally exhausted troops reached old French positions in the vicinity of the village of Erches. On arrival, they deployed in front of the village with 108th Brigade on the left, 109th Brigade on the right and 107th Brigade in reserve, two miles to the rear in the village of Guerbigny.

26 March 1918

The 26th March is of great importance from a strategic perspective; it was on this date that an emergency Anglo-French conference was held at Doullens, attended by the French President Clemenceau, Prime Minister Poincare, Generals Foch and Petain. Lord Milner (a member of the British War Cabinet) Field Marshal Haig, Chief of General Staff General Lawrence and Chief of Imperial General Staff General Sir Henry Wilson.[66] At this meeting is was decided (as had been pressed for by Lloyd George for some time) to appoint General Foch as the overall Commander of Allied Forces on the Western Front. The appointment was proposed by Lord Milner and agreed by all present. Ironically, it took the German Offensive to force this move, which had been resisted by successive British Commanders in Chief for over three and a half years. The current incumbent, Field Marshal Haig had initially opposed this course of action however, in the desperate circumstances which prevailed, he saw the wisdom of the move. If nothing else, this removed a degree of responsibility and no small degree of pressure from Haig and placed it at the feet of General Foch. Following the meeting, Sir Henry Wilson commented:

> Douglas Haig is 10 years younger tonight than he was yesterday afternoon.[67]

A follow-on meeting then took place where it was agreed by both French and British attendees that in light of the current offensive, the town of Amiens was to be protected at all costs. Amiens was of primary importance not just to the French but to the

65   Falls, *The History of the 36th (Ulster) Division*, p. 220. There is evidence that Falls was perturbed that as a fluent French speaker, he was not called upon in a liaison role.
66   General Sir Henry Wilson had replaced General Sir William Robertson as Chief of Imperial General Staff in February 1918.
67   Major General Sir Charles Edward Callwell *Field Marshall Sir Henry Wilson. Bart, GCB. DSO* (London: Cassell & Company, 1927), p. 78.

British as it was the logistics and rail hub for the entire Picardy Region. Any reinforcements being brought to the area to assist in halting the German offensive would be routed through the town.

The decision to defend Amiens at all costs placed added importance on the ability of the 36th (Ulster) Division and 30th Division to plug the gap between the French and British lines around Roye. That this task fell to two Divisions who had been fighting and marching constantly for five days and were seriously depleted, showed the paucity of resources available to the British. To compound matters for the 36th, as we have already seen, they had no artillery with which to support their defensive efforts.

The area in which the Ulster Division found themselves was known by the French as the 'plain of Santerre', a vast area of agricultural land which was flat and featureless, except for villages and farming communes scattered about it. On the morning of 26 March, the Division was defending an area roughly in the shape of a triangle around 6 miles north-west of the town of Roye. This triangle comprised the villages of Erches and Andechy along one axis with the village of Guerbigny, two miles to the rear.

The problems with coordinating a defence between the armies of two nations had again been exploited by the Germans who had entered the town of Roye from the north-east in the early hours of the morning, brushing aside the weak defences of a French Cavalry Division.

It had rained on the night of 25/26 March and again in the morning there was a heavy mist. At 8:00 a.m. the Ulster Division received orders to take up a defensive line from L'Echelle-St-Aurin on the River Avre, north past the western outskirts of Andechy, to meet with 30th Division on the main Amiens-Roye Road. This put them directly in the line of the German advance. The 109th Brigade was to occupy the line from the River Avre towards Andechy with 108th Brigade on their left, 107th Brigade remained in Guerbigny. By the time 109th and 108th brigades manoeuvred into position, the Germans had already taken the village of Andechy. Worse still, the 108th Brigade line was intended to extend on the left to woods known as Les Grands Bois, a good defensive position in the otherwise featureless landscape, but the Germans beat them to it and had established a machine-gun position there. To support the defensive line, 107th Brigade was moved to a position to the rear of 108th Brigade from the village of Erches towards the village of Bouchoir where it was hoped to gain touch with 30th Division. The rapid advance of the Germans however, ensured that this link could not and would not be established.

The line held for most of the day. There were probing German advances which were repulsed by machine-gun and Lewis gun fire, but no major attacks. The commanding officer of 9th Royal Irish Fusiliers, Lieutenant Colonel Philip Edward Kelly from County Mayo, was wounded and command of the battalion passed to Major John George Brew. In a lull in the attacks, Major Brew went across to the positions of 1st Royal Irish Fusiliers on the right to consult with the commanding officer, Lieutenant Colonel Michael Furnell. Both men then went to 109th Brigade HQ to inform Brigadier General Hessey of their intention to withdraw when darkness fell. Whilst there, they met the Division's Staff Officer, Lieutenant Colonel Place. The proposed

Map 15   Area of Operations 26th and 27th March 1918.

retirement was agreed, and all three men left in Lieutenant Colonel Place' staff car for Erches to brief General Griffiths, 108th Brigade of the plan.

In a letter to his wife on 28 March, Major General Nugent outlined what then occurred:

> In the evening, I sent my GSO (1) Col Place out to see one of the Brigadiers who was close by but told him to return from there. He took one of the cars, saw the Brigadier, but instead of coming back, he took 2 CO's of Battns with him and went off to see General Griffith, another of my Brigadiers (108th) who was on the left near a village called Erches. It seems he drove straight into a cavalry party of Germans and was captured with both CO's. One of our men saw the thing happen, he was captured too but managed to escape and brought the news.[68]

With dusk approaching, parties of Germans had easily infiltrated the Division's lines. Records indicate that some were dressed in captured French uniforms which sowed seeds of doubt in the minds of the defenders and gave the Germans a crucial advantage. The three officers and their driver were all captured, and their initial fate was unknown. Towards the end of April however, information was received from the Red Cross that Major Brew had died of wounds. What had actually occurred remained a mystery until a number of years later, when Lieutenant Colonel Furnell, having been repatriated from a prisoner of war camp and having re-joined the Royal Irish Fusiliers, wrote to Major Brew's widow. The letter contains inaccuracies as to the exact date and the name of the GSO, but otherwise provides a picture as to the confusion which existed at the time:

> As you probably know your husband and I were commanding the 9th and 1st Bns of the Regt and on the evening of the 27th I think it was, our two battalions were holding a position in some old trenches where we had been heavily attacked all day and we had decided to withdraw both our battalions at dark we went to tell the General who was on our right what our intentions were when the General Staff Officer No 1 Col. Green of the Ulster Division arrived and said he would take your husband and myself to see our Brigadier in his motor. We went to see the Brigadier but on returning in the motor drove into an advance party of the Germans who opened fire and bombed the car. Col. Green was wounded, and we were all captured, after being searched we were being marched back to the German Headquarters by an escort when some Germans who evidently mistook us for British troops opened fire on us. Your husband was walking alongside me and was hit. I ran over towards the men who were firing thinking they were our troops as things were rather mixed up and it was dark, however I discovered they

68 PRONI D3835/E/2/17/14A: Farren Connell papers.

were Boche as they fired at me when I was a few yards from them. I then went back to your husband who was lying in the road. I found that he had been hit through the lung and as Col Green and the motor driver were already wounded it was impossible to move him without help from the Boche which they refused to give and only beat us with the butts of their rifles when we asked them to move your husband. We moved him to the side of the road and made him as comfortable as possible. He could not speak much, the Boche were trying to hurry us at the time so didn't have much chance of doing anything. Said goodbye to your husband and he was able to shake hands with me. When we reached German Headquarters, Col Green who spoke German told the German Commander about your husband and they told him they would send out for him but one can never believe a Boche. There was one of our doctors there also a prisoner and I asked him about your husband and he said that the best thing that could happen was for him to remain where he was as it was a frosty night and that might stop the bleeding. I never heard what happened to your husband afterwards and I didn't meet anyone who had met him in a German hospital but heard when I was released that he had died. I had met your husband many times in 1917/18 and was very sorry to hear that he had died. I was afraid at the time that it was a bad wound.[69]

Major John George Brew was a 41 years old married man from Carrickblacker Road, Portadown, County Armagh. Born at Gateshead, Northumberland, he was a Ship's Master before gaining employment with his father-in-law in the firm of James Clow and sons, Cornmillers. A member of Portadown Ulster Volunteer Force, he enlisted in the 9th Royal Irish Fusiliers on its formation as a Private and obtained his commission in December of that year. He was wounded on 1 July 1916 and had been second in command of the battalion since September 1917. Major Brew is buried in Roye New British Cemetery.

As this was happening the Germans had commenced an artillery barrage of Erches which obliged 108th Brigade HQ to move into the fields behind the village. The Germans who had infiltrated also came close to capturing the personnel of the HQ as the brigade war diary records:

At about 8:00 p.m. sniping suddenly began round Bde HQ and it was reported that the enemy were in the neighbourhood...Parties of Germans accompanied by mounted men suddenly appeared along the roads around Bde HQ and in the bright moonlight it was impossible to ascertain who were friends and who were foes. It is not clear where the Germans came through in force, but

---

69   Original letter held by the Royal Irish Fusiliers Museum, Sovereign's House, The Mall, Armagh. TNA WO 95/828/10: The war diary of 21st Entrenching Battalion confirms that there was a severe frost on the night of 26/27 March.

a number accompanied by transport apparently moved through Erches where the RE whom they first encountered believed them to be a French column until too late...Bde HQ was partially surrounded and fired upon with MG at close range. We broke through however and got away with documents etc, only the Signalling Officer being captured and the Brigadier slightly wounded. A considerable number of Germans might have been accounted for only for the difficulty of distinguishing friend from foe. The Germans moved along roads in the most obvious manner without precautions or concealment and were accordingly usually mistaken for our own transport and ration parties or for French.

This confusion as to the identities of parties on the move in the gathering dusk was commonplace across the front line. Given the proximity of French troops, the Germans of 1st Guard Infantry Division and 28th Infantry Division were quick to use all means at their disposal to gain an advantage. The war diaries of the units involved contain examples of this:

1st Royal Irish Rifles war diary – About 10:00 p.m. the enemy 1st Guards Division approached the village securing posts by use of French uniform. They kidnapped in one case the occupants. Desultory fire opened which later developed into bursts of MG fire of some intensity. Having made good the village, light trench mortars were brought up and our positions bombarded. On two occasions, the white flag was used to distract attention while MG crews operated on the

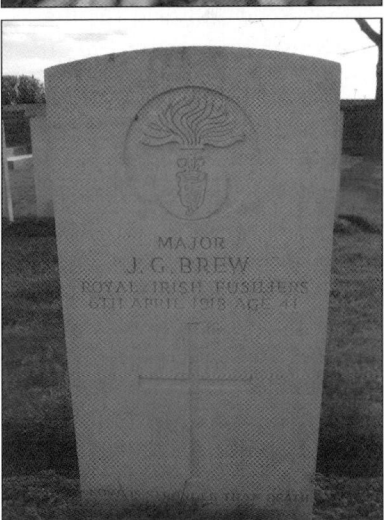

Major John George Brew 9th Battalion Royal Irish Fusiliers. (Great War Ulster Newspaper Archive) Headstone of Major John George Brew, Roye New British Cemetery. (Author's Collection)

opposite flank and considerable use made of the presumed presence of French vis. 'Don't fire, we are French' until it became necessary to warn troops to fire on <u>all</u> in front.

2nd Royal Irish Rifles war diary – The afternoon and evening passed quietly, but immediately after dark large columns of men and transport could be seen passing down the road from Erches-Guerbigny about 100 yards to the right of the position occupied by the battalion. For some time, these were believed to be French, but an officers' patrol got in touch with an Uhlan patrol and it was discovered they were enemy.

15th Royal Irish Rifles war diary – 10:00 p.m. A party of the enemy about 20 strong and more or less intoxicated was discovered owing to the noise they made outside the wire N of Erches. On being challenged they replied in French and English. Suspecting a ruse, we again challenged them and getting no reply opened fire on them wounding several.[70]

The chaos of the evening enabled the Germans to drive the 36th Division out of Erches, but the remnants of the Division consolidated their positions near the Guerbigny-Erches Road and held the line overnight despite supplies of food and ammunition being unable to reach them. The war diary of 12th Royal Irish Rifles, detailing the activities of the remaining men of the Quartermaster, Transport and Band who were under the command of 1st Royal Irish Rifles, wistfully recorded:

All available men were again collected and sent outside the village to fight a rearguard action to delay enemy's progress. Five officers and approx. 60 OR's were sent forward. Bandsmen were included, and the instruments were dumped at Erches and were not recovered.[71]

The fact that the band were still carrying their instruments five days into the withdrawal seem somewhat bizarre in the circumstances.

27 March 1918

This was the last day that the Division fought as a cohesive unit in the offensive.

As on the previous nights, a fog descended on the plain. Patrols sent out during the hours of darkness confirmed that the Germans were in Erches in substantial numbers. The 107th brigade war diary records the initiative shown on one such patrol:

One patrol of an officer and two men from 121st Field Company RE advanced towards the village and went to about 100 yards from the Quesnoy-Erches Road

---

70   TNA: WO 95/2502/3: 1st Battalion Royal Irish Rifles war diary, WO 95/2502/4: 2nd Battalion Royal Irish Rifles war diary, WO 95/2503/5: 15th Battalion Royal Irish Rifles war diary.
71   TNA: WO 95/2506/2: 12th Battalion Royal Irish Rifles war diary.

where it lay down and watched a large amount of enemy transport on the road. Wagons, limbers, about 20 Cavalry, some straggling infantry and one battery of Field Artillery. The officer even spoke to a man marching on the road and states that there is no doubt that he was a German.[72]

Once the Germans had consolidated their position, they lost little time in attacking the positions of the Ulster Division. At about 3:10 a.m. the positions held by the depleted ranks of 15th Royal Irish Rifles came under heavy bombardment. Confusion however still reigned on all sides due to the fog, but also due to the rapidly changing positions enforced as the Germans advanced and the British and French withdrew. Records indicate a number of instances which highlighted the problem:

- Lieutenant James Curley, 1st Inniskillings was leading a ration party bringing food and ammunition and heading for the front line when they were stopped by a party of Germans. The ration party broke through and managed to reach the Inniskilling's positions.[73]
- The 15th Royal Irish Rifles war diary records how at 5:00 a.m. a French cavalry patrol came from Arvillers and intended proceeding to Erches, the officer in charge unaware that it was in the hands of the enemy. Soon after a German cavalry patrol (five strong) came up from behind our lines. We killed one and wounded another and the remainder rode away.[74]
- At 5:30 a.m. a ration party from 2nd Royal Irish Rifles under CQMS Somers missed its way and got into Erches village where it was twice charged by cavalry patrols. The rations were however delivered, one man being wounded.[75]

From available records, the Germans were uncertain of the exact strength and location of British and French positions and perhaps prudently, sent out small parties – some of whom may have been those referred to above, to test the defences. As Falls recalls in the *History of the 36th (Ulster) Division* (1922) one such party, still using deception tactics, stumbled into a position held by a composite unit led by one of the few remaining Machine Gun Battalion officers, Captain Densmore Walker and got rather more than they bargained for:

Things were looking as black as conceivable. I suppose it would have been about 7:30 a.m. when the attack came. We heard shouting behind us and saw about

72   TNA: WO 95/2502/1: 107th Infantry Brigade war diary. Lieutenant Curley had been recommended for and was subsequently awarded the Military Cross for an action the previous day when he attacked an enemy cavalry reconnaissance patrol which had breached the lines during the hours of darkness. *The London Gazette*, 16 September 1918.
73   TNA: WO 95/2509/4: 109th Infantry Brigade war diary.
74   TNA: WO 95/2503/5: 15th Battalion Royal Irish Rifles war diary.
75   TNA: WO 95/2502/4: 2nd Battalion Royal Irish Rifles war diary.

a dozen men coming towards us in a line. One waved a white flag and they all shouted. Some said they were English, and we were relieved, some said that they looked like French, and I said that anyway we would fire on them which we did. They were perfectly good Huns! They took cover when we opened and then when we were really interested in them, the real attack came from Erches. He swarmed on to the road and came down the trench. This looked like the finish of it. There was a general movement backwards, but Evans prevented the machine gunners from dismounting the one machine-gun with 107th Bde and we got it into action on the top of the trench... This changed the aspect of things as the Huns checked...Fritz was legging it for Erches hard enough and by this time indeed they had all reached it. I don't know how big the village was but we might have rushed it... I think on the whole the Erches scrap went in our favour. We were few in numbers compared with the Huns. They were backed up by victory, while our men were terribly tired, hungry and dispirited... Our ammunition was about gone. For our MG we had three belts left when we retired. We were entirely surrounded, if only by Hun patrols and we only knew hazily what direction to make for. In the circumstances, to delay a force superior in numbers and morale for half a day was as much as could be expected. I reckon that the Boche should have wiped out our party at Erches, but we turned on him severely enough to persuade him to let us go quietly.[76]

Captain Densmore Walker was 24-years-old when this action occurred. From Adlington, Lancashire, he had enlisted in the King's (Liverpool) Regiment at the outbreak of war and received his commission in July 1915. Gassed in 1917, he survived the war and relinquished his commission in February 1919.

From around this time onwards, all remaining units of the Ulster Division came under concerted attack by infantry preceded by Artillery and Trench Mortar bombardments. These attacks were driven off and in one instance a composite unit of 1st Royal Irish Rifles and 121st Field Company RE, under the command of Lieutenant Colonel MacCarthy-O'Leary counterattacked and drove the attackers back. As their position was rapidly becoming untenable, this action in which the commanding officer was wounded for a second time, enabled the remnants of the party numbering four officers and 68 men, to execute a fighting withdrawal to the outskirts of Arvillers where they established a defensive line. At the other end of the Divisional line, 109th Brigade were holding positions close to the River Avre. After dawn, they came under sustained Artillery and Trench Mortar bombardment and some probing attacks by German units, but these were beaten off. Then at around 10:00 a.m. without warning to the British, the French on the right of 109th Brigade mounted an attack to retake the village of Erches. They were initially successful, but then the enemy regrouped and drove the French back beyond their start position. This left the Inniskillings positions

76 Falls *The History of the 36th (Ulster) Division*, p. 224.

exposed as on the left, the Germans had also forced a breach in the 108th brigade defences. To avoid being surrounded and cut off, the remaining men of the brigade were forced to retreat across the River Avre, as the brigade war diary records:

> 11:35 a.m. Orders were sent out at once to the left to bring back their flank but before they were received word came back from our right that the French across the river were falling back and our front line was heavily involved. Our left was being attacked from the rear and men began to come back and were directed to move towards the river and cross at once as it was feared that Guerbigny was in enemy hands. The withdrawal to the river was quite orderly, covering fire being given by various sections especially by a section crewed by the Brigade Intelligence Officer and Sergeant Instructors of 2nd Inniskillings who were the last to cross the river. Captain Bruce the Brigade Major, superintended this move and was among the last to leave… The Germans came on in large numbers particularly on the right and the shelling became very heavy whilst the MG fire was tremendous… The roads behind were all under fire but fortunately the Germans made no attempt to put cavalry through so troops retired steadily, ending the day at Bouillancourt.[77]

The lack of coordination in mounting a joint defence by French and British units as already highlighted by Captain Falls, was instrumental in necessitating the Inniskillings to withdraw, an issue which was the subject of understated comment in the 9th Inniskillings war diary:

> Throughout this day's fighting the lack of arrangements for liaison with the French was again most marked.[78]

At 12:15 p.m., an order was issued by XVIII Corps Headquarters, directing the relief of 36th Division, by the French 56th Division. Following relief, the Division was to consolidate at Hargicourt. This was most difficult to achieve as the majority of the Division was still in action at this time. To complicate matters, by 1:15 p.m. units of German cavalry were reported in Davenescourt, five miles from Hargicourt having exploited the gap opened up by the withdrawal of 109th Brigade. This put the German advanced units between the remnants of the Division and the proposed rendezvous.

The attacks on 109th Brigade on the right and 107th Brigade on the left and the subsequent progress made by the enemy, left the remnants of 108th Brigade exposed on both sides. The infantry attack was preceded by an intense Artillery and Trench Mortar bombardment, often at point blank range. The exhausted men of 1st and 9th

---

77   TNA: WO 95/2509/4: 109th Infantry Brigade war diary. Bouillancourt-la-Bataille is located seven miles from Guerbigny.
78   TNA: WO 95/2510/3: 9th Battalion Royal Inniskilling Fusiliers war diary.

Royal Irish Fusiliers held out as long as they could, but by 11:20 a.m. the 1st Royal Irish Fusiliers were surrounded and cut off. Of the already depleted unit, one officer and 19 men made it to the rear.

The 9th Royal Irish Fusiliers however, continued to hold out in an attempt to delay the German advance. The defence, no matter how spirited was only going to delay the inevitable. A valuable account of that day from Private John William Page[79] describes how the day progressed:

> About midday the Germans began to move forward, and things began to get uncomfortable for us because he started dropping them right on us and after each one had burst someone would shout out for stretcher bearers. By about two o'clock we were getting it hot and strong and chaps were getting smashed and wounded on either side of where I was. Shortly after two we found he was enfilading our left flank and we had to get out of the portion of trench we were in. We dashed across the road and flung ourselves in the continuation of it on the other side. That's where we lost most of our best, for the Germans had a machine gun trained right down this road and when about four or five of our fellows got on the road he opened up and down went the boys. Still, we couldn't stay where we were, or we'd get it in the back and the Germans behind us were drawing in closer. Very soon we should be inside the circle, so we decided between us to make a dash for it. It was a sporting chance and the only opening we had. Soon we would be as rats in a trap, so emptying our pockets of our letters and burying them anywhere in the trench we prepared for the dash across the road. We managed to go across one at a time at irregular intervals. A young officer went first, but as soon as he was about half way over he got one right in the head and fell down dead right in our path. The second chap started off and he tried crawling on his stomach. He was almost in the other side when he caught one in the ankle. Then a young Lance Corporal ran over but fell headlong into the other trench with one in the head. I went next and ran over bent right down and literally threw myself into the trench. I got a bruise or two, but at least I was safe – from that touch anyhow. I watched the next chap come over, he bent down like I did but got three right through the buttocks. He yelled like fury and my God when we got his trousers off he was like a slaughterhouse. Some more of our chaps got over all right but goodness knows what became of those we had left lying in the road. We found some more of our chaps were in this trench just farther along and we were glad to see them. Some of them had got some 'Ruby Queens' [issue cigarettes] so we were able to get a smoke. After about 10 minutes we had a look round with a periscope and could see the Germans advancing on

79   Private John William Page 43370 was from Middlesex. He had enlisted in the London Regiment being posted to the 1/7th (City of London) Battalion. He transferred to the Royal Irish Fusiliers in early 1917.

us not a thousand yards away. Our poor old periscope didn't reign long for a bullet went through it. One of our officers, Lt Henry by name, was in our trench so of course we asked him what he was going to do. He said 'Well chaps, you see our position, we are surrounded, and it would be madness to even attempt to rush it with thousands of these xxxxxxx's not a thousand yards away and all round us. I will tie my handkerchief on my stick and we must surrender'. He waved the handkerchief a few minutes and the German rifle fire fell off a bit. After a while it ceased, and someone shouted and when we looked over we saw a German officer coming towards our officer who had now climbed to the top of the trench. The German was accompanied by two big hefty soldiers with rifles and bayonet. After making some gestures to our officer making him understand that we were to disarm and file out of our trench with our hands above our heads. Our officer came back to us very downhearted and said, 'Well chaps, we're finished and we're prisoners. We couldn't have done any better if we had made a bid for it, there would only have been more loss of life to no beneficial purpose, so boys, we must make the best of it.' So, we all put our rifles, bayonets, ammo, bombs etc in the trench and filed out of the trench behind the officer, each one of us with our hands above his head. We walked towards the advancing Germans, their officer again coming towards us with about 25 German soldiers all of whom were jeering and laughing at us, but our boys were as good as they and laughed at them too. It was the same indomitable spirit that had carried the boys through some rough times and the same spirit was prevailing even though we were beaten so to speak. The German officer made us form up into fours and forming his squad of men all round us as escort we commenced to march back behind his troops.[80]

Private Page's officer was Lieutenant Albert William Henry aged 24, from Ely in Cambridgeshire. From an army family, his father had been a Serjeant-Major. Albert Henry enlisted in the Life Guards in November 1914 and obtained his commission in November 1916. He was posted to the 2nd Reserve Cavalry Regiment at the Curragh and in April 1917 joined the 2nd North Irish Horse in Belgium. When the unit was dismounted, he was one of the several hundred who were absorbed into the 9th Royal Irish Fusiliers. In his own account, he describes the rationale for the surrender of his party:

About 3:00 p.m. I was ordered by 2nd Lt Scott, Acting Adjutant, to take my Coy and take up position in a trench in rear of 1st RIF's position. This I did having several casualties from enemy MG's in getting there. By the time we had reached this trench, all the 1st RIF in front of our position had been captured. The trench we were in was a deep communications trench with no fire steps,

80   IWM: D.11326 Private J.W. Page papers.

therefore undefendable. There were four other officers with me at this time and from our position we could see that the enemy was in possession of a ridge about two miles in rear of us. We therefore had a consultation in which senior NCO's were included and in view of the fact that the men were all exhausted, having had neither food nor water since the morning of the 26th and that only a few had any ammunition, we decided that it was impossible to extricate ourselves from our position and that to avoid unnecessary casualties it would be better to surrender to the enemy, which we did at about 3:30 p.m.[81]

All cohesive resistance from 36th Division on 27 March finished around this time although some isolated parties continued to resist. What remained of 9th Royal Irish Fusiliers with a few men of 12th Royal Irish Rifles withdrew to Arvillers. With the order to withdraw to Hargicourt having been issued by the Division, its remaining assets were geographically split. To the north, 107th and 108th Brigades were in the vicinity of Arvillers and unable to move directly to Hargicourt as the Germans had advanced to block their path. To the south, 109th Brigade had crossed the River Avre and were moving parallel to the Germans in an attempt to reach the rendezvous before them.

In the event due to the German advance, the rendezvous location was changed from Hargicourt to Sourdon, a further seven and a half miles west where Divisional Headquarters was located. This proved unachievable on 27 March. What remained of 107th Brigade had to undertake a long and trying march via the villages of Hangest-en-Santerre, Le Plessier-Rouzainvillers and Mailly-Raineval, before the first elements of it arrived at Sourdon at around 7:30 a.m. on 28 March, the war diary of 21st Entrenching Battalion recording that, 'the men were done up but quite cheerful.'[82] The remnants of 108th Brigade, the largest party belonging to 9th Royal Irish Fusiliers, remained at Arvillers for the night. The Inniskillings of 109th Brigade remained for the night at Bouillancourt-la-Bataille.

28-31 March 1918

Throughout 28 March the remainder of 107th Brigade made their way to Sourdon, the remnants of 15th Royal Irish Rifles not arriving there until 7:00 p.m. The Division, having been relieved in its entirety by French forces, had the expectation of a period to obtain much needed rest and to reorganise. It was however, not to be. Writing to his wife on 29 March, Nugent described how the situation had developed:

I had to break off in a hurry yesterday as the Commander of the French 1st Army, General Debeney came to see me and to tell me that the Germans had

---

81   TNA: WO 339/80330: Lieutenant Albert William Henry service record.
82   TNA: WO 95/828/10: 21st Entrenching Battalion war diary.

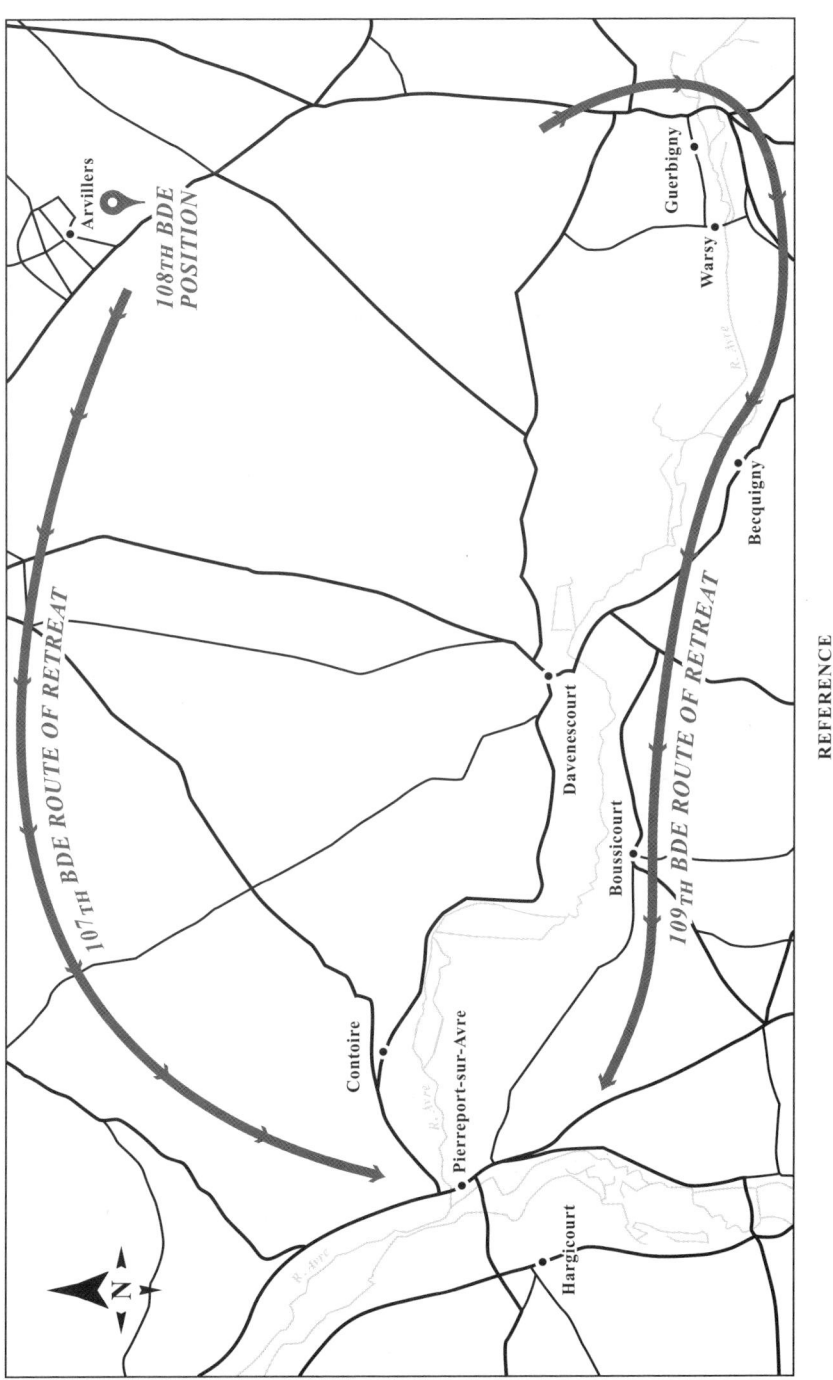

Map 16 Area of withdrawal 27th March 1918.

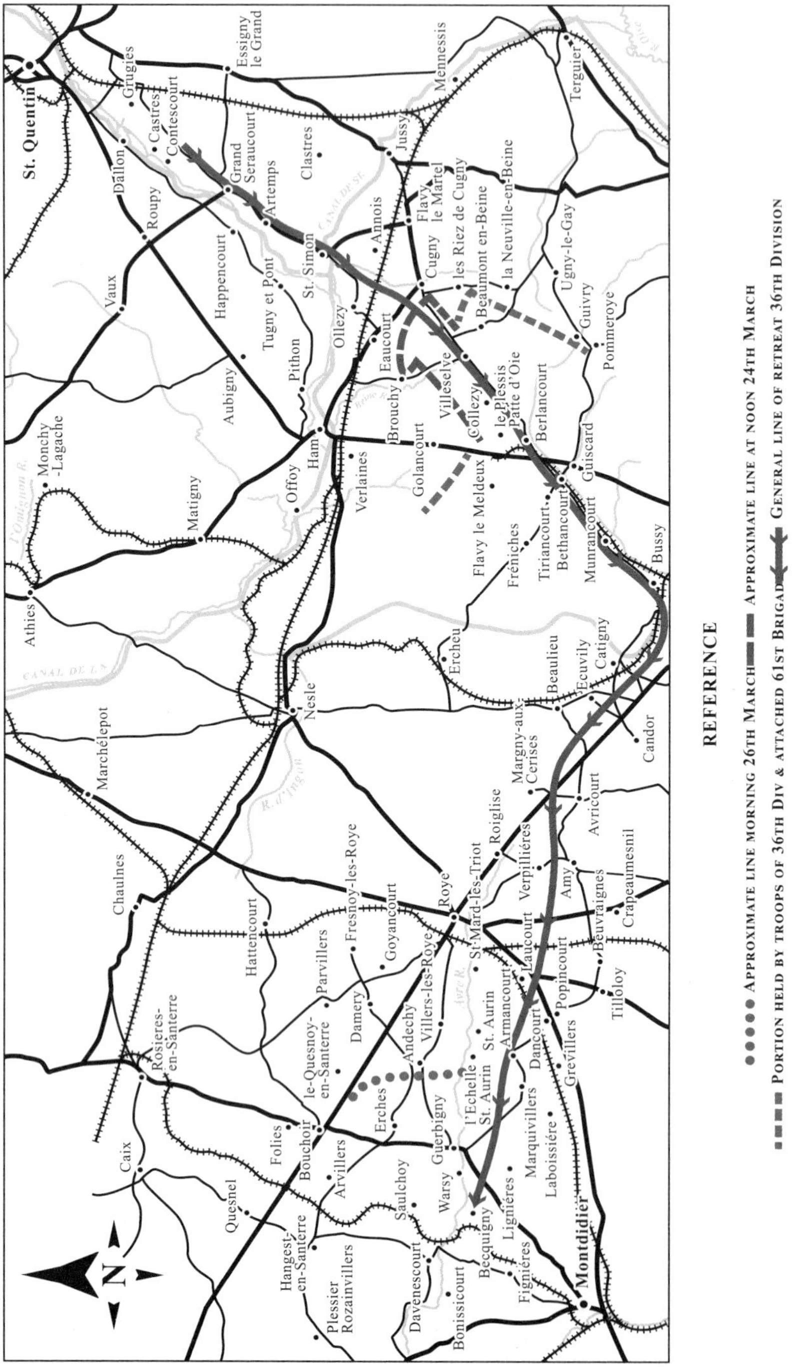

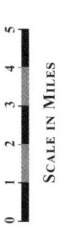

REFERENCE

●●●●● APPROXIMATE LINE MORNING 26TH MARCH ▬▬▬ APPROXIMATE LINE AT NOON 24TH MARCH

▬ ▬ ▬ PORTION HELD BY TROOPS OF 36TH DIV & ATTACHED 61ST BRIGADE ➤ GENERAL LINE OF RETREAT 36TH DIVISION

SCALE IN MILES

0 1 2 3 4 5

Map 17 Route of retreat.

broken in his line west of Montdidier and to ask for every man I had. I gave them of course and the poor devils who have been fighting for seven days without rest had to drag themselves out to a village called Coullemelle where we took up a position.[83]

The problem for Nugent was that all his three Brigades were in different locations – most of 107th Brigade was at Sourdon, 108th Brigade was making its way to Sourdon from Arvillers and 109th Brigade was at Chirmont also en route to Sourdon. All had to be instructed to make for Coullemelle as fast as possible, with most arriving there around 5:00 p.m.[84] By the time they had arrived however, they were informed that a counter-attack had taken place and the situation had been resolved. It was anticipated that the enemy might have carried out some form of attack from the nearby village of Mesnil-St-Georges in the early hours of 29 March, so the 36th Division troops were billeted in houses in Coullemelle on standby, the night being cold and wet.

As nothing had happened by the early hours of the morning, a reconnaissance party of 20 men from 1st Royal Irish Rifles under the command of Captain Harry Francis Tayler checked the nearby villages of Villers-Tourmelle and Cantigny but found only French troops there.

After seven days continuous fighting whilst conducting a withdrawal, this patrol was the last action in which the 36th Division was involved in in the opening battle of the *Kaiserschlacht*.

By the afternoon of 29 March, all three brigades had been released by the French and orders were issued to make for Saleux, on the southern outskirts of Amiens where arrangements were in hand to remove them by train from the battlefield. During this march through many small villages, the weather had turned inclement. Although the majority of troops had arrived by the evening of 30 March, no trains were available until the following morning. This necessitated a cold and wet stay at the side of the road for the exhausted troops. The next day, the first train departed at 9:00 a.m. and the second at 11:00 a.m. The personnel attached to 107th Brigade detrained at Gamaches, 40 miles away and marched to billets in a number of outlying villages. Both 108th and 109th Brigade personnel continued by train to the village of Eu near the French coast at Le Treport, a further six miles distant and when they detrained, marched to billets in surrounding villages, the 1st Royal Irish Fusiliers being billeted in the pre-war holiday resort of Ault-sur-Mer.

Whilst the officers and men were able to get some well-deserved rest, their commanding officer knew that the rest period was likely to be short. Writing to his wife on 1 April 1918, he shared the feelings of disbelief and utter exhaustion that many under his command must also have experienced:

83   PRONI D3835/E/2/17/15: Farren Connell papers.
84   The village of Coullemelle is four and a half miles south-east of Sourdon and seven and a half miles north-west of Montdidier.

One can hardly realise the nine days of nightmare really existed. I seem to want to do nothing but sleep. Everything passed so quickly, and the strain was so great, and one was so strung up that now the tension suddenly has relaxed, it seems as if I had never gone through the time.[85]

The feelings of exhaustion for all ranks were understandable. During the course of their withdrawal, the Division had retreated 167.8 kilometres, just short of 105 miles.[86]

85   PRONI D3835/E/2/17/17: Farren Connell papers.
86   TNA: WO 95/2502/3: Figures contained within 1st Battalion Royal Irish Rifles war diary.

7

Casualties

Excuse me taking the liberty of writing to you, but I have a boy in the 15th which I have not heard anything about since the battle commenced. He was attached to Battn. Hqrs as a runner he belonged to D Coy. I wrote the officer of his company and got no answer.[1]

      Extract from a letter sent by Mrs Margaret Johnston, Lilliput Street, Belfast in April 1918 to 2nd Lieutenant Samuel Douglas Irons enquiring about the fate of her son, Rifleman William Johnston 19/634 15th battalion Royal Irish Rifles.

If the remaining officers and men of the Division believed that they were in for a long period of rest and recuperation, they were sadly mistaken. A warning order was issued to the Division on 2 April, ordering them to prepare to move north to the area of Ypres the following day. The reason that the depleted Division was being ushered north with undue haste, emanated from a developing intelligence picture. The German High Command had correctly predicted that the Allies would send reinforcements to defend the strategically important town of Amiens. In doing so, they had weakened their position in other areas. The Germans then believed that the time was right to launch the next phases of their offensive which were codenamed *Operation Mars*, which took place around Arras and *Operation Georgette* at Ypres. The aim of *Operation Georgette* which necessitated hasty redeployment of the division, was to capture key supply routes and cut off the British Second Army at Ypres.

In order to combat this move, nine Divisions who had fought in *Operation Michael*, including the 36th (Ulster) Division, were rushed north to the area of the France/ Belgium border in the early days of April. In the two days available to the depleted units of the Division, much reorganisation had gone on. The most pressing issue was reinforcements to bring the frontline battalions up to somewhere near active service strength. Fortuitously, a ready-made supply was to hand, the three Entrenching

---

1   Original letter held by the Royal Ulster Rifles Museum, Waring Street, Belfast.

battalions that had been raised from the surplus personnel identified following the reorganisation of the Division some six weeks before.

Although all three Entrenching battalions had taken part in the defensive action of the last week of March, they had suffered less heavily than the infantry battalions of 36th Division. This was despite the fact that when they were designated as what were basically large working parties, they had had their Lewis Guns removed. For a frontline infantry unit, this deprived them of their main infantry support weapon and one which played an integral role in any offensive or defensive manoeuvres to be carried out by the battalion. The loss of their Lewis Guns was keenly felt by the men, but designation as an Entrenching Battalion had hidden benefits as the commanding officer of 23rd Entrenching Battalion, Lieutenant Colonel the Hon. Odo Vivian (Lord Swansea) commented:

> I should like to emphasize that when these battalions were made into Entrenching battalions they had their Lewis Guns taken away. Had they had Lewis Guns during the action they could have made their defence much stronger. They took one Lewis Gun from a demoralised Pioneer Battalion during the retirement and used it with good effect. The personnel of the battalion were in great form when they were working as an Entrenching Battalion. We did more infantry training when we were off digging than we were able to do when we were in the trenches.[2]

Perhaps being employed on labouring duties for a period of six weeks was as good as a rest from the rigours of the front line as suggested by Lieutenant Colonel Vivian, but the hypothetical question remains as to what difference if any it would have made, to have had the 3,000 men of these battalions available to construct defences on the Divisional front and bolster the Forward or Battle Zones? In hindsight, it would have been more effective to have left these battalions under Divisional, instead of Corps control and they could have been utilised to greater effect under a command system that was recognised by all.

As it was, over the first week of April, the three battalions were broken up and distributed to reinforce the existing battalions as indicated below:[3]

21st Entrenching Battalion
12 officers and 107 other ranks (formerly from 10th Inniskillings) to 2nd Inniskillings[4]
Three officers and 33 other ranks to 1st Royal Irish Rifles
Six officers and 133 other ranks to 2nd Royal Irish Rifles

2   TNA: WO 95/664/7: 23rd Entrenching Battalion war diary.
3   The figures are taken where they exist from battalion war diaries as there are discrepancies between the totals recorded by the battalions and those recorded by brigades.
4   TNA: WO 95/2510/2: This battalion received a further 308 reinforcements on 7 April.

Three officers and 340 other ranks to 15th Royal Irish Rifles

Major JD McCallum DSO took command of 15th Royal Irish Rifles, replacing Captain PM Miller, who had commanded the remnants of 15th Rifles with distinction since 21 March.

22nd Entrenching Battalion

There is little detail contained within the battalion war diary, but from what does exist it can be established that the battalion strength was 26 Officers and 750 other ranks at the start of the offensive. Some were undoubtedly killed, including the Commanding Officer, Lieutenant Colonel Blair-Oliphant DSO, who was severely wounded on 28 March and died on 6 April. The remainder appear to have been transferred in their entirety to 12th Battalion Royal Irish Rifles. The war diary of 108th Infantry Brigade indicates that eight officers and 330 other ranks left 22nd Entrenching Battalion for 12th Rifles.[5] The war diary of this battalion simply states, 'a reinforcement arrived from 22nd Entrenching Battalion.'[6]

23rd Entrenching Battalion

Four officers and 160 other ranks to 1st Battalion Royal Irish Rifles

Three officers and 123 other ranks to 2nd Battalion Royal Irish Rifles

Three officers and 120 other ranks to 15th Battalion Royal Irish Rifles

11 officers and 93 other ranks to 1st Battalion Royal Inniskilling Fusiliers.[7]

Apart from the redistribution of the officers and men of the Entrenching battalions, thousands more reinforcements were sent to join the battalions of 36th Division, further detail being available in the footnotes. At this stage, there was no pretence at trying to retain an Ulster or Irish ethos when allocating replacements. The drafts contained mostly 18 or 19-year-olds who hailed from across the United Kingdom and all with little or no experience of soldiering.

The move to the Ypres Salient necessitated a transfer from XVIII Corps to II Corps. The Commander XVIII Corps, Lieutenant General Sir Ivor Maxse, wrote to Major General Nugent on 4 April:

> Orders having been received for the move of the 36th Division from the XVIII Corps to another area, I wish to place on record my appreciation of the services rendered by the Division during the arduous operations and strenuous fighting which commenced on 21st March near St Quentin and terminated on the River

---

5   TNA: WO 95/2504/3: 108th Infantry brigade war diary.
6   TNA: WO 95/2506/2: 12th Battalion Royal Irish Rifles war diary. On 7 April, this battalion received a further draft of 434 replacements.
7   The 1st Inniskillings received a further 300 reinforcements on 6 April.

Avre, near Moreuil on the 30th March 1918…I wish to thank all ranks of the 36th Division for the fighting spirit they have displayed and to remind them that further deeds of gallantry will be required of them in the coming months. May good fortune attend them in all their future enterprises.[8]

By 8 April, a week after the end of the arduous retreat, the Division was back in the front line, having relieved the 1st Division near Poelcappelle, six miles north of Ypres. The fine words of Lieutenant General Maxse were however, of little benefit to the thousands of Ulster Division men who became casualties during the last week of March.

To try and accurately identify the total number of British and Commonwealth casualties during the offensive was recognised at an early stage to be an extremely difficult process. In the *Official History*, Edmonds (1935) observed:

Only the gross, uncorrected casualties, reported soon after events can be given, and the various sets available do not always agree, do not cover quite the same periods and do not sometimes cover all the arms of the service. To investigate the figures thoroughly… was quite beyond the powers of the small staff of the Historical Section. To take the Picardy battle of 21 March-5 April, the esti-mated casualties for cavalry and infantry alone from 21-31 March are given in the Adjutant General's War Diary as 4,477 officers and 119,985 other ranks… By adding together the casualties given in the Divisional and other War Diaries, some in the General Staff papers, some in the A and Q Staffs which seem to give the most reliable figures for the period 21 March-5 April, a higher total is reached – 178,000… By deduction of Missing who returned this becomes 160,000. Of this some 22,000 were probably killed, 96,000 wounded and 42,000 unwounded prisoners.[9]

But what of the casualties of the Ulster Division?

As is mentioned in the introduction, according to Edmonds (1935), the 36th (Ulster) Division sustained 7,310 casualties (dead, wounded and missing) during its period of involvement.[10] This figure was later revised in the following days when strag-glers and those mixed up with other units returned, to 6,109. This figure may not be even correct and is certainly disputed by the 36th Division historian who claims:

8   TNA: WO 95/2492/2: 36th (Ulster) Division war diary.
9   Edmonds, *Military Operations France and Belgium 1918*, Volume II Note 1 pp. 488-9.
10   Edmonds, Volume II, Note 1, p. 491.

The total casualties in the Division in the ten days from March 21st were 7,252. Of these 185 officers and 5,659 other ranks were reported missing. Perhaps four-fifths of these were prisoners of war, wounded or unwounded.[11]

However, what remains undisputed is that the Ulster Division sustained the greatest casualty total of any Division attached to XVIII Corps during their seven days of fighting:

Table 1 Casualties 21 March-5 April by Divisions in XVIII Corps

Division	Total Casualties
36th	6109
30th	5051
61st	5933
20th	5004

Figures reproduced from Edmonds (1935)[12]

In carrying out research for this book, efforts have been made to try and identify the number of men attached to the Ulster Division who were killed during the Division's involvement in the battle. At the outset, I wish to state that this should not be regarded as a definitive list. To provide some form of parameters, I decided to include all those who fell during the battle from the opening of the offensive on 21 March until the remnants of the Division arrived at their billets close to the French coast on 31 March. These dates automatically exclude those who died of wounds subsequent to these dates and those who succumbed to wounds or illness whilst incarcerated in German prisoner of war camps.

The main inhibitor to accurate research is the absence of original records. Research was therefore carried out primarily utilising the Commonwealth War Graves Commission website, the Ancestry website and the Soldiers Died in the Great War database. The latter contains the caveat: *The original versions of both Soldiers Died in the Great War 1914-1919 and Officers Died in the Great War 1914-1919 unfortunately contain many errors. They were made at the time.* For that reason, the figures elicited from the CWGC website have to be regarded as being closer to the correct figure. The word 'closer' is intentional as I and others involved in Great War research have come across many instances of errors within the CWGC database, which to their credit, the CWGC devote a team to analysing and researching eligibility for inclusion in their records. Focusing on those who served with the Division during this time period also excludes many men who, during the reorganisation of the British Army in January

11   Falls, *History of the 36th (Ulster) Division*, p. 232.
12   Edmonds, *Military Operations France and Belgium 1918*, p. 491

and February 1918 were posted to Entrenching Battalions which came under Corps control. As we have seen, of the three Entrenching battalions formed from disbanded 36th (Ulster) Division battalions, figures for 21st Entrenching battalion have been included for the period that they were attached to the Division, 23-31 March (prior to this they were attached to 30th Division, but lost touch with them in the confusion of the withdrawal). Totals of those killed whilst serving with the 22nd Entrenching battalion who came under 18 Corps command throughout – 47, and 23rd Entrenching battalion who came under the command of 30th Division – 14, have therefore not been included. A further complicating factor is that following the reorganisation in January 1918, records indicate that some men appear to have retained their original battalion affiliation. This is the case for men from 8th, 9th, 10th, 11th and 14th Royal Irish Rifles as well as 10th and 11th Inniskillings, and this affiliation appears in available records despite the battalions having been disbanded in February 1918. Given these limitations, the totals found are as highlighted below:

Table 2.

Unit	Recorded as Killed 21-31 March 1918	Notes
107th Infantry Bde		
15th Royal Irish Rifles	76	
1st Royal Irish Rifles	90	
2nd Royal Irish Rifles	133	
108th Infantry Bde		
12th Royal Irish Rifles	51	
1st Royal Irish Fusiliers	64	
9th Royal Irish Fusiliers	40	
109th Infantry Bde		
1st Royal Inniskilling Fusiliers	90	
2nd Royal Inniskilling Fusiliers	62	
9th Royal Inniskilling Fusiliers	107	
Divisional		
16th Royal Irish Rifles	31	
21st Entrenching Battalion	8	Battalion attached to 36th Division 23-31 March
36th Battalion Machine Gun Corps	28	
36th Divisional Signal Company	3	
RAMC		
110th Field Ambulance RAMC	1	

Unit	Recorded as Killed 21-31 March 1918	Notes
Royal Engineers		
121st Field Company	11	
122nd Field Company	5	
Royal Artillery		
153rd Brigade RFA	3	
173rd Brigade RFA	21	
61st Brigade		Brigade attached to 36th Division 21-25 March
7th Duke of Cornwall's Light Infantry	**30**	
7th Somerset Light Infantry	**43**	
12th King's (Liverpool) Regiment	**30**	
Retained numbers		
8th Royal Irish Rifles	1	
9th Royal Irish Rifles	2	
10th Royal Irish Rifles	3	
11th Royal Irish Rifles	5	
14th Royal Irish Rifles	19	
10th Royal Inniskilling Fusiliers	7	
11th Royal Inniskilling Fusiliers	2	
Total	**966**	

The situation around the accurate calculation of casualties from the Province of Ulster is a complex one. It will be recalled that at the formation of the Division in 1914, Lord Kitchener sent for Colonel Thomas Edgecumbe Hickman, an MP and President of the British League for the Defence of Ulster who acted as Inspector General for the UVF and stated, 'I want the Ulster Volunteers'.[13] It was on this basis that the Ulster Division was recruited, with units of the UVF enlisting en masse to form battalions and then Brigades of the Division. Whilst it would be unwise to claim that every member of the Division was an Ulsterman, the greatest proportion were. Following the horrendous casualties suffered on the Somme and coupled with the political machinations concerning recruiting in Ireland, it could be said that the Ulster presence and ethos began to diminish as soon as the Division embarked for France in October 1915. Certainly, by the time the German Spring Offensive of 1918 began, the Ulster ethos was much diminished. To illustrate this, I have carried out some analysis concerning fatalities and as highlighted above, this was not a straightforward exercise

13   Falls, *History of the 36th (Ulster) Division*, p. 3

due to missing and incomplete records. When these factors were taken into consideration, a total of 966 fatalities were identified of men attached to the Division who fell
in the period 21-31 March 1918. Of these, 103 belonged to the 61st Infantry Brigade
and for the purposes of this exercise were discounted, giving a total of 863. Of this
figure, 330 fell on the opening day of the offensive, 21 March. Each of the 863 fatalities were researched using the Soldiers Died in the Great War and Ireland's Memorial
Records databases to establish those who were 'born, resided or enlisted' in any of the
nine counties of Ulster. Of the 863, no identifiable records could be established for
nine. Of the remainder, research established that 442 men had such a connection with
the Province. This represents just over 51.2 percent of the fatalities. A further 49 or 5.6
percent were born in other counties of Ireland.

Given the limitations of the information available to carry out the analysis, if the
total numbers of those killed with Ulster connections are taken as representative of
the rest of the Division, it is possible that in March 1918, over three and a half years
after its formation, the Division could still, just, claim to be the 'Ulster' Division.

A list of all those identified as having been killed can be accessed via the following link
http://www.helion.co.uk/LWiM_Appendix.pdf

Analysis of the records of the fatalities also illustrates the efforts of military authorities to plug the gaps caused by the downturn in recruiting in Ireland. Of the 863
killed, 162 were men who had previously served in 25 different Regiments traditionally recruiting across England. Of these, 35 men had previously been attached to the
London Regiment and 52 had been attached to the Army Service Corps. The prepon-
derance of men from the Army Service Corps is of interest as these were men who
had enlisted as logistics personnel, drivers and other tradesmen and although trained
as infantrymen, would not have been used to the rigours of life and consequent risks
to life in a frontline infantry battalion.

A list of the previous Regiments and the number who died serving with the Ulster Division
is contained in Appendix I.

If the fate of just one of the infantry brigades is examined in closer detail, the
impact of the offensive on the organisation and effectiveness of the Division can be
recognised. Records pertaining to 108th Infantry Brigade are available and make for
interesting reading. On 1 March 1918, Brigade strength returns record the following:

Brigade Headquarters – 24
12th Royal Irish Rifles – 51 Officers, 1031 Other Ranks = 1082
1st Royal Irish Fusiliers – 51 Officers, 1195 Other Ranks = 1246
9th Royal Irish Fusiliers – 46 Officers, 1080 Other Ranks = 1126
108th Trench Mortar Battery – 2 Officers, 46 Other Ranks = 48
Total for Brigade – 3526[14]

---

14   TNA: WO 95/2504/3 108th Infantry Brigade war diary.

After the final action of 28 March, the Brigade war diary records the strength of the Brigade as 14 officers and 321 other ranks – 8.4 percent of the figure of 1 March. Obviously, this figure was taken when the withdrawal was still ongoing and there was confusion surrounding the locations of units. By 25 April, Brigade Headquarters had drawn up a narrative of the withdrawal which is contained within the Brigade war diary.[15] This narrative includes strength totals for each of the units comprising the Brigade on 31 March 1918. These totals were taken when those men who had been attached to other units in the withdrawal had returned and those lightly wounded had returned to their units. In the circumstances, these figures can be regarded as the most accurate available:

Brigade Headquarters – 23
12th Royal Irish Rifles – 16 Officers, 351 Other Ranks = 367
1st Royal Irish Fusiliers – 22 Officers, 461 Other Ranks = 483
9th Royal Irish Fusiliers – 21 Officers, 658 Other Ranks = 679
108th Trench Mortar Battery – 2 Officers, 24 Other Ranks = 26
Total – 1578[16]

This total shows that during the month of March and most likely in the final week, the Brigade lost 1948 officers and men, or 55.3 percent of their total strength.

Research has identified the following fatalities suffered by each battalion in the Brigade:

12th Royal Irish Rifles – 51
1st Royal Irish Fusiliers – 64
9th Royal Irish Fusiliers – 40
Total fatalities – 155

The Brigade war diary indicates that a total of 151 men were wounded.[17] This figure appears unusually low when compared with those killed. In Mitchell & Smith (1931) *Medical Services, Casualties and Medical Statistics of the Great War*, the ratio of killed to wounded in the British Expeditionary Force in France in 1918 was given as 1:7.8.[18] If this ratio is used, the total wounded within 108th Infantry Brigade would be 1209. Given that this equates to conditions from lightly wounded to life threatening wounds, this figure may be close to being correct.

---

15   TNA: WO 95/2504/3 108th Infantry Brigade war diary.
16   Ibid.
17   Ibid.
18   Major Thomas Mitchell & Miss GM Smith, *Official History of the War. Medical Services. Casualties and medical statistics of the Great War* (London: Imperial War Museum reprint of 1931 edition) p. 169, Table 6.

This leaves the issue of those missing, many of whom would also have been amongst the wounded. It is without doubt that the vast majority of these men were taken prisoner. Exact figures of those taken prisoner during the offensive are not available. Edmonds (1935) deduces that in the period 21 March-5 April, a total of 42,000 officers and men became prisoners, the greatest proportion of these being captured on the opening day of the offensive.[19] Respected commentators, Middlebrook (1978) and Lewis-Stempel (2014) agree with this assertion, calculating that around 21,000 prisoners were taken by the Germans on 21 March alone.[20] As we have seen above, Falls (1922) claims that 185 officers and 5,659 other ranks were reported missing with perhaps four-fifths prisoners of war, wounded or unwounded.[21] This would give a total of those in the Division taken prisoner as 4,675. Unfortunately, due to the unavailability of accurate records, it is impossible to state what the exact figure is, but if we regard 108th Brigade as being roughly a third of the Divisional strength, research indicates that they had a total of 1576 men recorded as missing, the great majority of whom it must be assumed ended up as prisoners. As roughly one third of the strength of the Division, if this figure is extrapolated for the whole Division, it gives a total of 4,728, reasonably close to Fall's 1922 assertion.

Records are available however, in relation to officers. Research indicates that 144 officers from the Division were taken prisoner between 21-31 March 1918.[22] If we relate these figures to 108th Brigade, the following numbers of officers from each battalion were taken prisoner:

12th Royal Irish Rifles – 25
1st Royal Irish Fusiliers – 17
9th Royal Irish Fusiliers – 13

A full list of all officers identified as having been taken prisoner is included at Appendix II.

The casualties of all descriptions suffered by 108th Brigade and the remainder of the Division represented a severe loss of experience which would prove impossible to replace. With the arrival of reinforcements hailing from throughout the United Kingdom, the 'Ulster' ethos of the Division was to be further diminished.

Figures alone however, cannot describe the full impact of the offensive on the Ulster Division. It is the stories of the men themselves which best illustrates the human cost, not only to the men at the front, but also those waiting at home.

Lieutenant Samuel Douglas Irons aged 21 was from Edenballymore House, Londonderry. He had originally enlisted in the Royal Irish Rifles as a Rifleman but

19   Edmonds, *Military Operations France and Belgium 1918*, Volume II, p. 491.
20   Middlebrook, *The Kaiser's Battle* p. 322.
21   Falls, *History of the 36th (Ulster) Division*, p. 232.
22   Ancestry, British Officer Prisoners of War 1914-1918 <http://www.ancestry.co.uk> (Accessed various dates November 2015).

had been commissioned in 1917 and posted to 15th Royal Irish Rifles. Following the retreat, he had the unenviable task of conversing with family members of those reported missing. On 23 April 1918, he received two letters from equally anxious mothers. The first is from Mrs Margaret Johnston of Lilliput Street, Belfast, concerning her eldest son, 20 years old Rifleman William John Johnston, 19/634:

> Sir,
> Excuse me taking the liberty of writing to you, but I have a boy in the 15th which I have not heard anything about since the battle commenced. He was attached to Battn. Hqrs as a runner he belonged to D Coy. I wrote the Officer of his company and got no answer. I heard of you coming through it and I wrote to see if you knew anything or could find out anything and let me know as I am very uneasy about him. His address was No 634 Rfm Wm Johnston D Coy 15 RIR attached Battn Hqrs, BEF France.
> I remain your humble servant, Mrs Johnston
> PS. His last letter was dated 19th March

The second letter was from Mrs Maryanne Nevin of Larne Street, Ballymena, enquiring about her only son, 22 years old Serjeant William Nevin, 18/239:

> Dear Mr Irons
> Your note of sympathy to hand for which I thank you. I had every doubt of my son being posted as missing, as I have had no news from him since the advance of the 21st inst. Again, I thank you for your kind information and any further news you may receive shall be thankfully acknowledged by me as news of any description are better than being kept in suspense. Any news I may receive I shall forward on to you.
> Yours sincerely,
> Mrs W Nevin[23]

For two mothers who had not heard anything from their sons in over a month, the anxiety of waiting for news as many other mothers were, must have been horrendous. As it turned out, there were two different outcomes.

Nothing was ever heard of Rifleman William Johnston again. He was presumed dead and is commemorated on the Pozieres Memorial to the Missing. In December 1919, his father, also named William John received £17-02-09s from the War Office, the balance of William's pay and allowances, which include a War Gratuity of £8-00-00.

23   The originals of both letters are held by the Royal Ulster Rifles Museum, Belfast and are reproduced with kind permission.

By contrast, there was more positive news in relation to Serjeant Nevin. He was amongst the many who were captured (ironically on his 22nd birthday) and he spent the remainder of the war at Lagensalza prisoner of war camp, Thuringia, Germany.

The chaos of the withdrawal resulted in many men being separated from their units, with most being able to re-join in subsequent days. Research has identified however, at least one case where the confused circumstances of the retreat may have provided a unique opportunity. Thirty-four-year old Private Peter Fleming 3594 was attached to the 1st Royal Irish Fusiliers. He was initially reported as 'Missing' on 21 March and then was subsequently 'Presumed Dead'. He has no known grave and his name appears on no memorial in France. In March 1920, his widow Mary from Dimsdale Street, Belfast, received a gratuity of £16-00-00 from the War Office from whom she was also in receipt of a pension of 33 shillings and ninepence per week for herself and four children. A year later in March 1921, the Royal Irish Constabulary reported that an attempt to locate Mary Fleming for the Infantry Records Office, Dublin, at the home address had failed and that it was reported that she had moved, possibly to Glasgow, but had not been in touch with any of her friends. Medal records show that Peter Fleming's British War Medal and Allied Victory Medal were issued and returned in 1923, presumably as the location of the next of kin could not be clarified. Records however indicate that in June 1939, a man called in person to claim the medals, which were handed over – the inference being that this person purported to be Peter Fleming. Enquiries must have been made into the circumstances of

Medal Index Card, Private Peter Fleming. (Open source)

the medal issue, for his medal index card was annotated; 'subsequently traced as a deserter.' Is it possible that Peter Fleming used the chaos of the retreat to his own advantage, and caused himself to disappear to start a new life with his wife and children? Research shows that Peter Fleming had already served in the Royal Irish Fusiliers for 12 years before the outbreak of war, being discharged on completion of his period of engagement in December 1913 and had re-enlisted for the duration of the war in June 1915. During his military service he had previously been absent without leave on three occasions. The truth of what happened to Peter Fleming in March 1918 remains a mystery.

For those taken prisoner, there were a range of experiences in captivity. As has already been seen, in the heat of battle the act of surrendering to an adversary high on adrenalin was a risky procedure, as Captain Miller of 2nd Inniskillings discovered when he was shot by a German who saw that he still had possession of a revolver. Despite the obvious risks of stray bullets, which appears to have been the cause of death of Captain Hugh Baillie, 16th Royal Irish Rifles, fighting to the last minute and then laying down your weapons was not likely to gain a favourable response from the attackers. In the circumstances of the offensive, there are numerous cases where those in command having fought well, realised the hopelessness of the situation they were in and communicated a wish to surrender. There are also cases where the Germans, realising their numerical superiority, decided to negotiate the surrender of a defensive position rather than commit troops to an assault which could only have one ending, but would result in futile loss of life.

The treatment of prisoners of war is an emotive subject and could provide sufficient material for a book on its own. Here however, I want to concentrate on the experiences of men from the Ulster Division for whom the battle did not finish at the end of March 1918.

Whilst much is known of German prisoner of war camps in the 1939-45 conflict, there has not been the same focus of attention of those in the Great War. Whilst meticulous preparation went into the plans for the prosecution of the offensive from the German side, research indicates that wholly inadequate preparations were made for the management of prisoners. It is an indisputable fact that the Germans were overwhelmed by the numbers of prisoners coming under their control and that both the German Army and the German civilian populace were short of supplies of every kind, and this is reflected in the varying experiences of men who found themselves, 'guests of the Kaiser.'

There were certain internationally agreed norms that governed the management and treatment of prisoners. The most recognisable was the Geneva Convention which was first agreed in 1864 and updated in 1906. The Hague Convention of 1907 agreed protocols for the conduct of war on both land and sea and along with the Geneva Convention provided a comprehensive set of rules on the treatment of prisoners. Both Britain and Germany had ratified these Conventions and as such had agreed to adhere to their requirements. In summary these included:

- Prisoners were the responsibility of the Government of the force that captured them
- Prisoners should be treated humanely
- Prisoners were to be clothed, fed, and accommodated on the same basis as the troops of the capturing government.
- Personal belongings were to remain with the prisoner
- Soldiers (but not officers) could be used as labour, but not excessively or in connection with operations of war and they were to be paid for their labour
- Medical personnel were not to be treated as prisoners of war, but if called upon were to continue their duties under enemy supervision.[24]

With these protocols in mind, it is of interest to read the accounts of some from the Division who were taken prisoner.

As previously seen, Captain Charles Miller 2nd Inniskillings was wounded and taken prisoner in the vicinity of Boadicea Redoubt on the morning of 21 March:

> At the time when my sight came back to me I was in a barn apparently attached to a German dressing station at some depot not far behind the lines as there was a constant movement of troops through it. I was at once marched off to join a lot of prisoners in another part of the small town and we were put into cattle trucks and started off for some unknown destination. The time that follows is very blurred in my memory. It seemed to be constant railway travelling, sometimes in Third Class compartments, sometimes in cattle trucks. In the former I had to stand up practically the whole time owing to the wound in my thigh. Why we were being carted all round Germany I don't know, but I imagine that all the prison camps were full, there was a complete breakdown in arrangements and they didn't know what to do with us. I was in a beastly state, filthy because there was hardly ever any opportunity to wash, bearded because there was no such thing as a razor available, arm in a sling, neck bandaged, barely able to walk, and all one side of my tunic caked with dried blood...This time we disembarked at Karlsruhe and I remember that some women on the platform had a spit at us, but very few women can spit straight.[25]

As an officer, Captain Miller was fairly lucky. Karlsruhe prisoner of war camp had been in operation for a number of years and had facilities in place where he was able to clean himself up and replace his underclothing. An officer's canteen was also available which was well stocked with necessities sent out by charitable and benevolent institutions in the United Kingdom. Karlsruhe was however, only a clearing camp

---

24   John Yarnall, *Barbed Wire and Disease: British and German Prisoners of War 1914-19* (Stroud: Spellmount, 2011), pp. 9-10.
25   IWM Doc.4118 Captain Charles C Miller papers.

and once his particulars were recorded and verified, he was sent to an officer's camp at Mainz which was to be his home for the rest of the war. The contrast with Karlsruhe was stark:

> This was a sort of fortress on a hill outside the town. There were three blocks of buildings each under the command of a German officer. I suppose the barracks were meant to accommodate about 250 men all told, but we were 600 officer prisoners plus about 50 Tommies who were detailed for the job of orderlies... Mainz was a pretty awful experience. To begin with there was the food question. So far as British prisoners were concerned it was a new camp and therefore a starvation camp, as no food could come from outside till friends and authorities in England were aware of its existence. All communication went by Holland and was censored, so it was certain that it would be a long time before the first British parcels could be received...To each officer there was an issue every five days of a medium size loaf of German bread and a small quantity of beet sugar... it was frightfully difficult to make it last five days, especially at night-time when one was overpowered by hunger and could not sleep. Every morning when the orderly summoned the room he brought in a large metal jug filled with what looked like coffee but was really a coffee substitute made from acorns and almost as bitter as quinine. That and bread carried you to midday... when you got a plate of gruel simply tasting of greasy water followed by some sort of relish which might be a small piece of dubious sausage or raw fish or sauerkraut made with slivers of swedes or mangels. At 6:00 p.m. you had a similar meal.[26]

This was still preferable to the experience of those in the ranks. Private Henry Emerson 41103, A Company 9th Royal Irish Fusiliers, was from the townland of Foglish, County Fermanagh, close to Fivemiletown, County Tyrone. Aged 31, he had served with the North Irish Horse and transferred to the Royal Irish Fusiliers in 1917 when they were dismounted. He was captured near Nesle on 28 March in what must have been a mopping up exercise by the Germans, as in his account Private Emerson states that his party had been cut off for two days before capture. Along with other prisoners he was marched eight miles to the town of Ham. Private Emerson and his comrades had had no food for three days during the withdrawal prior to their capture. In a report for the War Office he detailed his experiences:

> We were kept one day at Ham. I was never searched or interrogated at all... There were some wounded and men were told off to look after them. The wounded got very little medical attention and there were plenty of bad cases amongst them. We were given water to drink and were not interfered with. I was taken to St Quentin on 30th March. I remained there three weeks. At St Quentin

---

26 IWM Doc.4118 Captain Charles C Miller papers.

we were put in what had been a cottage or cow-house. There were French prisoners there as well. There were no beds or blankets given us and our clothes
were never off us. It was very cold weather and there was no heating apparatus,
not even a roof on the buildings. The food here was a small loaf of black bread
(1,400 grammes of bread to each four men) soup, very thin, once a day, preserved
turnips seemed to be in it; coffee made of burnt barley, tea in the evenings, only
it was not tea, no meat, no fats. There was only a small quantity of each kind of
food and all the men got very low on this diet. No clothes were taken away from
us. I was captured with just the clothes I stood up in. The work I had to do here
was burying the dead. I spent the whole of the three weeks at this. The guard
indulged in plenty of abuse and knocked us about, but I do not know any case
of any man being badly injured. The place we were accommodated in was called
Martin-Henri. We were in big rooms with the roofs all shattered and not wired
round. The latrines were old places dug out in the yard. It was very filthy and
dirty and there was no payment for work.[27]

The accommodation for Private Emerson and his fellow prisoners, was in L'Ecole
Henri Martin at St Quentin which ironically had been the venue for a meeting
between Field Marshal Sir John French and Marshal Joffre on 25 and 26 August 1914
to discuss tactics prior to the Battle of Le Cateau. The building continues to operate
as a High School today.

Another who was taken to St Quentin was Serjeant William Finlay MM, 15th
Royal Irish Rifles who was one of the battalion medics. As per the provisions of the
Geneva and Hague conventions, he was initially treated as a non-combatant by the
Germans:

I and the four RAMC chaps were detained at the hospital to assist with the
wounded. The first 2 1/2 days we were carrying wounded without food of any
description and then they awakened to the fact that if they wanted any more
work done they would have to feed us, so we were sent under charge of a Red
Cross man, or as the Germans call them Sanitators and we were served with a
good issue of thick soup made from horse flesh. I saw them cut the steaks off
some horses that morning. They had been killed by bombs some days previous
when our chaps made an air raid on St Quentin. It was horse flesh that was
always used except on some rare occasions. After about five days stop in a Field
Hospital where most of our time was spent digging graves and burying the dead,
we were transferred to the Palace of Justice which was turned into a hospital.
After my second day there I was attached as Orderly to a German Doctor and
was with him about three weeks and I must say that he was very good and saw

---

27   TNA: WO 161/100/445: War Office. Committee on the Treatment of British Prisoners
of War. Interviews and reports pp. 3194-96.

L'Ecole Henri Martin, St Quentin 2017. (Author's Collection)

that I got plenty of food. His meal hours was different to ours and the first day I was with him I was late for my meals and the cook told me that I would get none if I was not there at the proper time, so I went to the Doctor and told him I had got no food that day. Well, the Cook got a good dressing down and a good shaking as well for it and he told him never to refuse me food no matter what time I came for it, so I had more food than I could eat while I was with the doctor. Often after a stiff spell of work, he would say 'Mongay' and point in the direction of the cookhouse and would always ask when I came back if I got it. He was one of the few good Germans I met and when you did meet one such he was extra good. I will never forget that hospital, it was something frightful the wounds the Germans had incurred in their advance against our chaps. At that time, they were the winners but paid for it heavily in the loss of life and wounds. One German Officer wounded near Amiens told us that their losses compared to the British were five to one.[28]

28   PRONI: D4101 Serjeant William Finlay papers.

Palais de Justice, St Quentin 2017. Presently used as the centre for civic administration in the town. (Author's Collection)

Serjeant Finlay remained carrying out medical duties at the hospital for a month, before his circumstances changed for the worse:

> After about four weeks stay in the hospital along with the RAMC men, we were transferred to the Henri Martin Hospital which was the prison camp and there our hardships commenced. The first day we were not on rations and had to do eight hours plate-laying on the railway as our men had blown up part of the railway sidings at the station in an air raid. We done all sorts of little jobs, such as ammunition loading on limbers, road paving and unloading coal bricks from railway wagons and then one morning the British were fell in in two batches, one party sent off to scour the fields and trenches for dead and another party of which I was a member went off to a spot near Dalons[29] which was marked off as a cemetery. We were set to dig graves and loads of bodies arrived per day in various

---

29   This was the village of Dallon on the outskirts of St Quentin. The remains of 21 British dead buried there were consolidated in Savy New British Cemetery after the war.

stages of decomposition, some fully clothed and some partially clothed. All personal property was taken off them. Any that had their identification marks on them were buried each in his own grave on which was erected a wooden cross with grave number, his name and regiment in English or German. All who could not be identified were buried in a mound. A heavy post was erected, and a large circle described, and the earth dug out and piled up, then a circle of bodies heads to pole was made close around the pole. A foot of earth on top of them and then on top another layer of bodies until about six layers of bodies was made and over this about a foot of earth and then a fresh circle of bodies was commenced and soon the numbers of layers getting less until it sloped down on a level with the field and there it was, a huge mound of British and German soldiers buried together. I thought often of the wives and mothers at home who would never know how their loved ones were lost or where buried. We had about 14 days of this work and then one morning the interpreter instead of sending us off on our work, shouted 'Fall in. The English go to Germany.' About 70 of us were numbered off and the remainder sent to work. We were marched off to another part of the town and joined onto another large party that was waiting for us and so the party of 1000 was marched off, not to Germany, but back to the firing line to a place called Flavy-le-Martel. We had our so-called breakfast at 6:00 a.m. in the morning and marched all that day without food until we reached Flavy at 8:00 p.m. in the evening and then had to fall to and bring down the canvas from the station to a field where we were to erect our marquees. By that time it was dark and about 10:30 p.m. Coffee was served with a slice of bread and jam and we lay down in the field and made ourselves as comfortable as we could until morning. At 6:00 a.m. we were roused for breakfast and then commenced to put up our marquees. In the evening we were told off into two separate working parties, one party going out in the morning, the other going out at midday to relieve them.[30]

Whilst Serjeant Finlay was initially involved in labour that could be justified from a German point of view, Rifleman Robert McGookin from Larne was engaged in labour which was definitely contrary to the conventions:

We were brought to Cugny Wood to work at the erection of the large gun which shelled Paris, this gun was known as Big Bertha… Whilst on this job, our daily routine was as follows. At 4 o'clock in the morning the first batch of men was awakened and given a pint of what was a substitute for coffee, in colour the same, but of course neither sugar or milk in the stuff; a loaf of German bread was divided amongst twelve men which worked out at the rate of one small slice per man. This wasn't much to start on eight hours' heavy work. At a quarter to five we

30   PRONI: D4101 Serjeant William Finlay papers.

set off across the fields. We ate dandelions and plucked nettles which were kept in paper so that they could be boiled back in the camp. When we arrived on the scene to work, we took the places of the men who had been working during the night. They were lined up and marched back to camp. Some men were handed large plugging picks which were used to pack stones under railway sleepers. Now this was very severe work and I saw men drop, completely exhausted, only to be kicked or thumped with a stick back to work again. Other men had to carry sections of rails, cut trees and dig drains alongside the line. The largest party of men were taken to the gun pit, which when completed was twelve feet deep and fifty or sixty feet in diameter... The worst job of all was the tree cutting. If a man was considered to be resting too long, he either got a kick or two or a thump in the ribs with a rifle butt.[31]

Both Serjeant Finlay and Rifleman McGookin were among many men of the Ulster Division who had the misfortune to be detained for a time at the holding camp at Flavy-le-Martel, close to the village of Cugny which had been captured by the Germans in their advance on 24 March. This camp had initially been used by the British to hold German prisoners and as it lay in marshy ground was prone to flooding and had inadequate and unsanitary facilities. When the Germans took control of it however, they used it as a holding camp and serious overcrowding was the norm. So horrendous were the conditions and the treatment meted out to prisoners, that the camp commandant, Captain Emil Muller was one of the few Germans indicted at the Leipzig Trials, established in 1921 to try those suspected of war crimes. A Captain in the Reserve, Emil Muller had been a Barrister in civilian life and took over the management of the camp in April 1918. Claud Mullins was an English barrister who attended the trials as an observer, in his book *The Leipzig Trials* (1921) he described the conditions:

> The camp had shortly before been taken from the English during the March offensive and had been previously used by them as a camp for the temporary reception of German POW's. It was in a wretched condition. It lay in a marshy and completely devastated district, immediately behind the fighting line, where everything was still in constant movement. During the time the English had been in possession of it, it was unfit for human occupation...The Court opined that whilst German prisoners were only there for a few days at most, it was used by the Germans as a semi-permanent camp for well over 1,000 men who were doing heavy work. Description – The outside fence of the camp was only about 200 yards in circumference and the whole area of the camp soon became one large cesspool. The men rapidly got into a filthy and verminous condition and became afflicted with sores. The accommodation was utterly insufficient. The

---

31   Minford et al. *It wasn't all Sunshine*, p. 124.

thousand men were herded in three huts the approximate dimensions of which were 60 x 20 feet. There were no floor boards, and no bedding or camp utensils were supplied. The men had to sleep on the wet ground, and so crowded were the huts that there was not room for all to lie down. The court recognised that Muller had inherited this and had to do his best with it.[32]

Although cognisance was taken of the fact that Muller had inherited the camp in an atrocious condition, it was his behaviour towards the prisoners which was most damning:

> His attitude towards the prisoners was hard and over severe, sometimes even brutal...The court has heard of his ill-treating prisoners by hitting and kicking them. He allowed his staff to treat them in the same manner. Insults were hurled at them... and he habitually struck them when he was on horseback, using a riding cane or walking stick. He thrashed the prisoner Batey with his walking stick. This man became ill while at work outside the camp and although violently attacked by the sentries who did not believe in his inability to work, he refused to work any further. The sentries reported him to the accused on their return and Batey repeated that he was ill and emphatically asked for a doctor. The accused got furious over this as he thought Batey was a malingerer, he then belaboured him. Muller also rode his horse into lines of prisoners, injuring them. Several prisoners complained that Muller habitually took photographs of them even when they were in the agonies of illness. The court accepted that the accused took photographs, especially of the latrine when the prisoners were using it.[33]

Muller was found guilty of nine counts of ill-treatment and was sentenced to six months imprisonment. Muller however, could be regarded as a convenient scapegoat, for it was not only at Flavy-le-Martel where ill-treatment was endemic. Private Henry Emerson of 9th Royal Irish Fusiliers experienced harsh treatment whilst detained at a camp at Esmery-Hallon, south of the town of Ham:

> At Esmery-Hallon, we lived in an old building, no roofs, no beds, no blankets, no protection from the weather. I remained all the time I was there in this building. I had just the clothes I stood up in and nothing else. We worked here as engineers, cutting timber, digging holes and erecting an electric cable. We worked eight hours a day, no night work, no payment received. Worked the eight hours straight through without a spell. The latrines here were very bad, filthy and dirty and a very bad stench. There was plenty of ill-treatment from the guards,

32   Claud Mullins, *The Leipzig Trials: An Account of the War Criminals' Trials and a Study of German Mentality* (London: H. F. & G. Witherby, 1921), p. 67.
33   Ibid, p. 73

abuse and beating with rifles and kicking. This the guard did to anyone, not only when there was a refusal to work.[34]

Whilst in these camps close to the front, the prisoners were in a form of limbo. They had been reported missing and no efforts had been made by the Germans to record details or provide means to contact those at home. For most men of the Ulster Division, time in the initial camps lasted a couple of months and they were then moved to more permanent facilities in Germany. It was only on arrival at these camps that efforts were made at effective administration. Travel was however, a trial in itself and little cognisance was taken of those wounded as Sapper Alfred Henderson of 122nd Field Company Royal Engineers recorded:

We were loaded onto the familiar '40 Hommes ou 8 Chevaux'[35] wagons en route for hospital. In my truck about 15 or 20 of us were laid on the floor and

given one blanket each. The only light came through chinks and splits in the woodwork. A very rough ride with much shunting and jolting in the darkness... It was a great relief when the train finally stopped, and the doors were opened. It was daylight, possibly about 10 o'clock when we arrived in Maubeuge, it was found that there was three dead in the truck.[36]

Corporal Jim Donaghy, 9th Inniskillings from Drumahoe, Londonderry, had a similar experience whilst travelling to the prisoner of war camp at Stendal, in the northern German province of Altmark:

One day we were told that we were being moved to a new camp. They marched us to the railway and put us in cattle trucks for the journey. We didn't know how far we were going,

Corporal Jim Donaghy with his sister Bella.
(Photo courtesy of Jim Duff)

34   TNA: WO 161/100/445: War Office. Committee on the Treatment of British Prisoners of War. Interviews and Reports, p. 3195.
35   Translates as 40 men or 8 horses.
36   IWM Doc.11045 Sapper AE Henderson papers.

but it turned out to be Germany. The trucks were very cramped. You could sit in a crouched position and no more. We travelled all night and the next morning when the train eventually stopped at a station, several men in my truck were dead and others very ill. During all this time we hadn't been given as much as a drink or been allowed to stretch our legs or go to the toilet. We thought we had arrived at the camp and they allowed us to go to the latrine, but we were marched back to the same train a short time later. Each prisoner was given a slice of German black bread and a hot drink that was supposed to be coffee but tasted nothing like it. This was the first food in twenty-four hours. All prisoners boarded the train and we travelled for another day, again without so much as a drink. When we eventually arrived at the camp there were more dead in the truck and we were all in a poor state.[37]

On arrival, or in the days following, registration took place. For Jim Donaghy at Stendal POW Camp, this was carried out by the Red Cross, who also informed anxious families at home. In Sapper Alfred Henderson's case, it was the Germans themselves who undertook the task of registration:

29th April. Arrived at Zerbst (Military Hospital) south east of Magdeburg. It must have been the 2nd May, two days after we arrived that we had a visit from a German in uniform who spoke English perfectly. He recorded our details, name, Regiment etc. He also gave us an official postcard which we could send home. This card gave barest details only and says nothing of condition. I did not date it but the postmark is dated 10th May and it arrived home on 18th May. This was the first indication to my parents that I was alive.[38]

In the case of Sapper Henderson, the arrival of the postcard put an end to two months of agonised waiting for news. In many cases, notification that a loved one was indeed a prisoner of war alleviated financial hardship. This was due to the fact that when a soldier was reported missing, his pay stopped until the matter was clarified. In the case of those identified as

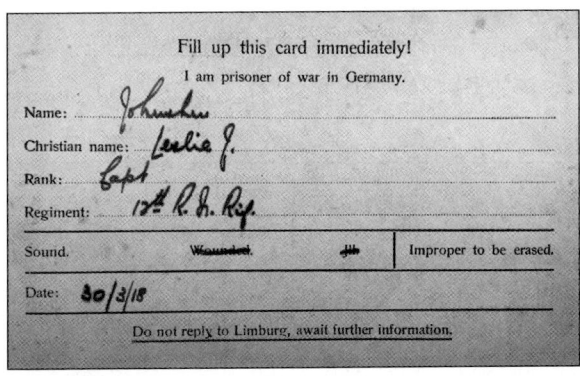

Prisoner of war notification Captain LJ Johnston 12th Battalion Royal Irish Rifles. (Royal Ulster Rifles Museum)

---

37 Mitchell, *Three Cheers for the Derry's*, p. 167.
38 IWM Doc.11045 Sapper AE Henderson papers.

prisoners, pay was backdated to the date they had been reported as missing.

The fact that prisoners were registered, meant that they were entitled to receive parcels to supplement the meagre food rations. Parcels could be sent out by families, but most often they were directed through committees who were organised specifically for the purpose. Amongst these was The Ulster Women's Gift Fund, established by the Ulster Women's Unionist Council. This Fund had been catering for the needs of prisoners from the Ulster Division since early 1915. They in turn were governed by The Central Prisoners of War Committee, based in London. Based in the Old Town Hall, Belfast, the Ulster Women's Gift Fund gave details of the contents which could be included in the parcels sent to POW's in a letter published to raise funds.

These parcels were a Godsend for men on a near starvation diet, although it is fair to say that at this stage of the war, German soldiers and especially civilians had similar diets. Sapper Alfred Henderson observed the privations of the German soldiers shortly after he was captured:

Prisoner of war notification Lieutenant Colonel Lord Farnham 2nd Inniskillings. (PRONI)

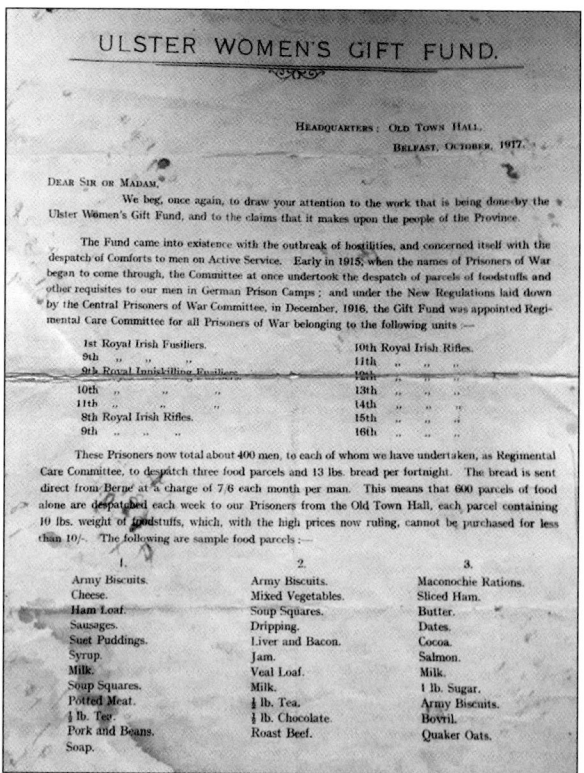

Ulster Women's Gift Fund advice in relation to parcels. (Royal Ulster Rifles Museum)

We received some ersatz coffee and a piece of black bread neither of which we thought much of but were glad of it all the same. Our next meal, the midday one consisted of vegetable soup, there were two or three scraps of stringy meat, never any butter, milk or sugar. It was however, the same that was issued to the other Germans. Our eyes were being opened to the quality and shortage of food being suffered by our enemies…Although I had been very apprehensive at what treatment I was likely to receive in the hands of my enemies I must record that up to now had been no different to that which I could have handed out to their own wounded. They received the same food as given to us. Only recently have I found out that the German soldier at that time of the war only saw meat nine times a month and he had to be on active service for that.[39]

The issue of work also determined how much a prisoner got fed. As Corporal Jim Donaghy recalled:

There was a rule that NCO's and above that, who didn't want to work for the Germans didn't have to. Most of us out of principle wouldn't work for them so because of this we were given just enough food to keep us alive and no more.[40]

In such conditions, food parcels weighing up to 14 pounds from home played a vital role in keeping men alive. The Central Prisoners of War Committee were able to monitor the flow of parcels as each parcel was signed for, as the receipt signed by Captain Leslie Johnston 12th Royal Irish Rifles at Pforzheim POW Camp shows.

Officers however, being spared from the obligation to work had usually enough food to keep body and soul alive and were also able to request comforts from home. In a letter to his wife on 21 April 1918, Lieutenant Colonel Lord Farnham, at the time at Clausthal prisoner of war camp, presented quite a shopping list for consideration:

Now in case my previous letter may have gone wrong, I am going to request some of the things that I require. Parcels of food through whatever is the most convenient parcels committee. Parcels to contain specially, Dripping, Bacon, Jam, Butter, Rice, Curry powder, Tea, Sugar, Chocolate, Quaker's Oats, Nestle's Milk (keeps the best) Fry's Cocoa, Cooks farm eggs – this is some form of concentrated eggs excellent for cooking. Preserved meat, Bottled Fruit and fresh where possible. Coffee, soap for washing clothes, also salt. Shaving soap. Safety Razor (this you can get at Barretts in a flat leather case containing Razor, brush and soap.) Also, patent Gillet strop… Of course, the razor must be a Gillet. There is also some way of sending out sole and heel leather once every six months. This is very necessary. Now about clothes. In my dressing room. One pair brown boots newly soled and

39   IWM Doc.11045 Sapper AE Henderson papers.
40   Mitchell, *Three Cheers for the Derry's* p. 167.

1 pair brown shoes to be soled before sending. Three pairs short, thin drawers, three thin vests. Some thin socks, three thin handkerchiefs, one thin uniform jacket. one thin pair khaki breeches – twill ones with buttons on and one pair of light khaki trousers. Large handkerchiefs, Slippers, Cholera belts.[41] A housewife containing darning wool and needle. Golden Syrup and Cornflour. Also, don't forget to make me some of your own shortbread. I would love that.[42]

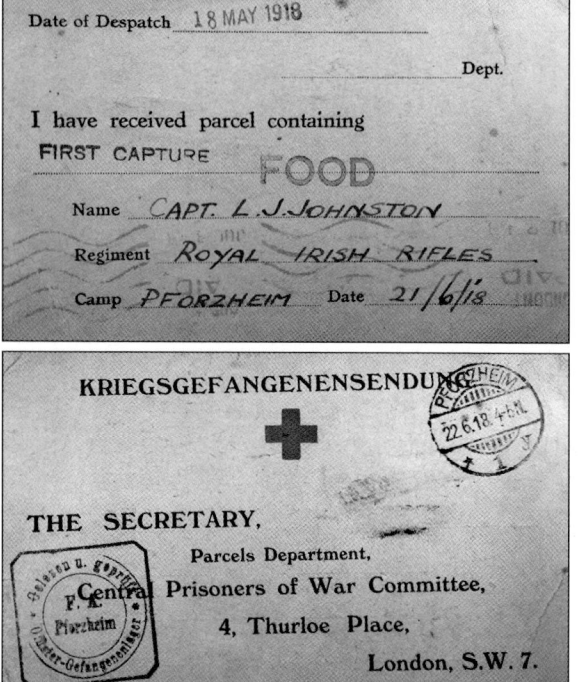

Notification of receipt of food parcel, Captain LJ Johnston Royal Irish Rifles and proof of receipt of food parcel. (Royal Ulster Rifles Museum)

There is no record to indicate whether or not the Lieutenant Colonel received all the items on his wish list. His company commander Captain Charles Miller, still imprisoned at Mainz, was similarly well catered for:

> For the clothing and footwear which I required, my Uncle Robert made himself responsible and he also sent me from time to time a small case of claret. This may sound absurdly luxurious for a prisoner of war, but it was just what I wanted as my blood was very poor and I had a beastly outbreak of boils.[43]

For those men who did work however, life could be a lottery. The most fortunate were sent to work on farms where with little supervision, relationships developed, and it was not uncommon for prisoners to share mealtimes with the farmer's family. These

---

41   A Cholera Belt was a strip of wool or flannel about six feet long and six inches wide which when wrapped around the stomach under a shirt was bizarrely as it may seem now, believed to prevent the disease.
42   PRONI: D3975/E/8/30/3 Farnham papers.
43   IWM Doc. 4118 Captain Charles C Miller papers.

however, were in the minority. Private Robert McGookin of the 12th Royal Irish Rifles whilst at Wittenberg POW Camp was set to work in a Chemical Factory, his job entailing the clearing of ashes from under the boilers – hot and dangerous work on a near starvation diet.[44]

Although most men were detained in prisoner of war camps throughout Germany, some men such as Serjeant William Finlay 15th Royal Irish Rifles, had a remarkably lucky break. Following his capture and initial detention in the St Quentin area, Finlay was transferred to Stendal prisoner of war Camp. At the end of August 1918 however, he was selected to be interned in Switzerland. The Swiss government and government agencies were heavily involved in humanitarian efforts throughout the Great War and operated a scheme whereby sick or injured prisoners from whatever belligerent country were interned for the duration of the war in facilities designed to aid their recovery. The cost of caring for the internees was paid by their respective governments. This was also beneficial to the Swiss, as in an indirect way they received recompense for the decline in their tourist industry. Compared to a prisoner of war camp, the facilities were luxurious. Records indicate that Serjeant Finlay was interned at the Alpine resort of Murren, Switzerland, where accommodation was provided in hotels which were otherwise empty. Finlay remained at this location until he was repatriated following the Armistice.

For the majority however, the daily grind in the POW camps continued. A few, including Private Henry Emerson 9th Royal Irish Fusiliers made successful escape attempts. Private Emerson and Lance Corporal Joseph Bennett 1st Royal Irish Fusiliers, from the Ravenhill Road, Belfast, had remained at various prisoner of war locations in France and had escaped together from Fresnoy-le-Grand near St Quentin on 15 September 1918.

Following the Armistice, those men of the Ulster Division taken prisoner were promptly repatriated, records indicating that nearly all had returned to the United Kingdom by the end of 1918. Not all were in the best of health. Rifleman

Private Henry Emerson 9th Battalion Royal Irish Fusiliers and Lance Corporal Joseph Bennett 1st Battalion Royal Irish Fusiliers. (Great War Ulster Newspaper Archive)

44   Minford et al., *It wasn't all Sunshine*, p. 139.

Andrew Steele aged 20, 12th Royal Irish Rifles from Cairncastle, County Antrim, had been captured with most of his battalion on 21 March and was repatriated on 24 November. His service record indicates that he went before a Medical Board at Dover on 27 November 1918 where it was discovered that he was suffering from, 'multiple wounds, debility and starvation.'[45] Rifleman Steele was however, one of the lucky ones. For some, there was to be no return home.

Some men, such as 20 years old Captain Gordon Deane, 1st Royal Irish Fusiliers, a Doctor's son from Loughgall, County Armagh, succumbed to wounds sustained during the offensive and died in a detention facility at Avesnes-sur-Helpe, France in April 1918.[46] Others fell victim to sickness. One of these was 20 years old Captain John Kemmy Boyle

Private Andrew Steele 12th Battalion Royal Irish Rifles. (Great War Ulster Newspaper Archive)

MC, 2nd battalion Royal Irish Rifles. Captain Boyle was the eldest son of Michael and Nora Boyle from Upper Gardiner Street, Dublin. He had been captured during the stand of the 2nd Rifles at Cugny on 24 March and was imprisoned at Cologne. The Anglican Chaplain at the camp forwarded a letter to the Casualty Department at the War Office outlining the circumstances of his death which occurred on 21 October – 3 weeks before the Armistice:

> I beg to inform you that I was at the prisoner of war camp at Cologne last October when Lieut. Boyle was taken from the camp to one of the hospitals suffering from pneumonia following on influenza. Within 48 hours he was reported dead.[47]

Captain Boyle was one of the tens of millions worldwide who died in the influenza pandemic of 1918-1919. Having been previously wounded on two occasions, it is likely that his constitution was weakened through these and the privations of a prisoner of war camp which weakened his ability to combat the illness. Captain

45   Ancestry <http://www.ancestry.co.uk> (Accessed 12 January 2016). Service record Rifleman Andrew Steele 18/969, 12th Royal Irish Rifles.
46   TNA: WO 339/36141: Captain Gordon Alexander Deane service record. The circumstances of Captain Deane's death were disputed by his family who had received a letter from him shortly after capture stating that he had been wounded in the legs and was progressing well. A later communication from the Germans indicated that he had succumbed to a gunshot wound to the stomach. The War Office concluded that Capt. Deane had indeed died as the Germans had stated and that he had lessened the severity of his wounds when writing to his family to avoid unnecessary distress.
47   TNA: WO 339/43888: Captain John Kemmy Boyle service record.

St Mary's RC Church War Memorial, Haddington Road, Dublin. (Author's Collection)

Boyle is commemorated on the war memorial at St Mary's Roman Catholic Church, Haddington Road, Dublin.

Along with the dead, wounded and those taken prisoner there were those who suffered in less obvious ways. Lieutenant Colonel Warren John Richard Peacocke DSO and Bar was at the time of the offensive, the commanding officer of 9th Inniskillings. Aged 28 and from Skevanish, Innishannon, County Cork, he had just returned from leave prior to the commencement of the offensive and during the with-drawal, he commanded the battalion with great skill and endeavour, particularly on 26 March when he organised a counter attack near Andechy.

The exposure to action and constant danger over three and a half years had however, taken its toll on Lieutenant Colonel Peacocke. Writing to his wife on 7 April, General Nugent stated:

> John Peacocke has had a nervous breakdown and I am replacing him in command of his battn. and he will probably go home at once for rest. He did most excel-lent work but was not really very fit when it began. One day two officers he was walking with were both killed by the same shell, one on either side of him, he

was untouched but greatly shaken. He was standing talking to Audley Pratt[48] the time Audley was killed.[49]

Lieutenant Colonel Peacocke was hospitalised as the result of his breakdown at No 14 General Hospital, Wimereux before being sent to England for convalescence. However, a month later in May 1918, his former brigade commander, Brigadier General Hessey DSO, wrote to the War Office on his behalf:

> I can say that Col Peacocke could not stand the strain of active service at present whereas if he could be given a term at home of some months duration his service will be most valuable later on. He is an excellent commanding officer and has done very gallant service. I feel sure that he will be of the greatest use to the Army at home for the present, but he is not fit to take up the work and strain of active service. If Col Peacocke had not gone sick on 6th April, I had intended to send him home before he completely broke down. I have a very high opinion of this officer who I have known intimately since October 1914.[50]

The brigade commander's representation appears to have been heeded, as Lieutenant Colonel Peacocke was posted to a reserve battalion of the Royal East Kent Mounted Rifles for the remainder of the war. He was discharged from the Army on 17 January 1919, his medical category being given as C1. This category meant that he was 'Fit for Garrison Duty. Able to walk, good eyesight and hearing.'

Lieutenant Colonel Peacocke returned to Skevanish House where he resided with his widowed mother. Unfortunately, the home was located in an area of West Cork where republican activity was rife during the War of Independence. On the evening of 21 May 1921, Lieutenant Colonel Peacocke was chopping wood in an outhouse when he was approached by two IRA members who asked for directions and then shot him twice in the stomach. Lieutenant Colonel Peacocke died of his wounds the following morning.[51]

---

48 Lieutenant Colonel Audley Pratt from Crossmolina, County Mayo, was the commanding officer of 11th Inniskillings and was killed by a shell on the morning of 16 August 1917 during the Battle of Langemarck.
49 PRONI: D3835/E/2/17/20A Farren Connell papers.
50 TNA: WO 339/14281: Lieutenant Colonel Warren John Richard Peacocke service record.
51 An examination of the circumstances surrounding the shooting can be found in Gerard Murphy, *The Year of Disappearances: Political Killings in Cork 1921-1922* (Dublin: Gill & MacMillan, 2011) pp. 224-31. It was alleged by the IRA that Lieutenant Colonel Peacocke was a member of an 'Anti Sinn Fein Society' and was passing information on republican activity and taking part in clandestine raids on the homes of suspected republicans. There is little concrete evidence to back this up. Two weeks after his murder, local IRA members returned to the scene and burnt down the family home which had been vacant from the attack.

As an officer, there are probably more records available to highlight the trauma which Lieutenant Colonel Peacocke suffered. However, as highlighted above, Rifleman Andrew Steele was suffering from debility when repatriated. This includes not only physical, but mental weakness, manifesting itself in exhaustion and lack of energy. There is no doubt that many men in the Division, in common with Lieutenant Colonel Peacocke and Rifleman Steele suffered not only physically, but mentally from their experiences in the last week of March 1918. Regarded as fortunate to be home with their lives, for these men there was no option but to 'soldier on'.

8

Aftermath

I find everyone is pleased with the Division and the way they fought, and I find we are considered to have had the heaviest fighting almost of anyone and the most difficult, as we had so often to move owing to the Germans breaking in on the Divisions to the right or left of us and because we did not get all the support from the French that we were supposed to get.[1]

A personal retrospective view of Major General Nugent
elucidated in a letter to his wife, 5 April 1918.

The Divisional Commander, Major General Nugent had little time to coordinate the re-structuring of the Division as it was thrust into action so soon after the withdrawal from St Quentin. Barely a month later, on 6 May 1918, he was replaced as Divisional Commander by Major General Clifford Coffin VC DSO.[2] Major General Nugent returned to England and was then posted to India as Commander of the Meerut Division of the Indian Army. His name however, is synonymous with the 36th (Ulster) Division, having been its Commanding Officer since pre-embarkation days in September 1915.

Major General Nugent was always intensely proud of his men and he greatly respected their efforts when backs were to the wall during the Spring Offensive. He predicted however, that no special cognisance would be taken of the Division's achievements, due to its association with General Gough's Fifth Army, a theme he elaborated on in a letter to his wife on 1 April 1918:

> I think it is very hard on the Division that the C in C has made no mention of them. I am afraid that the Divisions of the Fifth Army will get very little

1   PRONI: D3835/E/2/17/19 Farren Connell papers.
2   Major General Coffin was commissioned into the Corps of Royal Engineers and saw service in the South African War. He was awarded the Victoria Cross on the opening day of the Third Battle of Ypres, 31 July 1917 whilst commanding 25th Infantry Brigade.

acknowledgement. It was not their fault, but that of the dispositions which were made and which caused the sacrifice of so many battalions and so much loss of ground.[3]

His mood lightened however a few days later with the news of a reorganisation which was to see the disbandment of a number of Divisions due to losses:

> It is somewhat interesting and very significant that the two Divisions which were on either side of mine are not to be made up and may be broken up. There are a list of five or six in all to whom this may happen and they are notoriously Divisions which failed to do their duty. No Division I think suffered more than the 36th by the failure of the Divisions on either side to stick it out. I am thankful that my Division never gave way and never retired until they were ordered to do so.[4]

The stigma of guilt by association with General Gough's Fifth Army that he felt, was premature. It is no secret that Major General Nugent felt antipathy towards General Gough and did not rate him as a Commander, his dislike emanating particularly from what he perceived as Gough's mismanagement of the attack at Langemarck in August 1917, which caused severe and unnecessary losses to the Division. Having had time to reflect following the withdrawal, he vented his thoughts on General Gough's management as he did on most subjects, in a letter to his wife dated 7 April 1918:

> To think that so much of the losses and not only of men and material but of the ground it cost us six months and countless lives to win in 1916 should have been lost because of the incompetence of an individual.[5]

Suitable recognition of the Division's achievements during the withdrawal did come, particularly in Field Marshal Sir Douglas Haig's Sixth Despatch, which highlighted some of the successes of the Division during the withdrawal:

> 21st March. In this fighting the action of the 1st Battn. Royal Inniskilling Fusiliers, 36th Division, deserves special mention. This battalion held a redoubt in the forward zone near Fontaine-les-Clercs throughout the whole of the first day of the battle, and on the following day, after the troops on their right had withdrawn in accordance with orders, still maintained their position, although surrounded by the enemy. After a magnificent fight, in which all the enemy's attacks were repulsed with great loss, at 3:00 p.m. the officer commanding the

3   PRONI: D3835/E/2/17/17 Farren Connell papers.
4   PRONI: D3835/E/2/17/17 Farren Connell papers
5   PRONI D3835/E/2/17/20A Farren Connell papers

battalion sent back a small party of troops, who succeeded in getting through to our lines. The remainder of the battalion continued the fight to the end.

22nd March cont. To the east of this point, heavy fighting took place around Ollezy which the 36th Division, under command of Major General O. S. W. Nugent, C.B., D.S.O., regained and held until a late hour, and around Aubigny and Brouchy, both of which villages, however, fell into the enemy's hands before nightfall.

26th March. As the British forces retired westwards however, the French troops on their right were gradually forced back in a south-westerly direction beyond Roye, leaving a gap between the French and British Armies of which the enemy took immediate advantage. To fill this gap, the 36th and 30th Divisions, which on the previous day had been withdrawn to rest, were put once more into the battle and speedily became involved in heavy fighting about Andechy and to the north of that place. Though the enemy had penetrated behind them and had taken Erches, the troops of the 36th Division at Andechy maintained a most gallant resistance until the afternoon of the 27th March, thereby playing no small part in preventing the enemy from breaking through between the Allied Armies.[6]

This Despatch however, was not published until October 1918 by which time Major General Nugent was in India.

What impact then did the German Spring Offensive have on 36th Division?

By the end of 1917, the Division was, in common with most British infantry units, tired and depleted. The two years of constant offensive warfare had had a deleterious effect on its operational effectiveness. Although entirely a volunteer Division with a core of officers and men with previous military experience, the offensive actions at the Somme, Messines, Langemarck and Cambrai as well as the attritional tours of frontline positions had thinned the ranks of those with front line experience and reinforcements sent to the front had little experience of soldiering, let alone warfare.

As highlighted earlier in the narrative, the Ulster Division was founded on a unique ethos of political and religious solidarity within the British Army, the only near comparable units being those of the 'Pals' battalions recruited from close-knit neighbourhoods or from workplaces particularly in the north of England, and the attrition which had taken place since its arrival in France had certainly diminished, but not totally eradicated this ethos. The fact that there was a dramatic slowdown in recruits coming from Ireland assisted in this process, as replacements were found from whatever source.

6   Field Marshal Sir Douglas Haig's sixth despatch <http://www.longlongtrail.co.uk/battles/british-field-commanders-despatches/sir-douglas-haigs-sixth-despatch-german-spring-offensives-1918/> (Accessed 20 July 2017).

The arrival of the regular battalions of the Royal Inniskilling Fusiliers, Royal Irish Fusiliers and Royal Irish Rifles throughout the winter of 1917-18 were welcome additions, but by early 1918, these battalions bore no resemblance to the professional battalions which had taken to the field at the start of war. Actions stretching from Mons in August 1914, via Gallipoli in 1915, through to Cambrai in November 1917 had seen these battalions completely reformed up to three times, and the majority of professional soldiers were dead, no longer fit to fight, or were prisoners.

Thrust upon the officers and men of the Division at the beginning of 1918 was the necessary reorganisation of the British Army to meet the coming threat. This was entirely due to the refusal of the Prime Minister, David Lloyd George to provide the Commander-in-Chief, Field Marshal Sir Douglas Haig, with the necessary manpower to meet the needs of the coming year. If proof was needed as to the folly of Lloyd George's decision it can be found in figures of reinforcements provided by Edmonds (1935):

> From 1 Jan-21 March 1918 – 174,379 British, Dominion and Labour Corps sent to France. 21 March-31 August 1918 – 544,005 sent. The obvious conclusion which could be drawn was that British forces in France could have been brought up to strength by 21 March if Government had willed it.[7]

The divisional and brigade system had been inculcated over many years and was second nature to those remaining officers and men who had experience of soldiering. The fact that many men were novices may have lessened the impact, but this was what they had been taught in their basic training – they knew no other way. If nothing else, the change from four battalions to three had an unsettling effect and it could be argued particularly so in the Ulster Division, with the disbandment of so many battalions with links to particular geographical areas of the province. As a volunteer Division, these geographical links were particularly strong and to many it felt like a betrayal, given the sacrifices that had been made over the previous two years.

When the reorganisation had taken place, the creation of the Entrenching battalions and removing them from Divisional control was a scheme that pleased no-one. From a purely practical point of view, it provided much needed labour when resources were not being sent out from the United Kingdom, but were these resources best utilised as envisaged? The evidence suggests that they were not, with all three battalions being engaged in the construction of railways, roads and aerodromes when concentration on defensive works were the glaringly obvious priority.

The three Entrenching battalions, 21st, 22nd and 23rd were all up to, or over strength in the short period they were engaged on labouring tasks. With the benefit of hindsight, these battalions would have been more effectively utilised under Divisional control, perhaps to alleviate the burden from the remaining battalions who were

---

7   Edmonds, *Military Operations France and Belgium 1918*, Volume II, p. 96.

engaged on labouring tasks in the periods out of the line when they were supposed to be resting. The idea of working as labourers was also an anathema to men who had joined the army to fight. Major Apperson, Royal Irish Rifles and attached to 22nd Entrenching battalion summed up the mood:

> As showing the spirit of the battalion, I should like to mention that all ranks took strong exception to the title [of Entrenching battalion] and never used it, and that the fighting ability of the battalion was not allowed to be impaired by its short absence from the line.[8]

One positive benefit of the establishment of Entrenching battalions is hinted at in Major Apperson's account, that training could be continued, which was not possible whilst on front line duty. The removal of the infantry support weapon, the Lewis Gun from the Entrenching battalions, was a short-sighted move which impaired the ability of the battalions to operate when called upon during the offensive. Perhaps the best comment that could be made on the decision to establish Entrenching battalions was that following the losses incurred during the offensive, they were immediately available as ready replacements, familiar with the Division and ready to fill the gaps left by those killed, wounded and taken prisoner.

As if the reorganisation was not enough to cope with, the imposition of an unfamiliar defensive system compounded feelings of uncertainty. Since the arrival of the British Expeditionary Force in August 1914, the Army, with the exception of an initial withdrawal at the end of August 1914, had been on the offensive. They were trying with the aid of their partners to remove the Germans from French and Belgian soil. This is evidenced by every major action through 1914-1917. Countless thousands of lives had been lost in honing offensive tactics which had to be learned by trial and error once trench warfare became inevitable.

Now, with the expectation of a massive German offensive, the Army was being asked to employ an totally unfamiliar defensive strategy, and what was worse was that they had six weeks to perfect it. The British Army was used to fighting in a linear fashion, a front line with layers of support in lines behind it which ran parallel to the front line. This was controlled by a battalion HQ, at most 400 yards to the rear. The benefits of this were that each battalion was in touch with its neighbours to the left and right, providing a continuous defensive line and each battalion could be controlled by its Headquarters who had sight of its Companies deployed forward of it. The new defensive system was a European concept and consisted of a Forward Zone consisting of a fortified Redoubt with outposts positioned around it. A Battle Zone, which could be up to two miles behind was the main area where any attackers were to be countered and a Rear Zone where reserves were congregated could be up to a further four miles to the rear. The pressure was on to ensure that this system was perfected prior the

---

8   TNA: WO 95/957/4: 22nd Entrenching battalion war diary.

German attack. However, as Captain Miller of 2nd Inniskillings highlighted, this led to micromanagement on a grand scale, as senior officers who should have known better decided to get involved and defences were often relocated a number of times to satisfy the ego of officers who were never going to be near them when the time came for action.

This micromanagement in addition to diminishing confidence in the men had more practical disadvantages. Time was short and wasting time reconstructing defensive positions left less time for the more important task of training the men in defensive operations.

To compound matters, the order that the enemy was to be engaged primarily in the Battle Zone, led to feelings of hopelessness to those detailed to man the Forward Zone. With typical army black humour, they were regarded as 'the sacrifice battalion'.[9] For a soldier about to face a determined enemy, confidence in your defences and defensive system was key. It is glaringly obvious that the men of the Ulster Division had no such confidence prior to 21 March.

Whilst the men of the Ulster Division were engaged in constructing defences in what should have been their rest periods from front line duty, the Germans were engaged in a massive training programme in offensive tactics, with each battalion undergoing an intensive three week course. The fact that the Germans had voluntarily ceded the ground on which the Ulster Division were constructing their defences and had mapped out that ground to the inch is indicative of the comprehensive preparations they were undertaking. Allied to this was the fact that they held the higher ground and were able to observe the British preparations. To use a card playing analogy, the Germans 'held all the aces' prior to 21 March.

With the demoralised state of the defenders and inadequate defences, it should have been expected that the confident Germans would sweep aside the Ulster Division on their way to achieve their objectives. However, that this did not happen is testament to the character and fighting spirit of the Ulstermen. When the infantry attack followed the massive artillery and trench mortar bombardment, it was assisted by the thick fog which blanketed the battlefield. Had there been no fog, the attackers would have paid a much heavier price from the machine guns based with the battalions in the Forward Zone. The fog also added to the success of the stormtrooper tactics of the attackers, in that they were able to bypass the Redoubts in the Forward Zone in many cases without being seen, with the result that these redoubts were surrounded before they knew it.

That the Redoubts in the Forward Zone did not immediately surrender says much about the character and fighting spirit of the defenders. Being 'thran'[10] is often described as an Ulster trait and it was displayed in great measure on 21 March. Despite the knowledge that they were surrounded, the 12th and 15th battalions Royal Irish

9   Minford et al, *It Wasn't all Sunshine*, p. 109.
10   An Ulster term meaning stubborn or obstinate.

Rifles and 2nd Royal Inniskilling Fusiliers in the Forward Zone held their positions long past the stage when they were recognised as untenable. Although surrounded, the three front line battalions continued to ensure that the Germans had to use vital resources to subdue them and it is no small achievement that when they were finally overcome, that senior German commanders congratulated the commanding officer's on their spirited defence. The defence of the right flank of the Divisional line at Essigny by 1st and 9th Royal Irish Fusiliers ensured that the German gains against the neighbouring 14th Division were not able to be fully exploited. Had the 1st and 9th Fusiliers' defences been breached on 21 March, it is quite feasible that the entire Ulster Division defences would have folded. Similarly, the counter attacks by 1st and 2nd Royal Irish Rifles in the afternoon and evening of 21 March ensured that even when the Forward Zone was breached that the Division's defensive line held.

This same spirit was evidenced on 22 March when 1st Royal Inniskilling Fusiliers also fought to the last man at Ricardo Redoubt and although sometimes withdrawing as part of a hastily prepared strategy and sometimes due to the ferocity of the German attack, the Ulster Division conducted itself to the highest standards of the British Army. The view of a non-combatant in this regard is of value. Father Gill, accompanying the 2nd Royal Irish Rifles throughout the retreat observed:

> On the whole, the retreat as far as I saw was orderly and without any panic on the part of the troops.[11]

The greatest crisis to face 36th Division during the retreat came on 24 March. Isolated and unaware of the order to retire, Captain Joseph Charles Bryans, the 2nd Royal Irish Rifles third commanding officer in as many days, declined to retire across open ground with no cover, which would have proved disastrous and instead led his men in a gallant last stand from which few escaped. Following on from this, the triumphant Germans swarmed across the countryside with the battalions of the Ulster Division and those attached from 61st Infantry Brigade falling back in disarray. This was the point where the withdrawal could have become a rout but for the extraordinary and timely intervention of the composite cavalry brigade of 3rd Cavalry Division, which undoubtedly saved the day. The intervention of the cavalry galvanised the desperately tired Ulstermen and gave them the space and impetus to reorganise.

From this point on, although still withdrawing, the men of the Division fought with renewed vigour and purpose. The actions of 26 and 27 March in the villages of Andechy, Erches and Guerbigny being evidence of this, where even though heavily outnumbered, counter attacks were carried out to frustrate the German advance.

By this time, there were signs that the great German advance was running out of steam. Having been subject to privations forced on them by the naval blockade of Germany, supplies of all types of goods were in short supply throughout Germany.

---

11   IJA/CHP1/27, p. 161.

The efforts to maintain a vast Army in the field meant that the lion's share of supplies was diverted to the military with the consequent lessening of supply to civilians who were existing on a near starvation diet. Even so, the German army was in a parlous state regarding supplies. On his capture on 21 March, Sapper Alfred Henderson 122nd Field Company, Royal Engineers was astonished at the state of the German soldiers:

> This was no conquering army – there were no demonstrations of rejoicing, no singing on the march... Uniforms were poor and ragged in some cases. No horses to the General Service Wagons which were being towed by teams of 20 or 30 soldiers. What were those tyres on the bicycles? I soon found out that the Germans had no rubber and were using some kind of coiled wire in lieu.[12]

In his iconic *Storm of Steel* (1929) Leutnant Ernst Junger, in action further up the line from the Ulster Division described the excitement as his unit, starved of normal rations came across a cornucopia of abandoned British supplies:

> The dugout was the height of luxury, even down to a little open fireplace with a mantel piece with pipes and tobacco on it, and armchairs pulled round in a circle. Merry old England! Of course, we didn't stint ourselves, but helped ourselves to whatever we fancied. I took a haversack, undergarments, a little flask full of whisky, a map case and some exquisite items from Roger & Gallet, no doubt keepsakes from some romantic leave in Paris. We could see that the inhabitants had left in a hurry. An adjacent space harboured the kitchen, we stared at in wonder. There was a whole crate of eggs, which we sucked on the spot, as eggs were little more than a word to us at that stage. On the shelves along the walls were stacks of canned meat, tins of delicious English jam, and bottles of Camp Coffee, tomatoes and onions, everything to delight an epicure's heart.[13]

Whilst it was no surprise that soldiers pocketed items that they came across, the effect on the psyche of the German soldiers on discovering the bounty available was unsettling. They had been fed on propaganda which portrayed the British as suffering from the same privations as they were, which were now exposed as lies. Allied to this was the fact that due to its rapid advance, the German Army was becoming a victim of its own success and was finding difficulty in supplying those leading the advance. In some cases, this led to a breakdown in discipline as highlighted in the 15th Royal Irish Rifles war diary entry for 26 March:

12   IWM Doc.11045 Sapper AE Henderson papers.
13   Ernst Junger, *Storm of Steel* (London: Penguin, 1961 reprint of 1929 edition) p. 243.

> 10 pm – A party of the enemy about 20 strong and more or less intoxicated was discovered owing to the noise they made outside the wire N of Erches.[14]

As these examples show, the physical state of the German soldier encountered by the Ulstermen during the retreat confirmed that even though they were retreating, the Ulstermen retained confidence that they were still a superior fighting force to the Germans.

By the time they withdrew by train to the French coast at the end of March, the men of the Ulster Division were certainly fewer in number and were desperately tired, but their spirit was not broken. The achievement of managing a retirement of over 100 miles over the period of a week was a colossal one and was primarily down the leadership skills of those few battalion commanders who remained effective. On a daily basis, displays of initiative and bravery by junior officers and NCO's helped maintain the cohesiveness of the Division on the move. Not everything however, went smoothly.

Problems with battlefield communication had bedevilled the British Army since the first days of the war in 1914. By 1918, through trial and error and the development of telephonic communication, battalion headquarters were able to communicate with forward posts and with brigade headquarters to the rear. This was a great improvement on the early days of the war. However, the Germans specifically targeted communications as part of their artillery bombardment and once the underground cables were cut, the signallers were unable to repair them under the continued bombardment. This rendered all telephonic communication useless and units were forced to rely on runners to pass messages, an inherently dangerous occupation, especially in the thick fog where the danger of getting lost or blundering into a party of attacking Germans was ever present.

On the morning of 21 March, battalion headquarters, Brigade and Division were therefore blind and had no idea what was happening, except that the Germans had mounted a colossal Artillery bombardment. The first report that 36th (Ulster) Division Headquarters had that a German infantry attack was following the artillery bombardment was at 11:45 a.m.[15] Emphasizing the failure of communications is the fact that this message came from a neighbouring Division, the 30th and not from any of the 36th Division battalions in the Forward Zone. Indeed, the war diary of 108th Brigade records that the first inkling of a German attack came from the 1st Battalion Royal Irish Fusiliers holding the Battle Zone at 12:25 p.m. nearly three hours after the attack was launched.[16] At this time the 12th Royal Irish Rifles in the Forward Zone had been surrounded and the attack on the Battle Zone was under way.

14   TNA: WO 95/2503/5: 15th Royal Irish Rifles war diary.
15   TNA: WO 95/2492/2: 36th (Ulster) Division war diary.
16   TNA: WO 95/2504/3: 108th Infantry Brigade war diary.

The lack of effective communications continued from this point for the remainder of the withdrawal and cost the lives of many men. It will be recalled that on 21 March, Second Lieutenant McFerran 2nd Royal Irish Rifles had set off in the direction of Grugies to ascertain the situation and was never heard of again. On 24 March at Cugny, runners sent forward to inform the 2nd Royal Irish Rifles to withdraw never reached them and consequently they held their position until overrun. The capture of Colonel Place, Lieutenant Colonel Furnell and Major Brew on 26 March was due to the fact that they were having to travel to discuss the situation in person as opposed to discussing matters by telephone.

The lack of communication extended throughout the Fifth Army and Brigadier General James Kilvington Cochrane, the commander of 61st Infantry Brigade which was attached to the Division from 21-25 March, was particularly scathing in his criticism:

> Divisional Commanders were to blame for not keeping Higher Commanders fully informed of what was taking place at the front. My personal experience was this: On the evening of the 21st I saw the 36th Div. Commander at Ollezy. I never saw him again during the operations, nor did I see one of his Staff Officers, nor did I receive any assistance of any kind from Divisional HQ. Also, I did not see a Staff Officer of any other formation. Mine was, I regret to say, not an isolated experience. As soon as telegraphic and telephonic communication with Brigades ceased to exist, Div. HQ in many cases became paralysed. They had become so wedded to a set piece type of warfare that when open warfare occurred, they failed to appreciate the situation and were unable to function independent of a fixed HQ. They glued themselves to a housed HQ miles to the rear and not in any kind of communication with their fighting commanders. Many were satisfied by saying, 'It is impossible to keep touch with my Brigade Commanders and in such a situation, the fighting is best left in their hands.'[17]

Due to the rapid pace of the withdrawal, it is perhaps unfair to suggest that the Brigade Commanders were ignored. There is evidence that Brigadier General Cochrane was in contact with 36th Divisional Headquarters on 24 March when it was possible that a rout may have taken place and it is the case that Major General Nugent sent Colonel Place, his Staff Officer, to liaise with Brigadier General Hessey, 109th Brigade on the evening of 26 March which led to his subsequent capture and the untimely death of Major Brew. In the disordered circumstances of the withdrawal, the loss of telephone and telegraphic communications forced officers and men to rely on more traditional methods, which worked, but at a cost.

17   TNA: CAB 45/192: Original letters, comments, personal accounts and extracts from War Diaries: Fifth Army.

It is remarkable that two days after reaching the relative safety of the billets on the French coast at the end of March, that the Division was in a position to travel north to participate in another large scale action. It should be remembered that around 50 percent of the fighting strength of the Division was gone, killed, wounded or captured. Fortuitously, experienced replacements from the Entrenching battalions were available to fill the gaps, and this fact is perhaps key in the ability of the Division to rapidly recover and continue as a cohesive and proficient unit throughout the remaining seven and a half months of the war.

The 36th (Ulster) Division had the misfortune to be situated opposite St Quentin where the main thrust of the German offensive was focused, and their defensive actions were greatly hampered by the heavy fog which occurred each morning until 26 March. Their misfortune was compounded by further matters beyond their control, including the political machinations which resulted in the withholding of reinforcements from the British Expeditionary Force and the consequent reorganisation of the Infantry battalions. The imposition of a new and untried defensive system was doomed to fail from the start – whatever the circumstances. Yet despite all the negatives, the British Army and the 36th (Ulster) Division in particular, passed this stern test. As the compiler of the *Official History*, Brigadier-General Sir James Edmonds (1935) was better placed than most to recognise the cause of the British resolve:

> It was the unconquerable British soldier who averted defeat. When the Germans were sweeping all before them it is questionable whether a single British soldier even entertained a thought of the possibility of ultimate defeat. There might be, to use the South African phrase of 1899, 'regrettable incidents', set-backs, even disasters, but it was everybody's fixed conviction that the Germans would, some day or other, collapse and that the Empire would somehow or other muddle through to victory.[18]

The Germans knew that they had to win and win comprehensively to avoid ultimate defeat. In the end they failed to do so. It was true that they had advanced around 40 miles and had seized large tracts of the Somme countryside, however, the majority of the ground seized was ground they had voluntarily ceded a year before and was of little strategic value. In human terms, the cost to the Germans had been unsustainable. No figures are available for an exact comparison with Allied casualties, but the total German casualties for the period 21 March – 30 April 1918 were 348,300. In acknowledging this, Edmonds (1935) states:

> It is evident from these figures and rough calculations that as in other great battles of the War, the losses on both sides were nearly the same.[19]

18   Edmonds, *Military Operations France and Belgium 1918*, pp. 483-4
19   Edmonds, p. 490.

With the massive resources of the United States about to join the war on the Allied side, Ludendorff's gamble in Spring 1918 can only be seen as a pyrrhic victory and one which ultimately ensured that the Great War would finish in 1918 and not carry on into 1919 as many had predicted.

From an Ulster Division point of view, the Spring Offensive of 1918 cannot be regarded as a defeat as has arguably been the prevailing perception. Whilst severely tried and tested, the resolve of all those in the Division to continue to fight and their loyalty to their comrades ensured that as new trials presented themselves in the Ypres sector in April 1918, the 36th (Ulster) Division was in a sound position to meet the challenge.

Hopefully, this account will go some way in explaining the facts of the Ulster Division's experiences in the final days of March 1918 to a wider audience. As I stated in the introduction in my first book, my rationale was to give greater exposure to the experiences of brave men whose story had not been told. For this book, the rationale remains the same. Hopefully, what I have written will go some way to honour all the men who fought with the 36th (Ulster) Division during a long week in March 1918.

Appendix I

Those who fell serving with the 36th (Ulster) Division having transferred from other Regiments

---

Army Cyclist Corps – 1
Bedfordshire Regiment – 5
Coldstream Guards – 1
Essex Regiment – 8
Hussars – 6
King's (Liverpool) Regiment – 3
Lancashire Regiment – 3
London Regiment – 35
Loyal North Lancashire Regiment – 1
Norfolk Regiment – 3
Northamptonshire Regiment – 3
North Staffordshire Regiment – 1
Notts and Derby Regiment – 5
Rifle Brigade – 3
Royal Army Medical Corps – 1
Royal Army Ordnance Corps – 5
Royal Army Service Corps – 52
Royal Artillery – 1
Royal Fusiliers – 8
Royal Sussex Regiment – 4
Sherwood Foresters – 2
Somerset Light Infantry – 1
Various Training Establishments – 4
West Yorkshire Regiment – 3
Yorkshire Regiment – 3

Appendix II

Officer Prisoners of War

Date Captured	Rank	Name	Battalion	POW No.	Date Repatriated	Died in Captivity	Cemetery	Country	Grave	Age
21 March 1918	Capt	TS Adamson	12th Royal Irish Rifles	4333	01 November 1918					
21 March 1918	2nd Lt	J Armstrong	15th Royal Irish Rifles	4373	14 December 1918					
21 March 1918	Lt	J Barker	36th MGC	4832	14 December 1918					
21 March 1918	2nd Lt	AT Bell	12th Royal Irish Rifles	4340	28 December 1918					
21 March 1918	2nd Lt	TA Blackwood	12th Royal Irish Rifles	4334	29 November 1918					
21 March 1918	Lt	WD Bradley	1st Royal Irish Fusiliers	4317	01 December 1918					
21 March 1918	2nd Lt	J Burnside	12th Royal Irish Rifles	4388	25 December 1918					
21 March 1918	2nd Lt	MG Cardozo	15th Royal Irish Rifles	4372	06 December 1918					
21 March 1918	Lt Col	CG Cole-Hamilton	15th Royal Irish Rifles	4363	14 December 1918					
21 March 1918	Capt	JES Condon	15th Royal Irish Rifles	4365	06 December 1918					
21 March 1918	2nd Lt	E Croker	16th Royal Irish Rifles	4382	28 November 1918					
21 March 1918	2nd Lt	GA Day	16th Royal Irish Rifles	4383	10 December 1918					
21 March 1918	Capt	GA Deane	1st Royal Irish Fusiliers	4396		11 April 1918	Avesnes-sur-Helpe Communal Cemetery	France	B4	20
21 March 1918	2nd Lt	JHK Freeland	16th Royal Irish Rifles	4381	28 November 1918					
21 March 1918	2nd Lt	JW Furbisher	16th Royal Irish Rifles	4380	28 November 1918					
21 March 1918	2nd Lt	WHK Gibson	16th Royal Irish Rifles	4385	28 November 1918					
21 March 1918	Capt	LSH Glanville	15th Royal Irish Rifles/RAMC	5333	01 November 1918					
21 March 1918	Maj	AH Hall	12th Royal Irish Rifles	4330	28 November 1918					
21 March 1918	2nd Lt	C Halliman	16th Royal Irish Rifles	4387	14 December 1918					
21 March 1918	2nd Lt	P Hilder	15th Royal Irish Rifles	4370	04 December 1918					
21 March 1918	2nd Lt	SC Hughes	15th Royal Irish Rifles	4369	06 December 1918					
21 March 1918	2nd Lt	WF Irvine	12th Royal Irish Rifles	4344	11 December 1918					
21 March 1918	2nd Lt	NF Irwin	16th Royal Irish Rifles	4386	14 December 1918					
21 March 1918	2nd Lt	EW Johnston	12th Royal Irish Rifles	4346	25 December 1918					

Date Captured	Rank	Name	Battalion	POW No.	Date Repatriated	Died in Captivity	Cemetery	Country	Grave	Age
21 March 1918	Capt	LJ Johnston	12th Royal Irish Rifles	4331	08 December 1918					
21 March 1918	2nd Lt	JAC Kennedy	12th Royal Irish Rifles	4345	06 December 1918					
21 March 1918	Lt	AJ Lamport	36th MGC	4831	01 December 1918					
21 March 1918	2nd Lt	GH Lemon	1st Royal Irish Fusiliers	4398	25 December 1918					
21 March 1918	Lt	SA Lynch	15th Royal Irish Rifles	4367	06 December 1918					
21 March 1918	2nd Lt	JG Malone	12th Royal Irish Rifles	4348	08 December 1918					
21 March 1918	2nd Lt	DJ McGilton	13th Royal Irish Rifles	4356	06 December 1918					
21 March 1918	Reverend	WF Morris	Att. 15th Royal Irish Rifles	5468	01 November 1918					
21 March 1918	Capt	H St J Morrison	12th Royal Irish Rifles	4332	18 December 1918					
21 March 1918	2nd Lt	J Morton	12th Royal Irish Rifles	4349	29 November 1918					
21 March 1918	Capt	WW Neville	1st Royal Irish Fusiliers	4395	25 December 1918					
21 March 1918	Lt	VE Osborne	36th MGC	4829		07 April 1918	Niederzwehren	Germany	H.J.10	25
21 March 1918	2nd Lt	AH Osborough	12th Royal Irish Rifles	4343	11 December 1918					
21 March 1918	2nd Lt	CJT Perkins	9th Royal Irish Fusiliers	4419	11 December 1918					
21 March 1918	2nd Lt	RJ Raggett	12th Royal Irish Rifles	4339	25 December 1918					
21 March 1918	2nd Lt	WQ Rea	16th Royal Irish Rifles	4384	17 December 1918					
21 March 1918	2nd Lt	LK Reid	15th Royal Irish Rifles	4371	06 December 1918					
21 March 1918	Lt	TB Reynolds	36th MGC	4830	14 December 1918					
21 March 1918	2nd Lt	J Robinson	12th Royal Irish Rifles	4341	11 December 1918					
21 March 1918	Lt	HW Root	36th MGC	4833		22 March 1918	Premont British Cemetery	France	V.A.25	27
21 March 1918	Lt	JT Saunders	36th MGC	4834	29 November 1918					
21 March 1918	2nd Lt	A Scott	15th Royal Irish Rifles	4374	06 December 1918					
21 March 1918	2nd Lt	CP Seath	15th Royal Irish Rifles	4375	11 December 1918					
21 March 1918	2nd Lt	T Shearer	12th Royal Irish Rifles	4347	11 December 1918					
21 March 1918	2nd Lt	JWJ Sloan	36th MGC	4835	10 December 1918					
21 March 1918	2nd Lt	A Smith	12th Royal Irish Rifles	4336	11 December 1918					
21 March 1918	2nd Lt	R Sprott	15th Royal Irish Rifles	4376	06 December 1918					
21 March 1918	Capt	JH Stewart	15th Royal Irish Rifles	4364	06 December 1918					
21 March 1918	2nd Lt	HD Swayne	12th Royal Irish Rifles	4337	28 November 1918					
21 March 1918	2nd Lt	HF Walden	12th Royal Irish Rifles	4342	11 December 1918					
21 March 1918	Lt	SH Walker	1st &2nd Royal Irish Rifles	4306	06 December 1918					

Date Captured	Rank	Name	Battalion	POW No.	Date Repatriated	Died in Captivity	Cemetery	Country	Grave	Age
21 March 1918	2nd Lt	TE Weall	36th MGC	4836	17 December 1918					
21 March 1918	2nd Lt	HL Weir	12th Royal Irish Rifles	4350		28 October 1918	Cologne Southern	Germany	VII.C.27	30
21 March 1918	Lt	TH Wilson	12th Royal Irish Rifles	4335	10 December 1918					
21 March 1918	Lt	W Wilson	15th Royal Irish Rifles	4366	06 December 1918					
21 March 1918	2nd Lt	JK Wylie	15th Royal Irish Rifles	4377	14 December 1918					
21 March 1918	Capt	RM Boyle	2nd Royal Inniskilling Fusiliers	2295	08 December 1918					
21 March 1918	2nd Lt	GM Burke	2nd Royal Inniskilling Fusiliers	2304	20 December 1918					
21 March 1918	2nd Lt	F Cinnamond	2nd Royal Inniskilling Fusiliers	2299		12 November 1918	Poznan Old Garrison Cemetery	Poland	II.B.5	25
21 March 1918	Lt	FW Davidson	2nd Royal Inniskilling Fusiliers	2298	01 December 1918					
21 March 1918	Lt Col	Lord AK Farnham	2nd Royal Inniskilling Fusiliers	2305	17 December 1918					
21 March 1918	2nd Lt	C Gregg	1st Royal Inniskilling Fusiliers	2278	01 December 1918					
21 March 1918	2nd Lt	P Hennessy	2nd Royal Inniskilling Fusiliers	2303	18 December 1918					
21 March 1918	Capt	R Hodgson-Jones	1st Royal Inniskilling Fusiliers/RAMC	5332	01 November 1918					
21 March 1918	Capt	JAS Hopkins	2nd Royal Inniskilling Fusiliers	2293	01 December 1918					
21 March 1918	2nd Lt	F Marchant	1st Royal Inniskilling Fusiliers	2277	18 December 1918					
21 March 1918	Lt	S McConnell	1st Royal Inniskilling Fusiliers	2276	28 November 1918					
21 March 1918	2nd Lt	SB McConnell	2nd Royal Inniskilling Fusiliers	2300	01 December 1918					
21 March 1918	Capt	J McMechan	1st Royal Inniskilling Fusiliers	2275	28 December 1918					
21 March 1918	Capt	CC Miller	2nd Royal Inniskilling Fusiliers	2296	29 November 1918					
21 March 1918	Lt	WV Morony	2nd Royal Inniskilling Fusiliers	2297	18 December 1918					
21 March 1918	2nd Lt	JF O'Brien	2nd Royal Inniskilling Fusiliers	2302	02 December 1918					
21 March 1918	Lt	JF Parkhouse	9th Royal Inniskilling Fusiliers	2330	29 November 1918					
21 March 1918	Lt	JF Power	2nd Royal Inniskilling Fusiliers/RAMC	5361	01 December 1918					
21 March 1918	Capt	RM Vaughan	2nd Royal Inniskilling Fusiliers	2294	10 December 1918					
21 March 1918	2nd Lt	G Watson	2nd Royal Inniskilling Fusiliers	2301	28 November 1918					
21 March 1918	Lt	W Clarke	15th Royal Irish Rifles	4368	25 December 1918					
21 March 1918	2nd Lt	TF Hall	1st Royal Irish Fusiliers	4399	28 November 1918					
21 March 1918	2nd Lt	LJ Harrison	1st Royal Irish Fusiliers	4411		17 April 1918	Niederzwehren	Germany	IV.L.9	29
22 March 1918	Lt	WG Baker	1st Royal Inniskilling Fusiliers	2283	25 December 1918					

Date Captured	Rank	Name	Battalion	POW No.	Date Repatriated	Died in Captivity	Cemetery	Country	Grave	Age
22 March 1918	Capt	TH Cockburn-Mercer	1st Royal Inniskilling Fusiliers	2281	11 January 1919					
22 March 1918	Lt Col	JN Crawford	1st Royal Inniskilling Fusiliers	2279	03 January 1919					
22 March 1918	Maj	EF Eagar	2nd Royal Inniskilling Fusiliers	2314	29 November 1918					
22 March 1918	Lt	BL Griggs	1st Royal Inniskilling Fusiliers	2282	18 December 1918					
22 March 1918	2nd Lt	SS Hunter	1st Royal Inniskilling Fusiliers	2284	25 December 1918					
22 March 1918	2nd Lt	RB McConnell	1st Royal Inniskilling Fusiliers	2287	25 December 1918					
22 March 1918	Capt	EEJ Moore	1st Royal Inniskilling Fusiliers	2280	01 December 1918					
22 March 1918	2nd Lt	W Price	1st Royal Inniskilling Fusiliers	2286	29 November 1918					
22 March 1918	2nd Lt	JP Robinson	1st Royal Inniskilling Fusiliers	2285	17 December 1918					
22 March 1918	2nd Lt	JH Connor	9th Royal Inniskilling Fusiliers	4420	25 December 1918					
22 March 1918	2nd Lt	R Monteith	12th Royal Irish Rifles	4351	28 November 1918					
23 March 1918	2nd Lt	JA Gibson	9th Royal Inniskilling Fusiliers	2333		27 September 1918	Cologne Southern	Germany	XIV.E.16	25
23 March 1918	Capt	GW Willock	1st Royal Inniskilling Fusiliers	2288	18 December 1918					
23 March 1918	2nd Lt	W Ferguson	12th Royal Irish Rifles	4353	29 December 1918					
23 March 1918	2nd Lt	G Foy	12th Royal Irish Rifles	4434	17 December 1918					
23 March 1918	Lt	AJE Gibson	14th Royal Irish Rifles	4359	13 December 1918					
23 March 1918	2nd Lt	HL Kempson	12th Royal Irish Rifles	4352	17 December 1918					
24 March 1918	2nd Lt	JMJ Martin	2nd Royal Inniskilling Fusiliers	2313	17 December 1918					
24 March 1918	Capt	JC Bryans	2nd Royal Irish Rifles	4307	29 November 1918					
24 March 1918	Capt	JK Boyle	2nd Royal Irish Rifles	4308		21 October 1918	Cologne Southern	Germany	VII.C.21	21
24 March 1918	Lt QMR	CHT Dawson	21 Entrenching Bn/10th Royal Irish Rifles	4322		23 April 1918	Sains du Nord Communal Cemetery	France	308	
22 March 1918	Capt	M Henehan	9th Royal Irish Fusiliers	4422	18 December 1918					
24 March 1918	Capt	RM Pryde	13th Royal Irish Rifles	4357	06 December 1918					
24 March 1918	Capt	T Slatter	9th Royal Irish Fusiliers	4421	01 December 1918					
24 March 1918	2nd Lt	E Strohm	2nd Royal Irish Rifles	4309	11 December 1918					
24 March 1918	Lt	DB Taylor	14th Royal Irish Rifles	4360	18 December 1918					
23-25 March 1918	2nd Lt	C Hind	15th Royal Irish Rifles	4378	01 December 1918					
26 March 1918	Lt Col	M Furnell	1st Royal Irish Fusiliers	4400	02 December 1918					
26 March 1918	2nd Lt	EH Gilmer	9th Royal Irish Fusiliers	4423	25 December 1918					
26 March 1918	Lt Col	CO Place	36th Infantry Division Staff		08 December 1918					

Date Captured	Rank	Name	Battalion	POW No.	Date Repatriated	Died in Captivity	Cemetery	Country	Grave	Age
27 March 1918	2nd Lt	T Bremner	9th Royal Irish Fusiliers	4426	18 December 1918					
27 March 1918	2nd Lt	N Clarke	9th Royal Irish Fusiliers	4427	18 December 1918					
27 March 1918	Maj	SUL Clements	1st Royal Irish Fusiliers	4401	29 November 1918					
27 March 2018	2nd Lt	HHEQ Coles	1st Royal Irish Fusiliers	4416	25 December 1918					
27 March 1918	2nd Lt	FLH Donaldson	9th Royal Irish Fusiliers	4428	25 December 1918					
27 March 1918	2nd Lt	BJ Eyre	1st Royal Irish Fusiliers	4403	25 December 1918					
27 March 1918	Capt	B St J Galvin	1st Royal Irish Fusiliers	4402	25 December 1918					
27 March 1918	Lt	H Gray	1st Royal Irish Fusiliers	4405	01 December 1918					
27 March 1918	2nd Lt	TS Haswell	1st Royal Irish Fusiliers	4406	25 December 1918					
27 March 1918	2nd Lt	AW Henry	9th Royal Irish Fusiliers	4320	25 December 1918					
27 March 1918	Lt	T Houston	1st Royal Irish Fusiliers	4404	18 December 1918					
27 March 1918	Lt	G I O'F Johnstone	9th Royal Irish Fusiliers	4424	10 December 1918					
27 March 1918	2nd Lt	CN McKenny	1st Royal Irish Fusiliers	4407	25 December 1918					
27 March 1918	2nd Lt	RM Moore	1st Royal Irish Fusiliers	4408	01 December 1918					
27 March 1918	Lt	JJ McE Pollock	9th Royal Irish Fusiliers	4425	04 December 1918					
27 March 1918	2nd Lt	J Scott	9th Royal Irish Fusiliers	4430	25 December 1918					
27 March 1918	2nd Lt	RL Smith	9th Royal Irish Fusiliers	4429	01 December 1918					
28 March 1918	2nd Lt	JS Adair	11th/13th Royal Irish Rifles	4328	25 December 1918					
28 March 1918	2nd Lt	WTW Elliott	11th/13th Royal Irish Rifles	4327	19 December 1918					
28 March 1918	2nd Lt	RE Glover	1st Royal Irish Fusiliers	4409	25 December 1918					
21–29 March 1918	Lt	CJ Armstrong	2nd Royal Inniskilling Fusiliers	2307	10 December 1918					
21–29 March 1918	Lt	TH Bird	2nd Royal Inniskilling Fusiliers	2308	01 December 1918					
21–29 March 1918	2nd Lt	DR Clark	2nd Royal Inniskilling Fusiliers	2309	18 December 1918					
21–29 March 1918	2nd Lt	JFR Darbyshire	9th Royal Inniskilling Fusiliers	2331	29 November 1918					
21–29 March 1918	2nd Lt	REW Irwin	2nd Royal Inniskilling Fusiliers	2312	14 December 1918					
21–29 March 1918	2nd Lt	JD McCullough	2nd Royal Inniskilling Fusiliers	2310	18 December 1918					
21–29 March 1918	2nd Lt	HH Murdoch	9th Royal Inniskilling Fusiliers	2332	01 December 1918					
21–29 March 1918	Lt	JH Wharry	2nd Royal Inniskilling Fusiliers	2306	17 December 1918					
21–29 March 1918	2nd Lt	FC Williams	2nd Royal Inniskilling Fusiliers	2311	29 November 1918					
31 March 1918	2nd Lt	AE Todd	15th Royal Irish Rifles	4379	06 December 1918					

Note: Appendix compiled utilising material from Ancestry <https://www.ancestry.co.uk> (Accessed various dates 2017).

Appendix III

Composition of 36th (Ulster) Division at its formation

107th Infantry Brigade
8th (Service) Battalion Royal Irish Rifles (East Belfast Volunteers)
9th (Service) Battalion Royal Irish Rifles (West Belfast Volunteers)
10th (Service) Battalion Royal Irish Rifles (South Belfast Volunteers)
15th (Service) Battalion Royal Irish Rifles (West Belfast Volunteers)

108th Infantry Brigade
11th (Service) Battalion Royal Irish Rifles (South Antrim Volunteers)
12th (Service) Battalion Royal Irish Rifles (Central Antrim Volunteers)
13th (Service) Battalion Royal Irish Rifles (1st County Down Volunteers)
9th (Service) Battalion Royal Irish Fusiliers (Armagh, Monaghan and Cavan
    Volunteers)

109th Infantry Brigade
9th (Service) Battalion Royal Inniskilling Fusiliers (Tyrone Volunteers)
10th (Service) Battalion Royal Inniskilling Fusiliers (Derry Volunteers)
11th (Service) Battalion Royal Inniskilling Fusiliers (Donegal and Fermanagh
    Volunteers)
14th (Service) Battalion Royal Irish Rifles (Young Citizen Volunteers)

Pioneer Battalion
16th (Service) Battalion Royal Irish Rifles (2nd County Down Volunteers)

Divisional Troops
Service Squadron, 6th Royal Inniskilling Dragoons
36th Divisional Signal Company Royal Engineers
Divisional Cyclist Company

Royal Army Medical Corps
 108th Field Ambulance
 109th Field Ambulance
 110th Field Ambulance
76th Sanitary Section RAMC
Divisional Train Army Service Corps
48th Mobile Veterinary Section

Royal Artillery[1]
153rd Brigade Royal Field Artillery
154th Brigade Royal Field Artillery
172nd Brigade Royal Field Artillery
173rd Brigade Royal Field Artillery
Divisional Ammunition Column, Royal Field Artillery

Royal Engineers
121st Field Company Royal Engineers
122nd Field Company Royal Engineers
150th Field Company Royal Engineers

---

1 The Royal Artillery for the Division was not formed until May 1915 and recruited men
 chiefly from the south and north-east of London.

Appendix IV

German Artillery Time Programme – 21 March 1918

4.40 am. First period, 120 minutes
General surprise fire on the enemy batteries, trench mortars, command posts, telephone exchanges, billets and bivouacs, beginning with a crash, and fired by all batteries and trench mortars (mixed gas and HE shell). After 20 minutes the trench mortars stop. At 5.30 am ten minutes surprise fire on the infantry positions, beginning suddenly from all batteries except super-heavy (against the First and Intermediate positions, HE only, against the second position, mixed gas, lethal and lachrymatory). During this 10 minutes, no counter-battery work.

6.40 am. Second, Third and Fourth periods
Each of ten minutes, during each of which a proportion of the batteries of the infantry groups check the range on named trench lines, whilst the rest fire on other defences.

7.10 am. Fifth Period, 70 minutes
Whilst counter batteries and long-range batteries continue to fire on their normal targets, the others bombard the infantry defences for effect, the areas being defined by a map. After 30 minutes fire, some howitzers in each group sweep the ground between the trenches of the First Position for 15 minutes; the other howitzers shell certain types of resistance for ten minutes and then sweep backwards; the Field Guns sweep the ground between the Second and Intermediate Positions for 10 minutes with Lachrymatory and HE shell.

8.20 am. Sixth Period, 75 minutes
Shooting as in the Fifth Period, with slight variation of targets for the long-range batteries; the same special bombardments after 30 minutes' fire, also with slight variation of targets.

9.35 am. Seventh Period

The 5 minutes before Zero. All howitzers fire as near to the front line of the First Position as is possible without endangering their own infantry; beyond them the light and medium trench mortars fire, and beyond them again the Field Guns, but only with HE; beyond them again the super-heavy guns, flanking batteries and heavy trench mortars fire on the second line of the First Position; long-range guns (other than flanking batteries) and some of the guns not to be used in the creeping barrage fire on the Second Position; the others continue counter-battery work. At the end of this period the infantry will assault without "hurrahs".

The barrage (fired in principal by the field artillery, 5.9-inch howitzers and light trench mortars), proceeds by deep bounds, the first bound being 300 metres, other bounds 200 metres for field artillery and 400 for the heavy artillery; after the first bound the field artillery to halt the barrage for 3 minutes, the heavy for 2; after the other bounds for 4 and 8 minutes respectively. Signals for advancing the barrage on emergency, 200 metres at a time, to be by use of green rockets and the small flame projectors; no signals for halting it.[1]

---

1   Artillery programme reproduced from Brigadier General James Edward Edmonds, *History of the Great War based on Official Documents. Military Operations France and Belgium 1918* (London: MacMillan and Co Ltd, (1935) pp. 159-160.

Bibliography

Books

Anglesey, Marquess of, *A History of the British Cavalry 1816 to 1919. Volume 8. The Western Front, 1915-1918; Epilogue, 1919-1939* (Barnsley: Pen & Sword Books Ltd, 2012).

Bickersteth, Lieutenant John Burgon, *History of the 6th Cavalry Brigade 1914-1919* (London: Forgotten Books reprint of 1922 edition).

Bowman, Timothy, *Irish Regiments in the Great War, Discipline and Morale* (Manchester: Manchester University Press, 2003).

Broome, Frank Napier, *Not the Whole Truth* (Johannesburg: University of Natal Press, 1962).

Burke, Damien (ed.) *Irish Jesuit Chaplains in The First World War* (Dublin: Messenger Publications, 2014).

Burrows, Brigadier General Arnold Robinson, *The 1st Battalion The Faugh-A-Ballaghs in the Great War* (Uckfield: Naval & Military Press reprint, n.d.).

Callwell, Major General Sir Charles Edward, *Field Marshal Sir Henry Wilson Bart. GCB. DSO.* (London: Cassell & Company, 1927).

Canning, William James, *A Wheen of Medals. The History of the 9th (Service) Battalion Royal Inniskilling Fusiliers (The Tyrones) in World War One* (Antrim: Canning, 2006).

Condon, Jim, *Officers of the Royal Inniskilling Fusiliers in World War 1* (Enniskillen: Royal Inniskilling Fusiliers Museum, 2003).

Cox & Co, *List of British Officers taken prisoner in the various theatres of the War August 1914–November 1918* (Uckfield: Naval & Military Press reprint of 1919 edition).

Cron, Hermann, *The Imperial German Army 1914-18: Organisation, Structure, Orders of Battle* (Solihull: Helion & Company, 2002).

Cusack, John MM & Herbert, Ivor, *Scarlet Fever. A Lifetime with Horses* (London: Cassell & Company Ltd, 1972).

Doherty, Richard & Truesdale, David, *Irish Winners of the Victoria Cross* (Dublin: Four Courts Press, 2000).

Edmonds, Brigadier-General Sir James Edward, *History of the Great War Based on Official Documents. Military Operations France and Belgium 1918* (London: MacMillan & Co Ltd, 1935).

Falls, Cyril, *The History of the 36th (Ulster) Division.* (Belfast. McCaw, Stevenson & Orr, 1922).

Falls, Cyril, *The History of the First Seven Battalions: The Royal Irish Rifles in the Great War* (Uckfield: Naval & Military Press reprint of 1925 edition).

Farndale, General Sir Martin, *History of the Royal Regiment of Artillery, Western Front, 1914-18* (Woolwich: The Royal Artillery Institution, 1986).

Fox, Sir Frank OBE, *The Royal Inniskilling Fusiliers in the World War* (Uckfield: Naval & Military Press reprint of 1928 edition).

Gliddon, Gerald, *VC's of The First World War – Spring Offensive 1918* (Stroud: The History Press, 2013).

Goes, Gustav, *Der Tag X. Die Grosse Schlacht in Frankreich (21 Marz–5 April 1918) Unter dem Stahlhelm. Bd 7* (Berlin: Verlag Tradition, 1933).

Gough, General Sir Hubert, *The March Retreat* (London: Cassell, 1934).

Gray, Randal, *Kaiserschlacht 1918: The Final German Offensive* (Oxford: Osprey Publishing, 2000).

Harris, Major Henry Edward Davis, *The Irish Regiments in the First World War* (Dublin: Mercier Press, 1968).

Hill, George Herbert, *Retreat from Death. A Soldier on the Somme* (London: Tauris Parke Paperbacks 2005).

Hoffmann, Rudolf, *Infanterie-Regiment 463. 7000 Niedersachsen im Grosskampfe der Westfront* (Bremen: H.M. Hauschild, 1930).

Hutton, Lieutenant General Sir Edward et al, *The King's Royal Rifle Corps Chronicle 1918* (Winchester: Warren & Son, 1919)

Johnstone, Tom, *Orange, Green and Khaki. The Story of the Irish Regiments in the Great War, 1914-18* (Dublin: Gill and MacMillan, 1992).

Jones, Henry Albert, *The War in the Air. Being the Story of the part played in the Great War by the Royal Air Force. Volume IV* (Uckfield: Naval and Military Press, 1934, reprint).

Junger, Ernst, *Storm of Steel*, (London: Penguin, 1961).

Lewis-Stempel, John, *The Life, Death and Glory of British POW's 1914-1918* (London: Weidenfeld and Nicolson, 2014).

Lucy, John Francis, *There's a Devil in the Drum* (Uckfield: Naval & Military Press, 1993 reprint of 1938 edition).

Kenrick, Colonel Neville Cyril Evelyn DSO, *The Story of the Wiltshire Regiment (Duke of Edinburgh's)* (Aldershot: Gale & Polden, 1963).

MacDonald, Lyn, *To the Last Man, Spring 1918* (London: Penguin, 1999).

Metcalfe, Nick, *Blacker's Boys. 9th (Service) Battalion, Princess Victoria's (Royal Irish Fusiliers) (Co. Armagh) & 9th (North Irish Horse) Battalion Princess Victoria's (Royal Irish Fusiliers) 1914-1919* (Woodstock: Writersworld, 2012).

Middlebrook, Martin, *The Kaiser's Battle: 21 March 1918, The First Day of the German Spring Offensive* (London: Penguin, 1983).

Minford, Catherine et al. *It Wasn't all Sunshine. An ordinary man's account of the First World War* (Larne: Larne Borough Council, 2012).

Mitchell, Gardiner S, *Three Cheers for the Derrys. A History of the 10th Royal Inniskilling Fusiliers in the 1914-18 War* (Derry: YES Publications, 1991).

Mitchell, Major Thomas John & Smith, Miss G M, *Official History of the War. Medical Services. Casualties and Medical Statistics of the Great War* (London & Nashville: Imperial War Museum and The Battery Press, 1931).

Moore, Stephen, *The Chocolate Soldiers. The Story of the Young Citizen Volunteers and 14th Royal Irish Rifles during the Great War* (Newtownards: Colourpoint, 2016).

Moorehouse, Brendon, *Forged by Fire. The Battle Tactics and Soldiers of a World War One Battalion. The 7th Somerset Light Infantry* (Staplehurst: Spellmount, 2003).

Mullins, Claud, *The Leipzig Trials. An account of the War Criminals' Trials and a study of German mentality* (London: Witherby, 1921).

Murland, Jerry, *Retreat and Rearguard Somme 1918* (Barnsley: Pen & Sword, 2014).

Murphy, Gerard, *The Year of Disappearances. Political Killings in Cork 1921-1922* (Dublin: Gill & McMillan, 2011).

Orr, David R & Truesdale, David, *Ulster Will Fight … Vol 2. The 36th (Ulster) Division from Formation to the Armistice* (Solihull: Helion and Company, 2016).

Perry, Nicholas (ed.) *Major General Oliver Nugent and the Ulster Division, 1915-1918* (Stroud: Sutton Publishing, 2007).

Seymour, Brigadier William W, *The History of the Rifle Brigade in the War of 1914-1918, Volume II, January 1917-June 1919* (London: The Rifle Brigade Club, 1936).

Shaw Sparrow, Walter, *The Fifth Army in March 1918* (London: Bodley Head, 1921).

Sheffield, Gary & Bourne, John (eds.) *Douglas Haig. War Diaries and Letters 1914-1918* (London: Weidenfeld & Nicolson, 2005).

Sheldon, Jack, *The German Army at Passchendaele* (Barnsley: Pen & Sword, 2007).

Taylor, James W, *The 1st Royal Irish Rifles in the Great War* (Dublin: Four Courts Press, 2002).

Taylor, James W, *The 2nd Royal Irish Rifles in the Great War* (Dublin: Four Courts Press, 2005).

Tardif, Phillip, *The North Irish Horse in the Great War* (Barnsley: Pen & Sword, 2015).

War Office, *Manual of Military Law* (London, 1907).

Westman, Stephen, *Surgeon with the Kaiser's Army* (London: Kimber, 1968).

Whitmore, Lieutenant Colonel Francis Henry Douglas DSO, *The 10th PWO Royal Hussars and the Essex Yeomanry during the European War 1914-1918* (Colchester: Benham & Co, 1920).

Wyrall, Everard, *The Duke of Cornwall's Light Infantry, 1914-1919* (London: Methuen, 1932).

Wyrall, Everard, *The History of the King's Regiment (Liverpool) 1914-1919* (London: Arnold & Co, 1935).

Yarnall, John, *Barbed Wire Disease. British and German Prisoners of War 1914-19* (Stroud: Spellmount, 2011).

Journals

Faugh-a-Ballagh. The Regimental Gazette of the Royal Irish Fusiliers
The London Gazette
The Sprig of Shillelagh. The Regimental Gazette of the Royal Inniskilling Fusiliers

Newspapers

Gazette des Ardennes
The Ballymena Observer
The Belfast Evening Telegraph
The Belfast Newsletter
The Daily Mirror
The Derry Journal
The Irish Times

Electronic Sources

Sir Douglas Haig's Sixth Despatch 1918 <http://www.longlongtrail.co.uk/battles/british-field-commanders-despatches/sir-douglas-haigs-sixth-despatch-german-spring-offensives-1918/>

Government Publications

Parliamentary Papers, Cd 9106 *Report on the Treatment by The Germans Of Prisoners of War Taken during the Spring Offensives of 1918* (London: 1918)

Private Papers

War Reminiscences of Fr HV Gill SJ DSO MC, 1914-1918 held at Irish Jesuit Archives (IJA) Dublin

Museums

Royal Inniskilling Fusiliers Museum, Enniskillen, County Fermanagh
Royal Ulster Fusiliers Museum, Armagh, County Armagh
Royal Irish Rifles Museum, Belfast, County Antrim
Cavan County Museum, Ballyjamesduff, County Cavan

The National Archives (TNA)

WO 95 Series. Divisional, Brigade and Battalion war diaries
WO 161 Series. Committee on the treatment of British prisoners of war: Interviews and reports
WO 339 & 374 Series. Officer's personal records
CAB 45 Series. Committee of Imperial Defence. Official war histories correspondence

Imperial War Museum (IWM)

D.6477 Gunner William Grant papers
D.11045 Sapper Alfred Henderson papers
D. 4118 *A Letter to my Daughters*. Captain Charles Miller papers
D.11236 Private John William Page papers

Public Record Office of Northern Ireland (PRONI)

D961/8 Newton and Anderson papers.
D1447 Stone Family papers
D3835 Farren Connell papers
D3975 Farnham Papers
D4101 Serjeant W Finlay 15th Battalion Royal Irish Rifles
Londonderry Memorial Records

Index

People

Places

Military Formations/Units